Crusaders and Revolutionaries of the Thirteenth Century: De Montfort

For Rosana and Russell,
heirs to the de Montfort tradition

Crusaders and Revolutionaries of the Thirteenth Century: De Montfort

Darren Baker

Pen & Sword
MILITARY

First published in Great Britain in 2020 by
Pen & Sword Military
An imprint of
Pen & Sword Books Ltd
Yorkshire – Philadelphia

ISBN 978 1 52674 549 1

A CIP catalogue record for this book is
available from the British Library.

Typeset by Mac Style
Printed and bound in the UK by TJ Books Ltd,
Padstow, Cornwall.

Pen & Sword Books Limited incorporates the imprints of Atlas,
Archaeology, Aviation, Discovery, Family History, Fiction, History,
Maritime, Military, Military Classics, Politics, Select, Transport,
True Crime, Air World, Frontline Publishing, Leo Cooper, Remember
When, Seaforth Publishing, The Praetorian Press, Wharncliffe
Local History, Wharncliffe Transport, Wharncliffe True Crime
and White Owl.

For a complete list of Pen & Sword titles please contact

PEN & SWORD BOOKS LIMITED
47 Church Street, Barnsley, South Yorkshire, S70 2AS, England
E-mail: enquiries@pen-and-sword.co.uk
Website: www.pen-and-sword.co.uk

Or

PEN AND SWORD BOOKS
1950 Lawrence Rd, Havertown, PA 19083, USA
E-mail: Uspen-and-sword@casematepublishers.com
Website: www.penandswordbooks.com

Contents

Preface

The de Montforts started out as foresters in an area just west of Paris. By the beginning of the twelfth century, they were an established baronial family on the Norman frontier, key players in the struggle between the kings of England and France. A hundred years later they were renowned crusaders, fighting for Christendom while carving out new principalities for themselves in the process. During the course of the thirteenth century, they acquired lordships from Wales to Italy to the Holy Land, built in large part on their military skills, religious zeal, and overweening ambition and opportunism. But then, like that, it was over. As the century came to a close, there was nothing left of the fortune and power they had accumulated. Their influence with kings, popes, emperors and sultans was gone, their place among the noble houses of Europe had vanished.

The fame and notoriety of the family nevertheless endured because of the historic Simon de Montforts, father and son, two of the earliest proponents of constitutional government in medieval Europe. Both men were crusaders and revolutionaries (the latter in the sense of their attempts to overturn the existing order) but their careers and fates stood in stark contrast to each other. The father undertook a religious crusade with political overtones, the son a political crusade with religious overtones. The father went after heretics, the son foreigners. Where senior was ultimately thwarted by the unwilling population he had conquered, junior enjoyed widespread support from the middling folk and peasants. He had mostly himself to blame for his downfall. Each man having died for his cause, senior was borne away and given an honourable burial. His son was frightfully chopped up into trophies on the battlefield, his name soon synonymous with disorder and outlawry. And yet the younger Simon is the one celebrated today, for the principles of democracy he supposedly espoused. His father, who was very much admired in his own day, is condemned as a fanatic out to destroy a whole people and culture.

What both men had in common were exceptional wives and devoted children who, in many ways, were equally capable and controversial. The cousins too were forces to be reckoned with, but there has never been a single volume that treated the lot of them, let alone together with these two commanding figures, who themselves have never shared the same pages. So when one day I was asked what historical book I would like to write next, my answer was instantaneous. It was no sooner agreed, however, than I began to wonder what lay in store for me. The biggest challenge was starting with a clean slate, which is to say basing this biography on source material and not on the work, and opinions, of the historians who preceded me. Fortunately many fine translations of thirteenth-century chronicles and texts have become available in recent years, especially in the case of the Albigensian Crusade. The other problem with bringing this extended family to a wider audience is the repetition of names that occur through the generations. There are eight Simons and nine Amaurys alone from beginning to end. Although the story about to unfold is ordered in a strictly chronological fashion, the assorted de Montforts, even those who make the briefest of appearances, have been given numeric suffixes. It may be an eyesore to some readers, but the alternative for those who lose the thread will be total confusion.

The family, friends and associates mentioned in my previous work on the de Montforts have my thanks and gratitude here as well. Two I would like to add are Danna Messer, who asked the question that became the book, and Laura Hirst, who took care of the production side of it during an extraordinarily difficult time. This spring of 2020 saw the coronavirus pandemic bring the world to a virtual standstill, but Laura patiently and skillfully made sure everything stayed on schedule and in the quality that this remarkable medieval family deserves.

Timeline

1000 – Indicative year of the birth of Amaury I, the first lord of Montfort

1087 – Death of Simon I, lord of Montfort, succeeded by his son Amaury II

1089 – Death of Amaury II, succeeded by his brother Richard, who is succeeded by their brother Simon II as the lord of Montfort

1093 – Marriage of Bertrade de Montfort to King Philip I of France

1104 – Death of Simon II, succeeded by his brother Amaury III

1117 – Death of Bertrade, she is buried at Hautes-Bruyères

1119 – Amaury III becomes the count of Evreux and lord of Montfort

1129 – Bertrade's son Fulk V of Anjou becomes the king of Jerusalem

1137 – Death of Amaury III, succeeded by his son Amaury IV

1140 – Death of Amaury IV, succeeded by his brother Simon III

1170 – Marriages of the children of Simon III in and around this year: Amaury V to Mabel, daughter of the 2nd earl of Gloucester; Simon IV to Amicia, daughter of the 3rd earl of Leicester; Bertrade to the 5th earl of Chester

1171 – Probable birth year of Simon V, his brother Guy I born sometime later

1181 – Death of Simon III, his son Amaury V becomes the count of Evreux, his other son Simon IV becomes the lord of Montfort

1185 – Death of Simon IV, succeeded by his son Simon V

1186 – Amaury V goes on crusade to the Holy Land

1188 – Amicia de Montfort marries William III des Barres

1194 – Death of Amaury V, succeeded by his son Amaury VI

1195 – Simon V marries Alice Montmorency, probable birth year of Amaury VII

1197 – Probable birth year of Guy II

1199 – Simon V and Guy I take the cross, Amaury VI becomes the 3rd earl of Gloucester

1202 – The Fourth Crusade musters in Venice, diversion to Zara

1203 – Diversion of the crusade to Constantinople, Simon V and Guy I leave for the Holy Land

1204 – Conquest of Constantinople, conquest of Normandy, death of Robert de Beaumont, 4th earl of Leicester, Guy I marries Helvis of Ibelin, becomes the lord of Sidon

1206 – Simon V returns to France

1207 – Simon V is made the 5th earl of Leicester, but stripped of the earldom by King John

1208 – Pope Innocent III launches the Albigensian crusade, probable birth year of Simon VI

1209 – Sack of Béziers, Simon V becomes crusade commander

1210 – Alice de Montfort joins the crusade, brings the children south

1211 – Simon defeats Raymond VI at Castelnaudary, the first siege of Toulouse, daughter Petronilla is born and baptised by Dominic de Guzman, Guy I joins the crusade,

1212 – Simon V elected king of England, issues the Statute of Pamiers

1213 – Simon V victorious at the battle of Muret, Amaury VI dies, Amaury VII is knighted

1214 – Amaury VII marries Beatrice of Vienne

1215 – Lateran V in Rome, Raymond VI is disinherited, Simon V becomes the count of Toulouse, death of his mother Amicia

1216 – Simon V defeated at Beaucaire, the revolt of Toulouse is crushed, Guy II marries the countess of Bigorre

1217 – The second siege of Toulouse

1218 – Simon V is killed in front of Toulouse, Amaury VII becomes the count of Toulouse and lord of Montfort, the siege is lifted

1220 – Death of Guy II outside Castelnaudary

1221 – Death of Alice de Montfort

1222 – Death of Raymond VI of Toulouse

1224 – Amaury VII cedes his rights to Louis VIII and leaves Languedoc

1226 – Louis VIII renews the Albigensian Crusade and dies later in the year

1228 – Guy I is killed in renewed fighting, succeeded as lord of La Ferté-Alais by his son Philip I

1229 – The Treaty of Meaux ends the Albigensian conflict, Raymond VII is recognised as the count of Toulouse

1230 – Simon VI goes to England, Amaury VII becomes the constable of France

1231 – Simon VI is granted the earldom of Leicester

1238 – Simon VI marries Eleanor Marshal, birth of Henry de Montfort

1239 – Amaury VII and Philip I go on crusade, Simon VI disgraced by Henry III, Amaury VII is captured in Gaza

1240 – Simon VI goes on crusade, his son Simon VII is born, Philip I marries Maria of Antioch and becomes the lord of Toron

1241 – Amaury VII is freed, he dies on return journey, succeeded as the count of Montfort by his son John I

1242 – English forces are routed at Taillebourg by Louis IX, birth of Simon and Eleanor's son Amaury VIII

1243 – Simon and Eleanor return to England

1244 – The loss of Jerusalem, destruction of the Christian army under Philip I, birth of Guy IV

1246 – Philip I becomes the lord of Tyre

1248 – Simon VI becomes the viceroy of Gascony, John I, count of Montfort, joins the crusade of Louis IX

1249 – Death and burial of John I on Cyprus, death of Raymond VII of Toulouse

1250 – Destruction of Louis's crusade in Egypt, Philip I is imprisoned and ransomed with the army, death of Guy III on the crusade

1252 – The trial of Simon VI, birth of Richard de Montfort

1254 – Queen Eleanor of Provence summons the first elected parliament

1256 – War of St Sabas breaks out in the crusader states

1258 – The reform period begins in England, the Provisions of Oxford are enacted, birth of Eleanor de Montfort

1259 – Simon and Eleanor obstruct the passage of the Treaty of Paris

1260 – Showdown between Henry III and Simon VI over parliament, second trial of Simon VI

1261 – Henry III repudiates the Provisions of Oxford, Simon VI goes into exile

1262 – Arbitration between Henry III and Simon VI in France

1263 – Simon VI returns to make war, seizes power and loses it

1264 – Civil war in England, Simon wins the battle of Lewes, installs a constitutional monarchy

1265 – Simon VI summons parliament with the broadest sweep of representation yet, the battle of Evesham, he and his son Henry are killed, Henry III is restored to power, Eleanor and her children Amaury, Richard and Eleanor leave England

1266 – Philip II leads Charles of Anjou's army in the conquest of Italy and Sicily, Simon VII and Guy IV escape from England, Richard de Montfort goes to Navarre and is never heard of again

1268 – Guy IV fights at the battle of Tagliacozzo, becomes the vicar-general of Tuscany

1270 – The assassination of Philip I in Tyre, succeeded by his son John II, death of Louis IX and Philip II on crusade in Tunis, John III succeeds his father Philip II as the count of Squillace

1271 – Guy IV and Simon VII murder Henry of Almain in Viterbo, Simon VII dies

1272 – Death of Henry III and Richard of Cornwall

1275 – Death of their sister Eleanor, her son Amaury and daughter Eleanor are seized and imprisoned by Edward I

1277 – John II ends the feud between Tyre and Acre

1278 – The marriage of Eleanor de Montfort to Llywelyn, she becomes the princess of Wales

1281 – Guy IV restored to favour in Italy

1282 – Amaury VIII is freed, his sister Eleanor dies in childbirth, her daughter Gwenllian is later placed in a nunnery

1283 – John II dies in Tyre, succeeded by his brother Humphrey

1284 – Humphrey de Montfort dies

1287 – Guy IV and John III are captured in battle with the Aragonese, John III is ransomed

1292 – Guy IV dies in prison, Amaury VIII has temporary wardship of his daughters

1300 – Amaury VIII and John III die

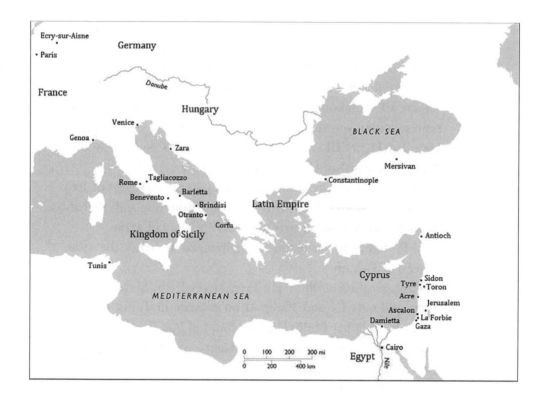

The Eastern and Western Mediterranean in the Thirteenth Century.

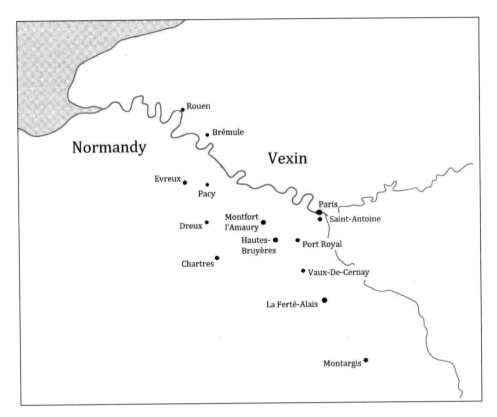

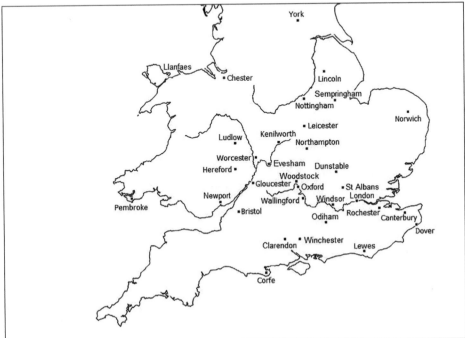

North-Central France and England in the Thirteenth Century.

Chapter 1

The Forebears
1000–1199

In medieval France the royal forest of Yveline lay about fifty kilometres west of Paris. The family of wardens and foresters who managed it eventually converted their hereditary offices into a local patrimony and lordship. By the eleventh century, one of their descendants had built a castle on a hilltop there. His name was Amaury, and because the castle was part of a natural fortress, it came to be called the 'strong mount of Amaury' or Montfort l'Amaury. It was to serve as the seat of the lords of Montfort who followed him.

Little is known about Amaury. The later notoriety of his family is likely behind the tradition that he was an illegitimate son of King Robert II of France and that his ancestry went back to Emperor Charles the Bald in the ninth century. The earliest mention of him only identifies his father as William, who came from the county of Hainault near modern-day Flanders. Whatever the true origins of Amaury de Montfort, by 1032 he had risen to become an adviser to Robert's successor, King Henry I.[1]

Amaury had three children with his wife Bertrade of Gometz. Their only daughter Eva was married to William Crispin, whose prominent family held a lordship on the border of Normandy and France. Eva and William were the parents of the famous Gilbert Crispin, who served as the abbot of Westminster Abbey for more than three decades after his appointment in 1085. Eva retired to the abbey of Bec, where Gilbert had been raised, and died there in 1099. A monk told of how she had appeared to him after her death and complained that she was undergoing sixty years of penance in the afterlife because she had been too fond of pet dogs and other trifles in her previous life.[2]

Of Amaury's two sons, he was succeeded by Simon, who had a son, Amaury II, and daughter, Isabella, by his first wife. In 1063, this first Simon de Montfort is found persuading William, the duke of Normandy and future Conqueror, to enlist the aid of certain exiled nobles for William's struggles against Maine and Brittany. One of the exiles was Ralph de Tosny, who later served as the Norman standard-bearer at the battle of Hastings. According to Orderic Vitalis, one night Ralph 'carried off' his younger half-sister Agnes to become Simon's third wife. In return, Simon married his daughter Isabella to Ralph. These two, Isabella and Ralph de Tosny, would become the founders of the English houses of Stafford and Tony.[3]

At the death of Simon I in 1087, his oldest son Amaury II became the lord of Montfort l'Amaury. His courage and feats earned him the nickname 'the Strong', literally making him Amaury de Montfort le Fort. He was killed in 1089 when, 'raging like a lion', he took on two men in combat and was run through with a lance. He was succeeded by his half-brother Richard, the oldest of the five children Simon I had with the abducted Agnes.

Richard was soon caught up in a quarrel between his half-sister Isabella and their aunt Helwise, the wife of William, the count of Evreux. In taking sides against his sister, Richard found her a worthy opponent. Orderic describes how Isabella de Tosny rode around 'in knightly armour and exhibited daring among belted knights and men–at–arms'. Richard was killed while trying to seize an abbey that belonged to the Tosnys and the unexpectedness of his death helped reconcile the two families.[4]

Richard de Montfort had three younger brothers: Simon, William and Amaury. In 1098, the new lord, Simon II, had to contend with an incursion from Normandy under King William II (Rufus) of England. Rufus's army was led by Simon's own younger brother Amaury III, and although Simon successfully defended Montfort l'Amaury, he was captured before the Normans withdrew. He is last heard taking part in the siege of Montmorency by the French army in 1101. Like his older brothers Amaury II and Richard, Simon II left no heirs. The next brother William was ineligible to succeed because he had been raised for a career in the Church. In 1095, he was made the bishop of Paris and died overseas on the crusade of 1101. The lordship fell to the younger Amaury III in spite of his disloyalty to his brother Simon.[5]

The campaign was one of the last for Rufus. In August 1100, he was shot dead while out hunting. His brother (and member of the hunting party) succeeded him as King Henry I of England, eventually the duke of Normandy as well. Henry would spend a good part of his reign trying to consolidate his control over the Norman frontier and nobody gave him more trouble with it than Amaury III. Ingratiating and ambitious, Amaury set out to do some consolidating of his own and used his ties of kinship to other regional lords and the French monarchy itself to make it happen. For these, he mostly had his flamboyant sister Bertrade to thank.

The youngest child and only daughter of Simon I and Agnes, Bertrade was raised by her aunt and uncle, Helwise and William of Evreux, who had no children of their own. She was still in their household in 1090 when Fulk IV, the count of Anjou, intimated to Robert Curthose, then the duke of Normandy and older brother of Rufus, that he would very much like to marry her. Since Robert was anxious for Fulk's support, he agreed to ask Bertrade's guardians about the possibility of such a union.

William of Evreux was aghast that he should give his niece in marriage to a man who had been married three times before, but he gave his consent when Robert met his demands for the return of certain lands. Bertrade bore Fulk a son, but she quickly became disenchanted with the marriage. Whether it was because of her husband's lecherous ways, his deformed feet or, as Orderic tells us, her worry that he would dump her like all his previous wives, she fled to King Philip I of France. Philip was 'carried away by lust for the married woman' and dumped his own wife Bertha for Bertrade. They were married in 1093 and had three children.[6]

Bertrade intrigued to put her eldest son with Philip on the throne in place of her stepson Louis. First, she plotted to have the crown prince arrested and detained while he was visiting the court in England. When that failed, she hired sorcerers to cast spells upon him. Finally, she resorted to poison. Louis survived thanks to the skills of a doctor trained by the Moors in Spain, but he remained grossly pale and fat until his death. The affair was exposed and Bertrade was forgiven only after humbling herself to become her stepson's handmaid. King Philip, says Abbot Suger, went into slovenly decline after that and 'did nothing worthy of the royal majesty'. He died in 1108 and Bertrade ended her days nine years later as a nun at the convent of Hautes-Bruyères, which she founded close to Montfort l'Amaury.[7]

Taking advantage of his sister's connections to the houses of Anjou and Capet, Amaury III encouraged his nephew Fulk V to make war on Henry I of England in 1112. They were joined by Amaury's uncle Count William of Evreux and cousin William Crispin III, but they waited in vain for help from King Louis VI of France. By the following year they were asking Henry for a truce and he pardoned the lot of them. When the childless Count William died in 1118, however, the king refused to allow Amaury to succeed to his uncle's county of Evreux.

Amaury found the snub intolerable and began inciting other lords to espouse his cause. In a scene that could easily describe his more famous descendants Simon V and VI, he rode about at night 'in breathless haste from one castle to another, keeping everyone in continual commotion by his restless activity'. Where he differed from his descendants was his response to the information that King Henry, furious at the news that Evreux had been betrayed to Amaury, marched up to the city and burnt it to the ground, churches and all. Instead of rushing to the aid of the garrison of Evreux, which still held out under the command of Bertrade's sons Philip and Fleury, Amaury sorrowfully gathered his troops and went home.[8]

Although he had appealed to Louis for aid, Amaury was not with the French army when they encountered Henry's forces at Brémule on 20 August 1119. It was William Crispin III, grandson of Eva de Montfort, who led the attack against the Anglo-Norman host and he got close enough to the English king to bring his sword down hard on the royal head. Henry was saved by his mail hood, while Crispin himself was only just saved from a mauling by Henry's household knights. The French were soon routed and in the confusion of their flight lost track of their king. Louis ended up alone in a forest and had to be shown the way out by a peasant. Once safely back in Paris, he was advised by Amaury not to take the defeat too hard.

> Such are the chances of war, and they have often been the lot of the most celebrated generals. Fortune is like a revolving wheel; it overturns in a moment those whom it has suddenly raised, and on the other hand frequently lifts higher those it has prostrated and rolled in the dust.[9]

It was a sentiment similar to the one expressed nearly a century and a half later by Amaury's great-great-grandson Simon VI, after he got the worst of his own struggle with an English king named Henry (III). The victory at Brémule allowed the English to press their siege of Evreux again. Amaury went to the king and agreed to surrender the castle in return for Henry's recognition of him as the count of Evreux. He thus became the first member of the house of Montfort to attain comital status.

But within a few years Amaury was in revolt again, this time over the harassment and general imposition of Anglo-Norman royal administrators. His impressive coalition included Waleran, one of the twin boys born to Robert I de Beaumont, who was both the count of Meulan and 1st earl of Leicester. Because Waleran was the oldest of the twins, he had received Meulan at his father's death in 1118 while his younger brother Robert II received Leicester. It was one of three earldoms that eventually brought the house of Montfort to England.[10]

In September 1123, Amaury and his allies, who again included his cousin William Crispin III and nephew Fulk V of Anjou, met to coordinate their conspiracy. Amaury led one of the initial assaults, but Henry was already on to them. Having suffered the tragedy of the White Ship (the drowning of his son and heir) the last time he left Normandy (in 1119), the king had returned in a vicious mood. He put together an army at Rouen and burnt towns and villages as he advanced towards the rebels. A line of the king's household troops encountered them in March 1124 at Rougemontier.

Against Amaury's advice to avoid a full-scale battle, the teenage Waleran was eager to prove himself and charged. Their horses were quickly felled by archers and the rebels were captured on the field. Amaury's captor, William de Grandcourt, was touched by his valour and the knowledge that if Amaury became a prisoner of Henry I, he might not ever win his freedom again. Grandcourt, says Orderic, decided to desert the king and go into exile with his captive. It was a lucky escape, because Henry had some prisoners banished, mutilated or blinded, and he kept Waleran, who had been his ward, in close custody for the next five years.[11]

King Louis VI had been unable to provide support because he had to repel a failed invasion from the east by Emperor Henry V. King Henry I launched his own invasion from Normandy, but Amaury alone, 'a man most keen in the art of war', says Suger, drove him back. In 1126, Louis marched against the rebellious count of Auvergne and relied on Amaury to lead the deciding charge. King and subject then quarrelled, however, after Amaury's father-in-law Stephen de Garlande, the chancellor and seneschal of France, fell from grace in 1128. This led to Amaury's estrangement from Louis and closer cooperation with Henry in the struggle between these two crowns. The last heard from him is in 1136, the year after the death of Henry I and the beginning of the struggle to succeed him. Amaury is seen giving support to his grand-nephew Geoffrey of Anjou as the latter moved to secure Normandy for his wife and contender to the English throne, the Empress Matilda. When Amaury III died in April 1137, he bequeathed to his heirs a lordship that was among the most powerful and influential along the Norman frontier. It might be said that under him and his sister Bertrade, the house of Montfort had arrived.[12]

The next generations of Amaurys and Simons

Amaury III had been married three times. There appears to have been no issue with his first wife Mabel. With his second wife Richilde, the daughter of the count of Hainault, he had two daughters. One became a nun at Hautes-Bruyères, the other was married to Hugh de Crécy, the son of the count of Rochefort, in about 1108. Hugh had a long history of depredations and in 1118 was forced to become a monk. His lands had by then come into the possession of the Garlande family and from them to Amaury through his third wife Agnes de Garlande.[13]

The three children of Amaury III and Agnes were Amaury, Simon and Agnes. The eldest, Amaury IV, succeeded his father as count of Evreux, but died young, in 1140. The following year his sister Agnes was married to Waleran, who like the de Montforts had come to support the cause of Geoffrey of Anjou in Normandy. The younger Agnes, now the countess of Meulan, had six sons and a daughter with Waleran and survived him by fifteen years, dying in December 1181.[14]

With the death of his older brother, Simon III became the count of Evreux and lord of Montfort. That made him, like his father before him, a vassal of the kings of England and France. In the war that erupted between Henry II and Louis VII in 1159, Simon surrendered his French castles to the English side. That cut off Louis's communications between Paris and Orleans and obliged him to seek a truce.[15] Simon's adherence to Henry II earned his three children lucrative marriages within the Anglo-Norman nobility. In 1170, his oldest son Amaury was married to Mabel, the oldest daughter of William Fitz-Robert, the 2nd earl of Gloucester. His next son Simon was married to Amicia, the oldest daughter of Robert III de Beaumont, the 3rd earl of Leicester and Waleran's nephew. His daughter Bertrade, named after her famous great-aunt, was given in marriage to Hugh, the 5th earl of Chester. Because Hugh and Simon III were kinfolk of Henry II, it was the king himself who gave the young Bertrade away.[16]

Hugh and his father-in-law went their separate ways when Henry was faced with a revolt in 1173 led by his adult sons Henry (the Young King), Richard and Geoffrey, and his wife Eleanor of Aquitaine. The old king put down this 'War Without Love' with great severity, including imprisoning the queen for the remainder of his reign. Like Waleran before him, Hugh had been a royal ward. He was taken prisoner at Alnwick in northern England and did not get his earldom back until 1177, dying four years later. His wife Bertrade II survived him by nearly half a century. The dowager countess of Chester died in 1227, aged about 71.[17]

Simon III remained loyal to Henry II during the uprising and was taken captive at the siege of Aumale by the rebels. His loyalty to the English Crown is further evidenced by his decision to be buried in Evreux Cathedral in Normandy as opposed to Hautes-Bruyères near Montfort l'Amaury, where his father, aunt and other family members were interred in the family crypt. Now referred to as 'the Bald', Count Simon died in March 1181. The mourners at his funeral included his sister Agnes and her son Count Robert II of Meulan.[18]

The lands of Simon III were divided between his two sons. The oldest, Amaury V, naturally received the better deal. He was made the count of Evreux, a vassal of the king of England, while his younger brother, Simon IV, became the lord of Montfort l'Amaury and owed his allegiance to the king of France. Two years later Amaury V stood in line to succeed as the earl of Gloucester after the death of his father-in-law William Fitz-Robert in 1183. But Henry II intended to endow his youngest son John with the earldom by marrying him to Isabella, the youngest of William's daughters. Amaury and his wife Mabel had to settle for £100 of English lands as compensation.[19]

In 1186, Amaury V can be found in the Holy Land. He was the first member of the de Montfort family to go on crusade since Fulk V of Anjou went to Jerusalem in 1120 and joined the Knights Templars there. If Amaury was at the catastrophic battle of Hattin the following year in 1187, he was among the few knights to escape and make it home, because three years later, in 1190, he was in Sicily as part of the crusade heading eastward under the new king of England, Richard I (Lionheart). Amaury appears as one of the witnesses to the peace treaty concluded by Richard with Tancred, the ruler of the island. What eventually became of Amaury V after that remains a mystery. He was dead by 1194, when his widow Mabel fined (paid an inheritance tax) for Evreux on behalf of their young son, Amaury VI.[20]

Like his brother, Simon IV would have been well into his forties by the time he came into his inheritance. He had been the acting lord of some of the family lands since 1165, probably with a view to his marriage to Amicia. He died in 1185, just four years after his father, and left behind two sons, Simon and Guy, and a daughter Petronilla. They were all minors as late as 1189. Their mother had since remarried and her dowry lands were under the control of her second husband, William III des Barres. He and Simon IV appear to have been comrades-in-arms. In 1180, they are found competing together at a tournament in Lagny-sur-Marne against the following of Henry the Young King and William Marshal.[21] The remarriage of Amicia to this famed warrior from the Norman Vexin was probably the work of King Philip II (Augustus), who wanted to keep the English heiress within the French fold.

Amicia and Barres had a son and daughter before he left with Philip in 1189 for the Third Crusade. Both the French and English forces had decided to winter in Sicily en route to the Holy Land, and one day they fell into a mock tournament using cane poles for weapons. King Richard and Barres had a long-standing personal feud and it soured the playful atmosphere of the tournament. The two were soon brawling, and when Richard found he could not get the better of Barres, he threw a fit and demanded that Philip send him home. Only with great reluctance, and some begging by the French, did the Lionheart relent and allow him to stay. He had to be happy for it, for Barres not only chose to stay behind after Philip abandoned the crusade, but proved his worth against the Turks during Richard's march from Acre to Jaffa.[22]

Doubtless Barres shared these exploits with his stepchildren. The oldest of them, Simon V, was born around 1171. He appears to have received some education at the nearby Cistercian abbey of Vaux-de-Cernay, where he learned to read Latin. He came of age between the end of the crusade and beginning of the war over Normandy that erupted in 1194 between former crusader kings Philip and Richard. His first seal shows an armoured knight on horseback, blowing a horn and accompanied by two hunting dogs. The image reflects his status as both a warrior and royal forester.[23]

As the new lord of Montfort l'Amaury, Simon V was expected to take Philip's side in the Norman wars. In 1196, he joined the French forces that prevented Richard from retaking the castle of Aumale, where Simon's grandfather Simon III had been captured three decades earlier. On the other side, his uncle Robert IV de Beaumont, the 4th earl of Leicester, was taken prisoner fighting for Richard. He was forced to give Philip 2,000 marks of silver and his castle of Pacy to obtain his freedom. Simon V and two of Robert's other French relatives stood surety for his promise not to try and retake his castle. If he did, they would lose their lands.[24]

Philip had already shown he was prepared to disinherit the de Montforts. After King Richard was captured on his way back from the crusade, Philip teamed up with Richard's brother John to seize Evreux from young Amaury VI and his custodians. They made their move in the spring of 1194, but by then Richard had been released and he quickly retook Evreux. Robert de Beaumont also tried to retake his castle of Pacy. Simon V was not made to pay for his uncle's indiscretion, both because the attempt failed and Philip had just been soundly beaten by Richard at Gisors (in 1198). He needed all the forces he could muster.[25]

One of Philip's knights captured at Gisors was Matthew Montmorency, who came from another illustrious baronial family of the Vexin. His namesake grandfather had been the constable of France under Louis VII and his grandmother was a natural daughter of Henry I of England.

Matthew had a sister named Alice and sometime during these years she and Simon V were married. The match was again in keeping with Philip's determination to maintain direct control over the families that straddled the Norman frontier. Simon V now had two relations by marriage, Barres and Montmorency, who were rising fast at the French court thanks to their military service (Matthew's recent setback notwithstanding). Philip was also promoting a similar class of new men in his civil service, and he married one of them, Bartholomew of Roye, to Simon's sister Petronilla.[26]

Two children had been born to Simon V and Alice as the century came to a close. They are first mentioned in a charter issued by Simon in February 1198 confirming the annual grant of 'a deer and fat wild boar' made by his ancestors to the leper community of Grand-Beaulieu des Chartres.[27] Meanwhile, the endless warfare between the two headstrong and vindictive monarchs of England and France had made it an unsettled time, as the imprisonment of Simon's uncle Robert and Alice's brother Matthew had shown. Preachers began taking to the countryside to call for a crusade as a way to put an end to the local misery. The most famous of them, Fulk of Neuilly, was known to point out sinners in the crowd and harangue them before onlookers. He now turned his ire on both kings and warned that one of them was going to meet an unfortunate end unless they made peace.[28]

In early 1199, Philip and Richard finally agreed to a truce. Then in April, Richard was killed during an inconsequential siege and succeeded by his brother John. The Treaty of Le Goulet worked out between Philip and John, now the king of England, called for Evreux to become part of the dower lands for John's niece, Blanche of Castile, who was to marry Philip's son and heir Louis. To get Amaury VI to quitclaim Evreux to the French, John allowed him to become the 3rd earl of Gloucester by right of his mother Mabel, who had died the previous year. In fact, Mabel's younger sister Isabella was already the countess of Gloucester. John, who was then in the process of divorcing Isabella, was ready to accept both Amaury and Isabella as the lords of Gloucester despite the inevitable conflict it was bound to cause.[29]

By this time, Fulk of Neuilly had ratcheted up the preaching of the crusade. He was especially active in the Île-de-France, which included Montfort l'Amaury. Whether Simon ever heard or met Fulk is unclear, but on 28 November 1199, he and his brother Guy attended a tournament at Écry-sur-Aisne. Sometime during the festivities, Count Theobald of Champagne, the host of the tournament, joined his cousin Count Louis of Blois in making a public display of taking the cross to fight in the Holy Land.[30]

Simon, Guy and other knights in attendance then followed their lead. They were probably less inspired by the examples of the counts themselves than by the allure of crusading and the benefits it brought. Avowed crusaders were given crosses of cloth to wear and indulgences for their sins. As pilgrims, they would get to see the holy places of the Bible. If they fell in battle, they were martyrs. If they came home, they were heroes. They could also win land and riches overseas, all that for making war against a nameless infidel instead of their neighbours. In all likelihood, the de Montfort brothers had already decided to go and the tournament simply offered them the opportunity of adding showmanship and chivalry to their religious duty and devotion.[31]

Such was Simon's standing at the time that his name appears third in the list of the barons taking the cross in Geoffrey of Villehardouin's contemporary account of the tournament. He did not enjoy the comital status of his forebears, but the elevation of his cousin Amaury VI as the earl of Gloucester allowed Simon to present himself as the singular head of the house of Montfort in France. Following Écry, he adopted as his own counterseal the one used by his grandfather Simon III, the last of their line who was both the count of Evreux and lord of Montfort l'Amaury.

The rider in the image was no longer a mounted knight, rather an ordinary forester. While perhaps a strange guise for a man to adopt on the eve of a crusade, it also reflected the pastoral mission of Fulk of Neuilly, who anticipated the preaching of the friars in the new century. But mostly it was a reminder of the glory days of the de Montforts that had been and were yet to be.[32]

Chapter 2

The Fourth Crusade
1200–1205

The crusades had been launched at the end of the eleventh century to recapture Jerusalem for the Christian faith. The conquests made in the Holy Land at that time were carved up into what became the crusader states. In 1129, Fulk V of Anjou, the eldest son of Bertrade de Montfort, left his county in France to his son Geoffrey (the father of Henry II of England) to become the king of Jerusalem by right of his second wife Melisende, the heiress of the kingdom. Turkish encroachment accelerated after Fulk's death in 1143, leading to a second, disastrous crusade under Louis VII and Eleanor of Aquitaine. Jerusalem was later lost in 1187 after the crusader states were routed at the battle of Hattin.

The Third Crusade was undertaken in response, but the Germans had no stomach for it after their emperor Frederick Barbarossa drowned in Asia Minor in 1190 during their march overland. Philip Augustus arrived in the Holy Land next, ahead of Richard the Lionheart, who had been detained by an unexpected dispute on Cyprus. Together the two kings took Acre, but then Philip went back to France and Richard was unable to retake Jerusalem on his own. Having made loads of enemies among the Christian lords, Richard was kidnapped on his way home in 1192 and had to be ransomed from the clutches of the new Holy Roman Emperor.

He was Henry VI, Barbarossa's son, and in 1194 Henry used that ransom money, some £100,000, to conquer Sicily, which he claimed through his wife Constance, the last of the legitimate line of Normans who had ruled the island for a hundred years. To placate the papacy, who wanted the Germans out of Italy altogether, the emperor made plans to go on crusade, but he died of a fever in 1197 while still in Sicily. The following year the new pope, Innocent III, enlisted Fulk of Neuilly to preach the crusade, but it was not until the tournament at Écry did the mobilisation of knights and nobles get underway.[1]

The experience of previous crusades informed the commanders to seek passage by sea and in early 1201 Venice was contracted to provide it. Within weeks of the emissaries returning from Italy with the treaty, Theobald of Champagne, still in his early twenties, was dead of an unspecified illness. To take his place, Simon V journeyed to Burgundy to recruit his friend Duke Odo III. Going with him was Matthew of Marly, a veteran of the Holy Land who had also been at the tournament.[2] He and Simon were well acquainted with each other. They had witnessed acts together, Matthew was the captor of Simon's uncle Robert de Beaumont, and he was himself the uncle of Alice de Montfort. In the event, Odo declined their invitation, and the leadership of the crusade eventually went to Boniface, the marquis of Montferrat, whose family had a long history of involvement in the crusader states.[3]

Simon V and his brother Guy had eighteen months to make preparations for what could only be an expensive and arduous undertaking. Like most pilgrims, they sought provisions for their souls and those of their men by making grants to various religious houses. Of the funds they raised, £150 came from pledging their mother's dowry property of Winterbourne Stoke in Wiltshire for three years. Abbeys and priories with links to the de Montfort family also made contributions. The priory of Saint-Thomas d'Épernon, which was founded by their ur-ancestor Amaury de Montfort in the eleventh century and where Simon I and his elder sons were buried, added £40 to their war chest.[4]

In April 1202, Simon said goodbye to his wife Alice, their sons and household, doubtless with the same emotions described by Villehardouin of these departures in general: 'Many were the tears shed for pity and sorrow at their departure, by their own people and by their friends.' Simon and Guy probably went to Chartres to muster with the troops under Count Louis of Blois.[5] They travelled through Burgundy and the Alps and arrived in Pavia just south of Milan. Venice was still 290 kilometres to the east across the Lombard Plain.

Other leaders like Count Baldwin of Flanders had already arrived in Venice and taken up encampment on the Isle of St Nicholas (Lido). They could instantly see that something was wrong. In accordance with the treaty, the Venetians had assembled a fleet to carry 33,500 men and 4,500 horses. They were supposed to set sail on 29 June 1202 but not even a third of the expected force had shown up by then. The sailing date was pushed back in case many were just tardy. Their commander Boniface did not arrive himself until August.[6] But now word arrived that Count Louis of Blois was hesitating in Pavia, unsure whether to continue to Venice or turn south and seek passage from a port in Apulia.

Villehardouin does not give a specific reason for the count's vacillation, but it probably had to do with the treaty with Venice. The emissaries who negotiated it had wildly overestimated the size of their army. By agreeing to pay two marks per man and four marks per horse based on the numbers given to the Venetians, the crusaders owed 85,000 marks total.[7] Whoever showed up would have to help pay the balance still owed. Not wanting to get stuck with the bill or run the risk they might not sail at all from Venice, many crusading contingents had gone to other ports.

Another problem arising from the treaty was the decision not to sail for the crusader states. The fleet would go to Egypt to strike at the heart of the Turkish power there. If they captured the great port of Alexandria, they would cut the Islamic world in half. They could then conquer Cairo and free Jerusalem coming up from the south, or failing that, swap Alexandria for Jerusalem. As much as this made a lot of sense strategically, the leadership had tried and failed to keep it secret for fear it would deter the rank and file who had their hearts set on going to the Holy Land.[8]

Simon V was probably one of them. The exploits of his uncle Robert de Beaumont and stepfather William des Barres in Acre and Jaffa would have filled him with the desire to follow in their footsteps. Soon to show he was a natural military leader, Simon could appreciate the current plan, but it would definitely take an army of more than 30,000 men for a long, gruelling campaign in Egypt. As future crusades showed, they had no chance with less than half that size.

Count Louis was something of a rash figure and would normally not have needed much persuasion to forget about Venice. But he was one of the three principals to the treaty, the other two being Theobald and Baldwin. It would be unconscionable for him to bail out now even if he believed the emissaries had been extremely naive in their negotiations with the Venetians. Assured of this, Baldwin dispatched one of the emissaries, Villehardouin himself, and another senior commander Count Hugh of St Pol, to Pavia to appeal to Louis's sense of honour. They were successful and the contingents from Blois, Chartres and Montfort l'Amaury arrived on the Isle of St Nicholas to a rapturous welcome.[9]

But the mood in the host again turned tense when news arrived that Fulk of Neuilly had died in May. He had been the inspiration for many to take the cross and his death coming on the eve of their departure seemed like an omen. The mournful spirit, however, gave away to accusations that the money he had collected for the crusade had been siphoned off by Church officials, if not by Fulk himself, when it should have gone towards paying for the fleet. In fact, it was used to help poor crusaders with their expenses or sent for the relief of the crusader states, which were still dealing with the aftermath of a recent earthquake.[10]

By end of the summer, it was clear the crusade was in serious trouble. The Venetian state could not defer payment because it had assumed great debt in putting together the fleet. Preparations had consumed the life and business of this city of 100,000 for more than a year. Just manning the ships alone required 9,000 men, almost as many as there were crusaders. In desperation, the baronial leaders took up a collection among the host, then added everything they themselves had, including their gold and silver vessels. The Venetians were happy to haul it all away, but after it was counted up, a balance of 34,000 marks remained.[11] Keeping the money and not sailing was never an option for the Venetians. It would not only make them look bad, but possibly leave them open to an attack by the disgruntled crusaders, by now angry and restless after spending a hot summer in a squalid camp. So they offered them a deal. They would sail and evenly split the forthcoming conquests. The crusaders would then pay the balance out of their own half of the spoils.

The city of Zara on the Dalmatian coast, where Richard the Lionheart had been forced to make landfall prior to his imprisonment, was proposed as the first of such conquests. It had once been a part of Venice's trading empire, but had defected to the kingdom of Hungary and was preying on Venetian shipping. All attempts to retake it had failed.[12] The Venetians hoped the sight of the fleet would induce the Zarans to surrender, but if not, the crusaders would be obliged to help them conquer it.

The offer deeply divided the baronial leadership. Zara was a Christian city and its overlord, the king of Hungary, was a sworn crusader. To attack it under the guise of a crusade would be the worst kind of sacrilege. This was the argument of the opposing camp, whose numbers included Simon and Guy de Montfort. Those in favour of the diversion were anxious about the money they had just paid the Venetians and the shame of going home with their vows unfulfilled. Even if they tried to seek other passage, they could never keep the host together as a fighting force as it stood now. As for attacking Christians while on crusade, they all knew that that precedent had been set when Richard the Lionheart conquered Cyprus on his way to the Holy Land. In the end, the situation was clear. Without the fleet, the crusade was doomed.[13]

That prospect won over Cardinal Peter Capuano, the papal legate, who had already gone through the camp and sent home the sick, the poor and the women. The crusade had to be preserved at all costs, even if it necessitated an attack on Christians. To maintain some semblance of propriety, the legate would not sail with them, nor would the overall commander himself, Boniface of Montferrat. Both left for Rome to explain the unfortunate turn of events to the pope. Meanwhile, the doge of Venice, Enrico Dandolo, took the cross and exhorted other Venetians to follow his example. He was now the de facto leader of the crusade, even though he was blind and 95 years old.[14]

Hearing what was afoot, Pope Innocent dispatched a letter forbidding the crusaders to attack Zara under any circumstance. The letter was given to an abbot, Guy of Vaux-de-Cernay, who was instructed to go with the fleet and use the letter to prevent the shedding of Christian blood.[15] It was probably at his behest that Simon and Guy de Montfort boarded the ships despite their opposition to the diversion to Zara. The abbot was an old friend of the de Montfort family, who were benefactors of his abbey. Simon had been educated there and the abbot may have served as his tutor or even guardian during his minority.[16] Doubtless Guy of Vaux-de-Cernay had shown the de Montfort brothers the letter and prevailed upon them to accompany him for support.

The fleet reaches Zara, Simon leads the opposition, a new diversion

The fleet was given a magnificent send-off in the first week of October 1202. It consisted of 50 war galleys with 120 rowers each, 150 transports ships for men and horses, and 200 lighter craft. A hundred trumpeters on the quayside sounded their departure while the priests on board chanted *Veni Creator Spiritus*. They shot across the Gulf of Venice and leisurely made their way south along the opposite coast, making numerous stops to take on supplies, to allow the horses out to graze and move about, and to put these Istrian port cities on notice about the might Venice was able to bring down on them should they fail to cooperate. The measured pace was also meant to give the Zarans sufficient warning of their arrival, which took place on 10 November 1202.[17]

As hoped, the inhabitants were overawed by the show of force. Two days later a deputation of citizens made their way through the siege engines set up outside the walls to meet the doge in his pavilion of vermillion samite. They offered to surrender the city in return for their lives. Dandolo told them he could make no agreement without first getting the consent of the crusaders. It seems fantastic that he did not seize the victory outright. He was under no obligation to the crusaders, who in any case would have welcomed an outcome that avoided bloodshed. It has been argued that he wanted the Zarans to stew for a while, to savour the victory that had long eluded him.[18]

The real reason was probably more sinister. It was vital to maintain control of the city after the crusade had moved on. This necessitated a bit of terror, to proscribe the Zarans at the heart of the policy that flaunted Venetian authority, perhaps the very people standing in the doge's pavilion at that moment. This was the consent he was after. The Venetians and the French would agree to the deal, move in and occupy the city, and then the crusaders would not stand in the way of the condemned being put to the sword.

As a leading baron, Simon de Montfort was likely present when Dandolo intimated his own terms for the capitulation. However strongly Simon argued against it, his compatriots were imminently more practical men, less bothered by their consciences. Their concern was to keep the crusade in business and that meant appeasing the Venetians. Simon was nevertheless confident they would turn away from the unscrupulous design if ordered to do so by the pope. Since the Venetians were not strong enough to take the city themselves, he and the other dissidents decided to undermine the scheme by paying a visit to the Zaran delegation. It was probably Simon who spoke for them.

'The pilgrims will not attack you', he assured them. 'You have no need to fear them. If you can defend yourselves against the Venetians, you will be safe enough.' Heartened, the envoys left. The dissidents then chose Robert of Boves, whose brothers Enguerrand and Hugh were among them, to go up to the walls of the city and repeat the same words for anyone within earshot to hear.

When the doge and baronial chieftains entered the pavilion, they found that the envoys had gone and that a stern Simon de Montfort and his party were ready to confront them. Guy of Vaux-de-Cernay spoke first. In the name of the pope, he forbade them to attack the city.[19] Anyone who did otherwise would incur the sentence of excommunication. Dandolo was furious. As sworn crusaders, the papal ban fell on him and his Venetians. They grew so angry that they would have killed the abbot on the spot had Simon not stepped forward to protect him.[20]

Dandolo decided it was better to ignore the dissidents and again present himself and his people to the chieftains as the injured party in all these affairs. Knowing that the pope forgave as much as he excommunicated, that what Innocent wanted most of all was for the crusade to stay intact, and that the riches of the city beckoned them, the chieftains, including Louis of Blois, agreed to help the Venetians. To ease their consciences, they claimed, according to Villehardouin, that they were doing it because Simon and his party had sabotaged the surrender and so had brought dishonour on the host.[21]

They were wrong if they had hoped the Montfortian dissidents would join them in the assault out of feelings of guilt. Turning to the few Zarans who had remained behind to hear the outcome of the proceedings, Simon told them, 'Whatever other (crusaders) may do, you will suffer no harm from me or mine'. He then led the other dissenters to some distance from the main body and set up their camp there. The message they sent by this act was that no real crusader had any business associating with those cut off from the Roman church and its heavenly sacraments.[22]

The chieftains probably grumbled the medieval equivalent of 'spoiled sports' and went to work helping the Venetians reduce the city's defences. Within a fortnight the walls began to crumble. On 24 November 1202, the inhabitants knew they could no longer hold out. They repeated their offer to surrender in return for their lives. This time it was accepted outright, but it made no difference. The Venetians and French spared no one or nothing as they tore the town apart. Not even the churches escaped their greed and defilement.[23]

Just days later they turned on each other. At issue was how the Venetians and chieftains had got the better of the spoils, leaving little to the common crusader. On top of that came the news that the sailing season was over and they would all have to winter in and around the ruins of Zara. They would not leave until spring, a whole year after most of them had left their homes. The rank and file soldiers were justifiably frustrated with the delays and pummelled the Venetians in a street battle that claimed nearly a hundred lives. Only with difficulty was peace restored and after that many of the commoners refused to have anything more to do with the unholy partnership. Some took flight aboard merchant ships. One that was lost en route took 500 crusaders down with it. Others who tried to make their way inland fell victim to local peasants and Zaran guerrillas.[24]

The de Montfort brothers and their party stayed put. The sack of Zara had been vile and unlawful, but they were still anxious to keep the crusade together. They even sent one of their own, Robert of Boves, who had earlier shouted encouragement to the Zarans on the walls, to join a baronial mission to Rome to seek absolution for the crusaders who had defied the pope. He would vouch that it was the Venetians who instigated the attack. The French had been unwilling accomplices. Once that absolution had been procured, the Montfortian dissidents could rejoin the host. The mission did indeed procure it, but Robert, who had sworn to return to Zara, figured he could no longer trust the leadership and took a ship to the Holy Land from Italy.[25]

In December, Boniface of Montferrat arrived in Zara along with Simon's friend Matthew of Marly, who had stayed behind in Venice on account of illness. Two weeks later, on 1 January 1203, a group of German envoys arrived. The chieftains knew all about their coming. A year earlier Boniface, fresh from his election as commander of the crusade, had stopped at the court of Philip of Swabia. Philip, the younger son of Frederick Barbarossa, had been elected the king of Germany following the death of his brother Holy Roman Emperor Henry VI. Boniface had long supported their family, the Hohenstaufens, despite the opposition of the papacy. He had come to Philip to discuss the participation of Germans in the crusade, but Philip had another guest with him, his brother-in-law from Constantinople, and the conversation quickly turned to him.[26]

He was Alexius, the son of the deposed Byzantine emperor Isaac II Angelus. Having made his escape, Alexius appealed to Philip of Swabia to help restore his father to the throne in Constantinople. There was little Philip could do about it, but, we can imagine, he pointed to the marquis and said, 'My lord Boniface here has a whole crusade at his disposal'. However far the crusade might be of service to Alexius, Boniface floated the idea when he visited the pope. Innocent was already unhappy that the commander of his crusade was associating with Philip of Swabia, who was occupying the throne of Germany against his wishes and so had been excommunicated for it. He strictly forbade Boniface to give any more thought to Constantinople. He was to use the crusade to reclaim Jerusalem, nothing else.[27]

Having himself received short shrift from the pope, Alexius stalked the crusaders as far as Verona. At the connivance of Boniface, he sent envoys to meet the counts of Flanders, Blois and other chieftains in Venice. They were intrigued with the scheme, but said nothing to the host or Venetians. While absent from the crusade, Boniface arranged to have Philip send his own envoys directly to Zara to make the pitch for Alexius. Now, in the presence of the doge and his officials, these German envoys claimed that if the fleet sailed for Constantinople, the show of force alone would regain the throne for Alexius and his father. In return, the Byzantine prince promised to raise a force of 10,000 men for the crusade, take over supplying the army, and give them 200,000 marks.[28]

The Venetians were for it. They were still seeking full compensation for the massacre of their people in Constantinople three decades earlier, and the conquest of Zara had done nothing to relieve the debt owed to them by the crusaders. The chieftains as usual saw it in practical terms. They were running low on supplies and the Venetians were still clamouring for their money. Diverting to Constantinople would take care of both problems.[29]

The Montfortian dissidents were appalled by the callousness of these men. First Zara, now Constantinople, it had become a crusade against Christians. Probably the most galling for Simon was Matthew of Marly throwing in his lot with this new diversion.[30] The proposal itself was ludicrous. Alexius brought no down payments or security with him, only promises. Constantinople was huge, dwarfing the largest cities of Europe, and it had never fallen to a siege. The pope would surely condemn it. In the letters that arrived from Rome at this time, Innocent was furious that they had proceeded to attack Zara against his explicit prohibition. While willing to overlook it on account of their predicament, he wanted it understood that in no way were they to attack other Christians and he wanted it preached throughout the army.[31]

But he was far away, across the Adriatic. Most of the clergy with the crusade were for the diversion. Their main reason was that Alexius also promised to bring the Greek church under the control of Rome. The pope could only approve of this union of Christian churches. Since that was still in the future, the bishops and abbots decided to keep the papal letters secret for fear it would turn the host against the plan. Guy of Vaux-de-Cernay knew of the letters and strongly preached to the men to keep the Holy Land in their sights, but among the clerical and baronial leadership he and Simon were in the minority. The Venetians and chieftains drew up a treaty with the envoys. Alexius was to arrive in April and they would sail for Constantinople.[32] The crusade had been hijacked for good.

Journey to the Holy Land, Guy I gets married, tragic end to the crusade

Reconciliation was impossible. The dissidents refused to have anything more to do with the 'sinners' and left to make their way to the Holy Land alone. The safest way was the longest, going north along the Adriatic coast, then down the Italian peninsula. They commenced the trek after securing safe-conducts from the king of Hungary. The size of their company may have been quite large. Simon's known outlays for the crusade were just over 274 marks (£183). Had all that gone to the Venetians, it would have covered passage and one year's provisions for fourteen knights and their horses, twenty-nine servants and sixty-six men-at-arms.[33] Perhaps not all of his men defected with him, but he would have been joined by other dissatisfied crusaders. They included family friend Simon of Neauphle, Robert Mauvoisin, and Guy of Vaux-de-Cernay and his nephew Peter, who was a boy at the time.

According to Peter's later account, they hired ships once they reached Barletta. That makes the total distance they covered since leaving Zara 1,300 kilometres. Barletta, which sits very close to the battlefield of Cannae, was not as common a departure point for crusaders as Bari and Brindisi further down the coast, but they were understandably anxious with already one year of the crusade behind them and absolutely nothing to show for it. It was from one of these ports that Simon and Guy's great-great-uncle William, the bishop of Paris, left with his crusading host for, ironically enough, Constantinople a little over a century earlier. From there they took an easterly inland route and were wiped out by the Turks at Mersivan in north-central Asia Minor in August 1101. William was probably killed in the massacre, for he is not listed among the bishops who escaped the slaughter.[34]

There is no record of their voyage from Barletta, but typical crusade seafaring routes suggest a stop in Corfu was possible. There they would have heard of how the Fourth Crusade had nearly come to an end when the fleet pulled into the island after leaving Zara. The crusaders were to spend three restless weeks on Corfu waiting for Alexius to show up. During that time a meeting of Greek and Latin prelates degenerated into insults, with the local archbishop declaring that he could see no reason for the Roman primacy of the Christian church other than the fact that Roman soldiers had crucified Christ.

When Alexius arrived, the Greek inhabitants rejected his pretensions to the throne by bombarding the fleet with stones launched from catapults. The French and Venetians retaliated by devastating part of the island. By now the plan for the latest diversion was well known throughout the host and the majority of crusaders denounced it. 'What do we care about Constantinople', they scoffed. They had only contempt for Alexius when the prince begged them on his hands and knees. It was only after Boniface and the other chieftains also begged and wept did they agree to go, but with sworn assurances they would leave Constantinople within a month of arriving there.[35]

For the Montfortian party, the first stage of their voyage would have hugged the coastline of Greece until they rounded Cape Malea, then headed south to Crete or across the Aegean Sea to an island off Asia Minor. From one of these points they sailed to Cyprus and on to Palestine. Like most arrivals, they probably landed at Acre, but they would not have been heartily welcomed. For one thing, the crusaders who preceded them there had brought diseases that resulted in a plague. This led to an outflow of survivors heading back to Europe. Two of the ships carrying them encountered the Venetian fleet going the other way. Although these fleeing crusaders were deemed treacherous for not having gone to Venice in the first place, they were still invited to join the expedition to Constantinople and 'conquer some lands'. Only one man accepted.[36]

More worrisome for Aimery de Lusignan, the king of both Jerusalem and Cyprus, were hot-headed crusaders coming in and stirring up trouble. Aimery had concluded a five-year truce with his Muslim neighbours in 1198, which may have informed the decision to sail to Egypt. The truce was still in effect when the 'errant' crusaders began arriving. In 1201, the dying count of Champagne had entrusted one of them, Renaud of Dampierre, with money to fulfil his (Theobald's) crusading vow. When Aimery refused to break the truce, Renaud took eighty knights north to force a passage to the crusader state of Antioch. They were waylaid by the sultan of Aleppo, and Renaud ended up spending the next thirty years in captivity. One report says that Simon de Montfort was with them but had escaped capture.[37]

King Aimery also had to deal with certain nut cases, like a relative of Count Baldwin by the name of Thierry. He had sailed with other crusaders from Flanders but had got no further than Marseille when they learned of the diversion to Zara. While the fleet wintered in the south of France, Thierry met and married the daughter of Isaac, the last Greek emperor of Cyprus. In the spring, after learning of the latest diversion to Constantinople, his fleet sailed for the Holy Land and Thierry took his wife, whose name is unknown, with him. Once in Acre, he decided to press his claim to the Cypriot throne by right of his wife. Aimery was not amused. 'Who is this beggar?' asked the king. 'He should leave and be quick about it if he values his life.' Thierry and his wife too left for Antioch.[38]

Few crusaders would have begrudged the man his attempt. There was nothing implicit in the code of crusading that ruled out personal gain, as the Fourth Crusade had made abundantly clear by that point. Aimery himself had gained the throne of Jerusalem through marriage to his wife Isabella, a granddaughter of King Fulk (making her a descendant of the house of Montfort). Many a knight would be grateful to marry into a principality or lordship in the east, even if it meant never coming home.

One prospect that became available was Sidon, a coastal fiefdom just south of Beirut. Reginald Grenier, the lord of Sidon, had recently died. His widow was Helvis of Ibelin, the half-sister of Queen Isabella. Since her son Balian was still a youth, whoever Helvis married would be the acting lord during his minority. In the aftermath of the truce coming to an end, Guy de Montfort seems to have distinguished himself in the skirmishing with troops of the sultanate, because in September 1204, he earned the hand of Helvis from Aimery and Isabella. The couple were about the same age, in their mid-twenties (her late husband had been forty years older) and they quickly had a son, Philip. Guy I settled down to life in the Holy Land.[39]

By then the Fourth Crusade was over. The Venetians and French had successfully installed Alexius on the Byzantine throne, but he was hated by his people for bringing the accursed 'Latins' into their city. When he was strangled by another Greek usurper, the Latins responded by storming Constantinople on 12 April 1204. Over the course of three days, the crusaders burnt one-sixth of the city, altogether one-third of the dwellings for half a million people, and nearly the Hagia Sophia itself. They murdered priests, men and boys, raped nuns, women and girls, stripped all the palaces and churches of wealth and relics, with even the Latin clergy eagerly getting in on the plunder. Scrolls were looted or destroyed, bronze statues from antiquity melted down for coin. Much of the ancient world was lost in this singular devastation. Villehardouin was nevertheless proud and dared to make a bold statement in his chronicle: 'And well does Geoffrey of Villehardouin, the Marshal of Champagne, bear witness, that never, since the world was created, had so much booty been won in any city.'[40]

Innocent was happy at the time because it finally imposed the supremacy of the Roman church. Not until the following year, when the details of the destruction reached him, did he react with shame and disgust. The crusader states would also suffer as word of the Byzantine conquest lured away much of their manpower. Those who had shunned the diversion now wanted to share in the spoils. Even the legate, Cardinal Peter, who had not seen the crusading army since it sailed from Venice, hurriedly left the kingdom of Jerusalem to get in on the action. They were gladly welcomed. A whole empire had been conquered and reinforcements were needed to keep it all together.[41]

Simon de Montfort would not be one of them. The crusade had been a monstrosity from the get-go and he wanted no part of it. Killing Christians, defiling churches, thumbing their nose at the pope every step of the way. Perhaps he spent his three years in the Holy Land participating in building projects, defensive works, even ministering the sick, all as an act of atonement for his former comrades. If so, he was unable to save them. Count Louis of Blois and Boniface of Montferrat were shortly killed defending their conquests in Greece. Baldwin of Flanders, who had been elected the new emperor, disappeared inside a Bulgarian prison. Matthew of Marly succumbed to illness in Constantinople in 1205, as did Dandolo, albeit in his 98th year. Before his death, the shrewd old doge wrote a letter to the pope justifying the hell they had unleashed. While admitting that 'a great massacre of Greeks had taken place,' his tone was unrepentant. They had nothing to be sorry for.[43]

Chapter 3

Inheritance and Heresy
1206–1209

As the de Montfort brothers were leaving on crusade, war was about to erupt again between England and France. It went back to Richard's death three years earlier and his lack of an heir apparent. He had named John as his successor before succumbing to gangrene, but the two of them had a nephew, Arthur of Brittany, with a better claim to the throne. Philip Augustus was as eager as ever to drive the Plantagenets out of their Continental domains, Normandy first and foremost, but was not quite strong enough for it. The Treaty of Le Goulet of 1200 settled it for the time being, but then John divorced his wife Isabella, the heiress of Gloucester, and married another Isabella, the far younger heiress of Angoulême. In doing so, he offended the powerful Lusignan family of Poitou, who had their sights set on the well-endowed girl themselves. They formed a league with Philip and the disaffected Arthur and struck in the summer of 1202.

John captured Arthur and the Lusignans, but then alienated his allies and scandalously treated his prisoners. Several knights were starved to death and Arthur vanished, probably murdered at his orders. As John's overlord, King Philip declared his fiefs forfeited and attacked. He forced the submission of Norman barons loyal to the English monarchy, not at all worried that these men were essentially traitors. Philip was planning to discard them anyway, calling them little better than soiled toilet paper.[1] The summer of 1204 saw the crusading chieftains celebrating their conquest of Constantinople and the king of France his own conquest of Normandy, Maine and Anjou.

The Anglo-Norman aristocracy now had a tough choice to make. By swearing allegiance to Philip, they stood to lose their lands in England, or in France for remaining loyal to John. Amaury VI de Montfort chose Philip, probably because John had given him only a meagre amount of the earldom of Gloucester that Amaury had inherited from his mother. He held just twenty knights' fees out of more than 300. He was stripped of his English lands as a result, but gained them back in October 1204 after the loss of Normandy. He was one of the few lords allowed to hold land of both kings, and as a mark of this distinction he called himself the count of Evreux and earl of Gloucester. He likely preferred the French title, as his aunt, John's ex-wife Isabella, continued to call herself the countess of Gloucester.[2]

The situation was much more complicated for Simon's uncle Robert IV de Beaumont, the 4th earl of Leicester, whose holdings were far more extensive. He held 120 knights' fees in Normandy alone. In September 1203, John gave him the earldom of Richmond in the north, recently confiscated from the count of Brittany, as compensation for Robert's losses on the Continent. The following April, Robert joined William Marshal and other magnates on an embassy from John to Philip to seek peace. He and Marshal took the opportunity of cutting their own deal. They offered the king of France 500 marks (£333) each to defer the decision on their allegiance. Philip took the money and gave them a year and a day to decide. In the end, Robert did not have to make the painful decision. Still in his mid-forties, he took ill and died on the night of 20 October 1204.[3]

Robert left a widow Loretta, whose parents William and Maude de Braose were later repressed by John with great cruelty. She was probably still a teenager at his death and the union produced no children. As the eldest of Robert's two sisters, Amicia de Montfort claimed the title to the earldom and began styling herself the countess of Leicester. Like her brother, she made her own deal with Philip Augustus. She transferred all of Robert's holdings in Normandy, including the wealthy honor of Breteuil, to the French royal demesne in exchange for the castle of Saint-Léger and forest of Yveline. In this way, she increased the dominions of Montfort l'Amaury at the loss of what had been lost anyway. She agreed to compensate her sister Margaret with her share of their inheritance in England.[4]

The real loser was Amicia and Margaret's mother Petronilla. When she wed their father, the 3rd earl of Leicester, in the mid-1150s, she was the heiress to the honor of Grandmesnil in Normandy. She had to leave

France for married life in England much as her daughter Amicia had to leave England for married life in France. With the conquest of Normandy, Grandmesnil was lost to her, but it so happened that the original lands of the earldom of Leicester came from an Englishman named Ivo de Grandmesnil. He was at best a distant cousin of hers, but the namesake coincidence represented an opportunity just the same. Petronilla made a claim for the earldom of Leicester as a Grandmesnil heiress and offered King John a fine of 3,000 marks (£2,000) to recognise it.

At this point Margaret and her husband Saher de Quincy could see they were going to be left with nothing. They challenged her mother and upped the ante with a bid of 5,000 marks. Petronilla's claim to the earldom was quickly found to be bogus and in March 1205 Saher was put in effective control of the estate. The division between the sisters still awaited the arrival of Amicia, but eighteen months after Robert's death and she had still not shown up. She may have been worried it might upset the good deal she had with her liege lord Philip Augustus. Finally, her son Simon V returned from the east, so she sent him to England in her place.[5]

Simon was a French vassal, but Philip allowed him to pursue the claim to Leicester, probably out of respect for his loyalty during the Norman wars and his unblemished service as a crusader. King John did not stand in his way, either, presumably because Simon had not taken part in the conquest of Normandy. He issued him a safe-conduct to come to England and paid his expenses after he arrived in June 1206. Sometime after that, Simon did homage to John and officially became the 5th earl of Leicester.

There was much about the division of the earldom that Simon did not like, but he was given lands with a respectable net yield of £237. Then, in mid-February 1207, John ordered them seized until he received the money 'which the earl owes us'. He was referring to the fine that Simon evidently refused to pay. It is unknown what amount John was seeking, only that Simon rejected it, either out of principle over the fairness of the division or, more likely, it had been grossly inflated. On 22 February, Simon was formally dispossessed of Leicester. He had probably gone home by then, disillusioned by the rapacity and deceit that confronted him during his first and only trip to England.[6]

In all likelihood this was the outcome John had been striving for. His recent failure to recover his lost Angevin lands convinced him his barons were not to be trusted. In getting rid of Simon, he not only had one less potentially troublesome baron to worry about, but was also able to profit from his lands. Indeed, royal custodians raised £308 from the sale of woods in Simon's half of Leicester during the next two years of the confiscation, something his son would bitterly recall more than fifty years later.

Naturally it all had to look very legal and official, hence John's initial cooperation. Saher de Quincy himself may have been in on the scheme. John had created him the 1st earl of Winchester by the time the final settlement of the estate was published on 10 March 1207, and the king made sure to compensate him and Margaret for her lost Norman lands out of Simon's share of Leicester, even out of Amicia's English dowry.[7] Saher may have known that John intended to slap Simon with an outrageous fine, much like the 20,000 marks the king later demanded from Geoffrey de Mandeville to marry his ex-wife Isabella of Gloucester. Ironically, when the barons decided they had had enough of John's arbitrary way of doing business and sought to impose Magna Carta on him, Saher de Quincy was one of their leaders.

Simon's trip across the Channel did get him what he probably wanted most, a comital title. Whether he was in possession of his English estates or not, he was the earl of Leicester and now began to fashion himself so in combination with his longstanding title of lord of Montfort.[8] By this point he was a man in his mid-thirties, who had spent nearly all of the past five years away from Montfort l'Amaury. Only two members of his pre-crusade affinity were still around. If the others had journeyed with him overseas as is likely, they had died there or perhaps stayed behind with his brother. His mother Amicia served as his regent of the lordship in his absence, acting independently but securing his consent and ratification whenever possible.

This arrangement probably brought her into conflict with her daughter-in-law Alice, but Simon's relations with his wife's relatives seemed to have suffered none over his break with her uncle Matthew of Marly during the crusade. He cooperated with his brother-in-law Matthew Montmorency in the management of Alice's dowry at Conflans, and in February 1207, probably just after his return from England, he was appointed as arbitrator in a case brought by Montmorency against the royal abbey of Saint-Denis. Simon must have had a reputation for fairness and integrity if the monks of the abbey were willing to let someone with close links to the plaintiff decide the outcome of the case.[9]

The spread of heresy, a new crusade

During the Fourth Crusade, Simon de Montfort would have encountered Christians in Dalmatia who had a completely different view of Christianity than he did. For him, it was about believing in an omniscient God, his son Jesus Christ, and in the Trinity which they formed together with the Holy Spirit. But these other people practiced a sect of dualism that denied that the material world had been created by God. They claimed it was the work of Lucifer, who was either a fallen angel or, in the minds of absolutists, a deity equal to God in the eternal struggle between good and evil. In seeking to overcome God's supreme authority, Lucifer lured other angels to Earth, a new world he had created below. Once seduced, they were trapped inside the bodies of fleshy creatures and started to populate the planet. The angels thus became the souls of these walking and talking 'skins' who longed to escape the state of matter in order to rejoin the spiritual world.

A messenger was dispatched to reclaim them, but not in any incarnated form, else he too would become imprisoned. In this sense, Jesus was merely a phantom presence who preached salvation of the soul before returning to the heavenly host. To carry on his work, he left behind a church imbued with the Holy Spirit, but naturally there could be nothing material about it. The sacraments that soon came to define the Catholic Church were more of Lucifer's perfidious guile. They were false instruments devised to corrupt the purity of the true Christian mission. Being material in any case, they were inherently evil. Anyone seeking salvation through the ritual of mass, the cross and veneration of relics and the Virgin Mary was on the wrong path indeed.

Although dualism went back to the early days of Christianity, this particular form, which in itself had many offshoots, arose in the Balkans in the tenth century. The Slavic inhabitants, recently converted by

Greek missionaries, found there was much they liked about the Paulician dualism planted there by a large Armenian settlement. The sect that subsequently achieved dominance throughout the region took on the name of Bogomilism, meaning 'beloved of God'. For them, the true god of the Old Testament was Satan and all the world around them was evil. Good existed only in the spiritual realm. They avoided animal products and tried to abstain from sex because procreation created prisons for more souls. The crucifix and other objects of Catholic worship filled them with horror and disgust.[10]

Bogomilism had spread throughout Dalmatia by the time the Fourth Crusade arrived. The pope's attempts to prod the king of Hungary into crushing the sect had been unsuccessful. Zara, a mercantile port city, may have been an exception. It is unlikely Innocent III or Simon V would have gone out of their way to save its inhabitants if they subscribed to beliefs that were anathema to them. The Zarans even tried to fend off the crusaders by hanging crosses over their walls, something no right-minded Bogomil would ever do, least of all to save their skins. Simon and his party probably came across their communities as they made their way north to re-enter Italy. Peter of Vaux-de-Cernay writes that their journey was full of 'hardships and unbelievable labours', suggesting they may have come into personal conflict with them and their preaching.[11]

Simon was certainly familiar with dualist sects before leaving on crusade. They had become established in northern Europe over the past century, imported, some said, by Frenchmen returning from Constantinople after the First Crusade.[12] The Church had only itself to blame for the inroads they made. Bloated and ornamented clergymen living in sumptuous palaces had left it struggling with the image of a corrupt institution. The heretics underscored what set them apart from their Catholic brethren by calling themselves Cathars. Derived from the Greek word *katharos*, they were the 'pure ones' as opposed to the debauched and negligent priesthood.

There were, moreover, other sects. In 1173, around the time of Simon's birth, Peter Waldo of Lyon renounced riches and luxury for poverty and squalor. He and his like-minded followers preached that the Church needed a good spiritual cleansing, not with holy water, because such sacraments were useless, but by divesting itself of property and going back to the fundamentals. While perhaps not going as far as the Cathars, the Waldensians and other heretical groups were open in their contempt for ecclesiastic tradition and authority. Venerable fathers like Bernard of Clairvaux, who had done much to reform and reinvigorate the Church, thought reason would bring them around, but he was exasperated after his own missions failed. 'If they prefer to die than believe', he gasped, 'then let them die'.[13]

It was medieval lay society that first took extreme measures against them. Ordinary Catholic worshippers might agree that the salvation of the soul was everything and that the world was bleak and, if not evil, certainly sinful, but they made the best of it with song, dance, meat and sex whenever possible. Atonement for whatever frivolity and good life they enjoyed was no problem because the sacraments also appealed to their senses. Looking at Jesus on the cross and partaking of his body and blood during mass were spiritually fulfilling in a way anybody, not just a priest, could feel and understand. Lazarus, the Resurrection and Ascension, were affirmations that miracles existed in the material world, that hope had a real place in their lives. Now, according to this new interpretation, it was all nonsense and superstition. Baptism by water, the tithes they paid, the pilgrimages they made, all had been for nothing. They were not necessarily damned because of it, but those who persisted in such foolishness could expect a torturous path to salvation. Their souls would have to undergo repeated reincarnation until they were deemed cleansed of their flirtation with the devil's worship.

Local communities were sufficiently outraged by this blasphemy and denigration of their beliefs and set out to lynch and burn the heretics themselves, without waiting for the sentence of any court. The heretics probably would not have sought protection from the authorities in any case. Some souls, they believed, had been created by Satan himself to run his world. They inhabited the skins of princes and prelates and would be revealed and extinguished in the final struggle. There was no sense turning to these 'demons' for help.[14] The secular arm had a long history of clamping down on heresy in any case, seeing it as a disrupting and corrupting influence on society. Nearly two centuries earlier in 1022, as Amaury I de Montfort was beginning his rise at court, three heretics in Orleans, one of them the confessor to the queen, were given full judicial treatment before being taken outside the city walls and burned.[15]

The combination of church, state and the mob made northern Europe an inhospitable environment for heresy, but the south of France was a different story. Indeed, Languedoc was a whole different world. It was famous for manners and romanticism, which they celebrated in their own language, Occitan, and in the fancy dress, entertainment and general splendour of courtly life missing from the north. Cathars and Waldensians would have found this preoccupation with goods and fashion decadent and superficial, but southern society was also very fluid and tolerant, partly due to the crusade trade. Jews could find positions of authority there unheard of elsewhere.

But Languedoc also had its dangerous side. Unlike the north, where bureaucratic centralisation and primogeniture had strengthened feudal bonds, the great estates in the south had been divided up within the family, creating an independent, fragmented caste of petty lords who warred with each other despite their ties of kinship. With no regular knight-service to summon, they relied on foreign mercenaries to do their dirty work. These warriors, usually from Flanders or Catalonia, had no fixed address or loyalty. A local lord might hire them to seize a castle or rough up his neighbour, but business being what it is, the mercenaries might come for him the next day after getting a better offer from the neighbour.

Successive popes railed against this practice, not least because the clergy tended to suffer from the depredations. The southern nobility often targeted church property and money for their own use, leaving some parishes so poor they had to be abandoned. This creeping poverty forced local bishops to spend more time on doing their books than ensuring villagers received proper spiritual care. Some prelates even hired their own mercenaries to take back what was theirs or defend what was left of it. It was in this atmosphere of war, desolation and neglect that the heretics found their most fertile crop.[16]

For one thing, their preachers made a lot of sense. No good and just God would create a world of such glaring violence and inequality, of endless toil, hunger and sadness. It had to be the work of Lucifer. If material deprivation was the key to their salvation, then the peasantry had spent their whole lives on the right trajectory. Nobody was telling them to give up Jesus as their saviour, just to look at the cross he was nailed to for what it was, an instrument of torture, unworthy of their belief. The Holy Spirit was still theirs for the taking, all they had to do was want it. It was all straightforward and simple and easy to understand, in part because it was understandable. Heretical ministers preached the Gospels to them in their own tongue, not in any of that Latin rot, which not every priest himself was sufficiently fluent in.

The only hard part seemed the actual purification process itself. Cathar initiates had to undergo a long period of rigorous living and devotion before the elders baptised them in the Holy Spirit. They had to swear off all sex and food of animal origin (because they were the product of sex), they had to promise to never lie or take an oath (because it was like putting a lien on the soul), and they had to never, ever renounce the faith, even if death by fire awaited them. The ceremony culminated in the *consolamentum*, where the minister placed his hands on the shoulders of the initiate, who read aloud the Lord's Prayer. Having thus been 'consoled' for the life they had previously lived, initiates now submitted themselves to poverty and total commitment. They walked about in black robes and barefoot, typically with a similarly consoled companion, preaching the mission and everywhere being received with awe and reverence. In the eyes of the Church, they were the perfect heretics.[17]

These 'perfects' as they were called included females, which was not surprising given the greater prominence of women in southern society than in the north, but few Cathars of either sex aspired for such austerity in their lives. They were content to be believe and wait until the end of their days to receive the *consolamentum*, when they could no longer rise from the deathbed. There were enough of these faithful (*credentes*) by the middle of the twelfth century to start organising themselves into an official religion. In 1167, they held the Catholic equivalent of a convocation in the town of St-Felix-de-Caraman near Toulouse. The honoured guest was a Bulgarian 'pope' from Constantinople named Niquinta. Apparently he had been summoned there because the Cathars could not agree among themselves about their own doctrine. He informed them that the dualist churches in the east were all separate and distinct, yet did nothing contradictory to each other. 'They are at peace among themselves', he told the gathering. 'You do likewise.'[18]

Several attendees received the *consolamentum* from Niquinta's hands. One of these new perfects, Robert, was named the bishop of France. He not only came from the north, as his title suggests, but from Épernon, which lay on the road to Chartres on the southwest fringes of the Montfort lordship. The oldest religious house in the family, the priory of Saint-Thomas, had been founded in Épernon by Amaury I in the eleventh century.[19] At the time of the Cathar convocation in Saint-Felix, Simon III was the count of Evreux and lord of Montfort. What if any action he took against heresy is unknown, but given his family's religious connection to Épernon, it is unlikely he would have allowed Robert to return there with notions of turning Montfort l'Amaury into a Cathar diocese. Nothing more is heard of Robert after his appointment.

In 1179, Simon V was a young boy, just commencing his education at the abbey of Vaux-de-Cernay. In March of that year, the Third Lateran Council opened in Rome. In addition to the usual announcement of reforms, the Church condemned heretics and mercenaries and called on secular rulers to suppress them both. But it was a losing cause. By the turn of the century, nearly every baronial family in the south was connected to heresy in some form or other. When a local knight told the bishop of Toulouse of his own reawakening in the Catholic faith, the bishop was sceptical because he had not expelled heretics from his lands. The knight explained that he and others were powerless to do it. 'We were brought up with them, there are many of our relatives amongst them.' And besides, he added, 'We can see their way of life is a virtuous one'. This blanket protection not only allowed the heretics to live freely in the open, but to taunt and ridicule the Catholic Church with contemptuous names like the Whore of Babylon.[20]

In Pope Innocent III, the Cathars found themselves faced with a pope it would have been better not to call names. After his election in 1198, he promoted a policy for Languedoc that was summed up in the phrase 'the business of peace and faith' (*negotium pacis et fidei*). Inclined to blame his bishops and priests for being lazy and uninspired, Innocent launched an intensive preaching campaign in the hope of crushing the twin abominations of mercenaries and heretics. He dispatched legates and abbots to win back the fallen. Dominic de Guzman, the later canonised founder of the Dominicans, attempted to succeed where St Bernard had failed a half century earlier, but nearly a decade on and not much progress had been made.[21]

Innocent turned his fury on local lay leaders, accusing them of tolerating, even sympathising with the Cathars. He especially had Raymond VI, the count of Toulouse, in mind, but like the other lords in the fractious region, Raymond was unable to impose his authority on his vassals. Not that he would have wanted to in any case. The heretics were everywhere, connected to practically every family, even members of the Catholic clergy. Raymond's personal history, which included five wives, suggested he simply lacked the vigour and conviction to tackle the problem.[22] To papal officials, his inaction amounted to wilfulness, and in March 1207 he was excommunicated. In a letter of more than 13,000 words, Innocent warned him, in no uncertain terms, to get his act together.

> God may suddenly strike you down, and his anger deliver you to everlasting torment. Even if you are permitted to live, do not suppose that misfortune cannot reach you. You are not made of iron. You are weak and vulnerable, like other men. Fever, leprosy, paralysis, insanity, incurable disease may all attack you like any other of your kind.[23]

To show that he meant business, Innocent wrote to Philip Augustus of France, urging to him to consider a crusade against the heretics. 'Let the strength of the crown and the misery of war bring them back to the truth.' In December 1207, Raymond invited two papal legates to come to Saint-Gilles to discuss the terms of lifting the sentence over him. One of them was Peter of Castelnau, who had laboured long and hard in the region and had accumulated an abundance of threats and hatred as a result. When Raymond kept hedging, Peter declared that the meeting was a waste of time and left despite Raymond's insistence that they try to break the impasse. In his anger, Raymond saw Peter off with a warning to watch his step. On the morning of 14 January 1208, as Peter and his party were approaching the River Rhône, a lone horseman galloped up from behind and ran the legate through with a sword.[24]

The crusade begins, Béziers is sacked, Carcassonne surrenders, Simon is appointed leader

In 1170, nearly four decades before these events, Raymond's father-in-law Henry II of England had used intemperate words that led four of his knights to murder the archbishop of Canterbury. The killer of Peter of Castelnau was said to have been one of Raymond's knights, a loyal servant who also thought he was doing his lord a favour by getting rid of an annoying churchman. Neither his identity nor proof of Raymond's involvement in the murder has ever been established, but Innocent believed there were 'sure indications that he must be presumed guilty of the death of that holy man'. Raymond might have staved off disaster by making a show of seeking justice for the legate and stepping up the fight against heresy, but in the end he did nothing. On 10 March 1208, the pope proclaimed a crusade against him and the heretics.[25]

'Forward then soldiers of Christ!' he thundered. He expected the king of France to lead the crusade, but the response he received was not hopeful. France was on a war alert in the north, said Philip Augustus. King John aimed to wrest Normandy back and had entered an alliance with his nephew Otto of Brunswick, who was then the papal favourite to become the next Holy Roman Emperor. Philip claimed he dared not lead an army south while he had 'two great and dangerous lions on his flanks'. He also gave the pope some legal advice. He should initiate proceedings against Raymond, who was the king's cousin and vassal, before condemning him outright. It was a harsh rebuke for the lawyerly pontiff. Early in his career, Innocent had studied theology in Paris among the Masters, a circle of reforming clergymen who looked to the law first and foremost to justify religious action. He should not have left himself open to a lecture in due process that he himself was apt to give others.[26]

After consideration, Philip allowed a couple of ranking nobles, along with 500 knights, to join the crusade. Senior among them was Odo III, the duke of Burgundy. His father Hugh had made a name for himself during the Third Crusade and had died at Acre, but Odo, it will be remembered, chose to sit out the Fourth Crusade. He immediately thought of his friend Simon de Montfort, who had tried to get him to join that earlier crusade. Odo wrote a letter and gave it to Simon's mentor Guy of Vaux-de-Cernay to deliver it to him in person.

According to Guy's nephew Peter, the abbot found Simon at the church in Rochefort just southeast of Montfort l'Amaury. Simon was moved to pick up a psaltery and put his finger on the first line. He then handed it to Guy and asked him to read it. 'For (the lord) shall command his angels on your behalf to guard you in all your ways. They shall bear you up in their hands, lest your foot stumble on a stone.' It suggested that Simon, should he undertake the crusade, would have guardian angels watching over him. Subsequent events, Peter assures us, will show that this moment was not coincidence, rather divine intervention.[27]

The last crusade had taken Simon away from home for four years. Since his return, he and Alice had added two more children to their family, a daughter Amicia and son Simon. Crusading in the south would be less burdensome on them because Languedoc was a few days' ride away and the term of service only forty days. While it would be a crusade against Christians, it was justified by the Paris masters on the grounds that heretics who subverted Church doctrine could be compelled to convert through preaching or spiritual weapons like excommunication. If both failed, force and confiscation could then be deployed. The peaceful persuasion had been going on there for more than half a century, and lately Catholic preachers had adopted the pastoral approach of the Cathars and Waldensians to win the heretics back, all to no avail. Simon would have heard all about it from Guy of Vaux-de-Cernay, who had been one of a dozen abbots preaching in the south and was in close contact with the Paris circle.[28]

The army mustered at Lyon on 24 June 1209. It was the feast day of St John the Baptist, another biblical figure held in contempt by the heretics. Conscious of the misguidance of the last crusade, Innocent was determined to control this one from the centre as much as possible. To that end, overall command of the army was given to the senior legate in the field, a southern churchman from Catalonia named Arnaud-Amalric. As the abbot of Cîteaux since 1201, he was the head of the Cistercians, the order of white monks founded by St Bernard, which had done the most to combat heresy. Arnaud-Amalric had been at it himself for the past five years. In his *The Song of the Cathar Wars*, William of Tudela describes how the abbot 'went up and down the heretics' country, preaching to them and begging them to repent. But the more he begged them, the more they laughed at him and scorned him for a fool'.[29] Now, with an army of Franks from the north, Arnaud-Amalric set out to teach them a little humility.

The target was supposed to be Toulouse, but Raymond, having found no support or allies anywhere, agreed to be reconciled to the Church. This called for him to accept every condition imposed on him, including dismissing his mercenaries. But then he went further and asked to join the crusade. It was a cynical ploy to shield his own lands from the coming war and destruction, but Innocent would not deny Raymond now that he had so completely capitulated. Arnaud-Amalric saw it as a sham, but the pope ordered it and so he obeyed. There were plenty of heretical hotspots elsewhere and the target was now switched to the domains of the Trencavel family south of Toulouse.[30]

The viscount there was Raymond's nephew, Raymond-Roger, and in the preceding years the two neighbours had been more at war with each other than at peace. Raymond had proposed that they close ranks against the Church, but when they could not agree, Raymond went over to the Church to make sure it was his nephew's lands that suffered and not his own. Learning of his uncle's treachery, Raymond-Roger tried to negotiate, but the other legate, Milo, rejected his entreaties. By this time Arnaud-Amalric had put his army on the road for Béziers.

'God be my witness, it was an enormous force', says William of Tudela, although his estimate of 250,000 is more than ten times the actual size. The viscount dashed ahead of them to warn his subjects. He conferred with the inhabitants of Béziers, then left for his other stronghold of Carcassonne seventy kilometres further west, taking some heretics and the entire Jewish population of the town with him.[31]

Located on the River Orb about ten kilometres from the Mediterranean coast, Béziers was reckoned strong enough to force a protracted siege. The first to arrive outside its wall were the camp-followers and servants who set up the tents and bivouacs for the army. The bishop of Béziers rode out past them to meet Arnaud-Amalric and the other chieftains in the rear, then returned with a list of heretics who should surrender themselves. If they refused, the other citizens were advised to evacuate and leave the heretics to their fate. The town leaders were convinced the army would be unable to provision itself in the heat of summer and rejected their offer. Some Catholics nevertheless left when the bishop did.[32]

The next day was 22 July 1209. Seeing how the main body of crusaders was still not in position, some members of the garrison opened the gate and charged at the camp-followers, even releasing a volley of arrows at them. They thought it would be fun, and perhaps it was until they captured one of the servants, slew him and threw him off the bridge. The chief of the servants was enraged by it and ordered his men to pick up whatever they could find and attack. As the defenders bolted back inside the city, the camp-followers swarmed after them with sticks and tent poles and in a short time managed to breach the gate. The arrogance of the garrison turned into fright as they fled with the civilians for the safety of the cathedral. Béziers had fallen in a matter of hours, taken as if by miracle.

The camp-followers had already claimed the town and the riches inside it when the knights rode in. Despite having done nothing to secure the victory, the mounted warriors clubbed these men of low-birth out into the streets and seized all the goods and houses for themselves. One of these ungrateful wretches was Simon de Montfort, for he is found in possession of at least one house in Béziers after the army had moved on. The camp-followers and servants took out their anger and disappointment on the civilian population and set fire to the cathedral and parts of the town.[33]

A letter sent by the legates to the pope says that none of the townsfolk were spared, which led to the later invention that Arnaud–Amalric had given orders to 'kill them all'. He probably did not arrive on the scene until after the sack was over. Of the roughly 10,000 inhabitants, it is impossible to know how many were killed or how much of the town was destroyed before order was restored. The speed and suddenness at which it was taken naturally suggested a slaughter had taken place and the thought of something similar awaiting anyone who resisted the crusaders was enough to open the way to Carcassonne.[34]

As the siege of that imposing fortress with twenty-six towers got underway on 1 August, Simon is seen in action for the first time. He led the assault that took one fortified suburb below the walls. When the crusaders were then repulsed in their assault on the other suburb, he alone, with a single squire, risked a hail of stones coming from above to rescue a knight who had fallen with a broken leg.[35]

King Peter II of Aragon was Raymond-Roger's nominal overlord and arrived with a company of 100 knights to negotiate a peaceful end. Just then sitting down to a dinner of roasted meat, the crusaders invited the king to join them. Arnaud-Amalric told him that he would only allow Raymond-Roger and eleven others to leave the town with their possessions, but the rest had to surrender. Peter angrily replied, 'That will happen when donkeys fly'. Raymond-Roger was prepared to have his men skinned alive than accept the terms, but after the king left, the heat and lack of water began to take its toll on the town, which was swollen with refugees. After two weeks of the siege, Raymond-Roger came out to parley. Eager not to lose Carcassonne to pillage and fire, Arnaud-Amalric agreed the townsfolk could leave in peace, but only with the barest of clothes on their backs. They walked out with nothing but their sins, says Peter of Vaux-de-Cernay, with most going north to Toulouse, others south to Aragon.[36]

With the exception of horses and mules, the spoils became the war chest of the crusade and were placed under guard. The chieftains decided that the next course of action was to depose Raymond-Roger, who had freely given himself up as a hostage, and to elect one of their own as the new viscount. He would be given all the Trencavel lands, but encumbered with the responsibility to continue the war against the heretics. The offer was made to the ranking nobles, first to the count of Nevers, then to the duke of Burgundy, but neither wanted what was going to be a long, brutal assignment with no foreseeable end in sight.

A committee of seven, consisting of four knights, two bishops and Arnaud-Amalric, took up the matter and unanimously agreed that Simon's pedigree, integrity and crusade experience all recommended him for the job. But he was no fool, either, and flatly refused. The duke and legate fell on their knees and begged him, but to no avail. Peter of Vaux-de-Cernay says it took a direct order from Arnaud-Amalric for him to accept the 'burden and the honour', while William of Puylaurens has Simon himself saying 'God's business should not be frustrated for the want of a single champion'.[37] The legates announced his appointment in their letter to the pope.

So that this land which God has given into the hands of his servants may be preserved for his honour and the honour of the Holy Roman Church and all Christendom, the nobleman Simon de Montfort, a man well known (we believe) to your holiness, most courageous in arms and most devoted to the faith, desirous of applying his every effort to persecuting heresy, has by common consent been chosen leader and lord of the territory.[38]

At this stage it might be worth noting the personal qualities and appearance of the new commander of the crusade, then approaching forty years of age. William of Tudela says Simon was generous, kind, honourable, pleasant, and a good horseman. Peter of Vaux-de-Cernay, who all but worshipped him, describes him as tall and muscular, with strikingly handsome features and a splendid head of hair. He adds that rarely has an individual been endowed with so many gifts at once, 'whether naturally present or provided by God's grace'.[39]

Although the reader is assured that these advantages did not instill excessive pride in Simon, it is entirely possible that he really wanted the job. He had a growing family, relatively modest fiefdom in the north, and leadership skills that had been underappreciated during the last crusade. It must have still gnawed at him how the renegade French barons who conquered Constantinople in defiance of the pope had been showered with praise and absolution by Innocent afterwards. His own 'numerous successes against the pagans' in the Holy Land, conducted in full obedience to the pope, went unnoticed.[40] The way he may have seen it, the Church owed him.

Consideration should also be given to a charter issued by Simon in August 1209 granting three houses he had confiscated from the heretics to Arnaud-Amalric and his abbey of Cîteaux.[41] There is no way of knowing if the grant was made before his election, in effect him lobbying the legate, or after it as thanks for his promotion. Assuming he did make Arnaud-Amalric and the barons beg him, there was probably more to it than wringing recognition out of them. The crusaders were given indulgences and other benefits for a forty-day term of service. With that now at an end, Simon wanted to make sure he received adequate support in men and material. In both, he was disappointed at the outset. The count of Nevers departed after falling out with Odo, and the knights guarding the war chest made off with nearly 5,000 livres (£1,250) of it.[42]

Odo agreed to watch over Carcassonne while Simon made his first foray as the new viscount. Together with Raymond of Toulouse, who was still with the crusade, he worked out a plan to neutralise the *castra*, the hilltop fortresses or fortified settlements used by the petty lords to harbour heretics or harass the countryside. Many had been deserted out of fear of the crusaders. These were either destroyed or occupied with as many men as could be spared. Having secured Castres sixty kilometres to the north, Simon made a stab at Cabaret on his return. It was located high on a craggy ridge and defended by the aged Peter-Roger, a Cathar sympathiser who had overseen much of the recent defence of Carcassonne. The attempt ended in failure.

In early September, Odo and his men went back to Burgundy. That left Simon with roughly 250 mounted troops, mostly recruited from France, but some of them Aragonese mercenaries. Several of the thirty knights who remained had close connections to him. They included Alice's cousin Bouchard, the son of Matthew of Marly, and Philip Gorloin, whose family were retainers of the de Montforts. Philip, who may have served with Simon on the Fourth Crusade, was later made the seneschal of Carcassonne. Another veteran of Zara and the Holy Land, Robert Mauvoisin, was dispatched to Rome with a letter from Simon to the pope. In it, the new commander of the crusade promised to reinstate the collection of tithes and other ecclesiastical taxes in lands under his control, but complained that, despite the promises of support, he had been all but deserted by the crusaders. He nevertheless set off from Carcassonne both to secure the submission of his new subjects and seek out and destroy the heretics.[43]

Chapter 4

Lest Your Foot Stumble on a Stone
1209–1211

Simon de Montfort's first-known encounter with the Cathars was actually a miracle. A perfect and his initiate were brought before him near Castres. After taking counsel, Simon decided to burn them. The initiate panicked and asked for mercy, promising to be a good Catholic in the future. After a heated discussion, Simon sided with those who insisted the man had come too far with his heresy. Both men were bound with chains and tied to a stake.

This was not the first use of burning at the stake in the crusade. A smaller army had already moved through the Agenais northwest of Toulouse. According to William of Tudela, this host 'condemned many heretics to be burned and had many fair women thrown into the flames, for they refused to recant however much they were begged to do so'. The Church had provided no fixed guidelines to secular authorities on the punishment of heretics except to insist that it be 'fitting'. Burning them to death had always been the conventional way, both because the flames purged them of their sins and it resembled the hell they found themselves in.

In this particular case, Simon justified burning the novice because, if he was truly repentant, the flames would expiate his sins; if he was not, it would be his 'just reward for perfidy'. The fire was lit, but while the perfect was consumed by the flames instantly, the initiate broke out of his chains and escaped with just singed fingertips. Peter of Vaux-de-Cernay does not say what became of the man after that, but since he calls his escape a miracle, Simon and the others probably did so too and spared the heretic his life.[1]

Prosecuting the war on heresy seems to have guided Simon's initial strategy. From Carcassonne he marched twenty-six kilometres west to Fanjeaux, where Dominic had based his preaching activity, and from there seventeen kilometres southwest to Mirepoix, which had hosted an assembly of 600 perfects a few years earlier. The large Cathar population fled before their arrival and Simon gave Mirepoix to one of his knights, Guy de Lévis, to hold as a fief. Lévis was Simon's adjutant, or marshal as he was called then, and this younger son of an indebted family needed enfeoffment in the south both as incentive to stay on and means to support himself far away from home. Such grants naturally provoked comment that northerners like him were just out to confiscate the property of the heretics, which was true in a certain sense, but then that was the whole point of the crusade. Of the twenty-four knights who formed the core of Simon's retinue, nine received land from him.[2]

The troops next moved twenty-two kilometres further west to take possession of Pamiers, the home of many Waldensians, at the invitation of the local abbot. Then, near the end of September, they marched 100 kilometres northeast to Albi, the city that gave the Albigensian Crusade its name. Heresy was actually less a problem there than it was further south thanks to the efforts of the local bishop, William Peyre. Simon was more or less putting in an appearance in the northernmost extent of his new lands, and he reflected his lordship of the surrounding region in the new title he gave himself, lord of Albigeois.[3]

Simon's reputation for being everywhere at once starts during this period, for he now headed ninety-seven kilometres due south to Limoux. He captured several nearby fortresses, hanging some of the inhabitants, then moved thirteen kilometres northwest to Preixan on the road back to Carcassonne. It was a fief of another Raymond-Roger, the count of Foix, whose wife and sister were heretics. Raymond-Roger now arrived to come to terms with Simon and hand over his youngest son to him as a hostage for his compliance. It was the same with Aimeric de Laurac, the lord of Montréal. His mother and sisters were ladies perfect, but Simon took him at his word that he would remain loyal to the crusade.[4]

The troops were back in Carcassonne when the lord that Simon had displaced, Raymond-Roger Trencavel, fell ill with dysentery and died on 10 November 1209, aged 24. To act honourably and dispel suspicions of foul play, Simon had his body laid out for his people to mourn over and pay their respects. He was then off again, this time fifty-three kilometres east for Narbonne near the coast. Simon had been summoned by King

Peter of Aragon, the overlord of the lands he now held, to meet him there. Together they rode eight-five kilometres northeast along the coast to Montpellier, another of Peter's fiefs. It may have been Simon's idea to go there. It was the home of young Trencavel's widow Agnes and it was during this visit that Simon came to an arrangement with her for her dowry lands, namely paying her 25,000 sous (£312) outright for them plus 3,000 (£38) more as an annual pension.[5]

The real point of Simon's mission was to gain the king's recognition of him as his new vassal. This was important to Innocent because the pope's whole concept of the crusade rested on a new doctrine. It used to be that in the case of excommunicates, the Church called on secular leaders to seize their lands, but since Philip Augustus had failed to act against Raymond of Toulouse, Innocent and his lawyers devised the precedent of 'liability to seizure'. This allowed any good Christian, not just the overlord, to seize the lands of the excommunicate. The only but significant requirement was that the good Christian had to respect the rights of the overlord, meaning he had to get him to recognise his seizure of the lands. Simon needed Peter to acknowledge that the Trencavels were out and the de Montforts in.[6]

The king and crusader spent two weeks together, but Peter refused to take Simon's homage. Peter hated the heretics and had tried to get young Trencavel to stamp them out, but the crusade had wrought its destruction on his lands and attacked his people. While passing Béziers on the way to Montpellier, it is possible he directed Simon's attention to the charred remains of the city and growled, 'Just look at it!' Good Catholic though he was, the king felt the Church had gone amok in its war against heresy. He refused to sanction it by accepting a usurper from the north as his new vassal.

Peter even set out to sabotage Simon by telling the local lords to resist him and promising them aid if they did. As Simon was returning from Montpellier in late November, several did renounce their fealty and attacked. Two of his knights from Île-de-France, brothers Amaury and William of Poissy, were besieged and captured. Another group of knights led by Bouchard of Marly were ambushed on their way to make another attempt at storming Cabaret. One was killed and Bouchard was made a prisoner by Peter-Roger. Meanwhile, the murder of a local abbot and lay brother appeared to have been orchestrated by Raymond-Roger, the count of Foix, who also deserted at this time, as did Aimeric of Montréal.[7]

Simon had gone to the extreme to placate the southern lords. Giraud de Pépieux had sworn allegiance to the crusade and was rewarded with certain fortified towns near Minerve. When a prominent French nobleman killed his uncle, Simon had the killer buried alive in the southern tradition, but Giraud was not satisfied. He turned coat and overwhelmed the Montfortian garrison at Puisserguier. While Simon gathered up a relief force, Giraud set fire to the castle and threw the soldiers into the moat with straw and debris and set it alight in the hope they would burn to death. Simon was able to rescue them, but not the two knights, whom Giraud took to Minerve. There he gouged their eyes out, cut off their ears, noses and upper lips, stripped them of their clothing and kicked them out into the cold. One died, the other was led to Carcassonne by a peasant.[8]

The desertions and loss of more than forty towns and fortresses in such a short space of time were one thing, but the cruelty and ruthlessness of these men, his new subjects, who had only recently knelt before him and sworn on their honour, had to weigh on him heavily. Peter of Vaux-de-Cernay describes how the adversity was enough to lead a normal man to despair, but Simon simply put all his faith in God.[9]

Ironically, the southern lord Simon got on best with was the count of Toulouse. In September 1209, Raymond had been excommunicated by the legates again because he had failed to fulfil the terms of his reconciliation. Toulouse was also placed under interdict because the city council refused to hand over a list of suspected heretics. Convinced the legates were out to get him, Raymond went to Rome to plead his case and that of Toulouse in person. His meeting with the pope went well and Innocent did him the honour of showing him the cloth used by St Veronica to wipe the sweat off Jesus's face as he carried the cross.

Raymond had to know the presentation of the cloth was meant as a test of his faith, for everyone knew an authentic heretic despised the cross. When he deigned to touch it, in effect proving he was Catholic, Innocent absolved the inhabitants of Toulouse on the spot.[10] Raymond still had to defend himself against the charges of the legates, but he found Simon ready to assist him. Learning that Raymond was next on his way to Paris to see Philip Augustus, Simon ordered his subjects in Montfort l'Amaury to put themselves at the count's service. Upon his return, the two counts agreed that their children should marry in the future, Raymond's 10-year-old namesake son and Simon's daughter Amicia.[11]

The military reversals had left the men at Carcassonne miserable and depressed that winter. They took great comfort in the arrival of Abbot Guy of Vaux-de-Cernay, who 'soothed their fears and anxieties'. He had come to participate in another preaching campaign, but the churchmen had had no more luck than their previous attempts. Arnaud-Amalric himself went as far as the Agenais to the northwest of Toulouse, but the heretical communities there were as contemptuous of him as ever. According to William of Tudela, they scoffed when the legate spoke. 'There's that bee buzzing around again!'[12]

It was Alice de Montfort who turned the fortunes of the crusade around. Simon had sent for her, apparently telling her to recruit a company of knights and join him in the south. In early March, Simon went to meet her at Pézenas, about twenty-five kilometres northeast of Béziers, but on their way together to Carcassonne he learned of another betrayal that put his men in jeopardy. Since they were close to Capendu, he left Alice there and raced to the trouble spot. Their children were probably with her, for they soon start to appear in the south. The older boys Amaury VII and Guy II were in their teens, while the younger pair Amicia and Simon VI were still toddlers.[13]

Simon and his men rode thirty-six kilometres northwest, past Carcassonne, to Bram. They took it after three days and found among their prisoners a French clergyman who had swapped sides. On Simon's orders, he was defrocked, dragged behind a horse and hanged. Of the over 100 other prisoners, he decided to mete out the same cruelty to them that Giraud had done to his men and so had them blinded and their faces mutilated. He left one man with a single eye so he could lead the others, a sorrowful pack, to their compatriots at Cabaret. It was Simon's way of informing the southern lords that he and the crusaders were ready to carry on the war according to their rules. But it was a beastly business and Peter de Vaux-de-Cernay takes pains to insist the commander never took delight in torture or the like. He uses the words of Ovid to describe Simon's nature as such: 'A prince slow to punish and quick to reward, who grieved when driven to be hard.'[14]

With just a few knights at his disposal, Simon began another sweep around the territory, first going thirty-two kilometres southeast to hit Montagne d'Alaric, then sixty-seven kilometres southwest of Carcassonne to raid Foix. He almost singlehandedly chased the garrison there inside the fortress, then destroyed surrounding vines and crops before leading his men fifty-one kilometres northeast to Montréal. The southerners appealed to King Peter for help, but they were unwilling to meet the king's demand that they surrender all their castles to him. That would be like ceding all control of their lordships to another dedicated Christian warrior. The king might no sooner chase Simon out of Languedoc than turn on the heretics himself. Peter settled for playing the peacemaker and arranged a truce between Simon and the count of Foix.[15]

Around 24 June 1210, the first anniversary of the crusade, Simon set out to invest Minerve thirty-five kilometres northeast of Carcassonne with a fresh supply of men from as far away as Germany and Friesland. Since the fortress was encircled by deep ravines, the crusaders pummelled it with siege engines, some with names like Bad Neighbour. With the walls crumbling and water running low, William of Minerve came out to discuss surrender terms with Simon. Suddenly Arnaud-Amalric showed up out of nowhere. Considering the legate to be his superior, Simon deferred the final decision to him. Arnaud-Amalric felt the heretics inside should die, but as a cleric he could have no part in condemning them. He was therefore relieved when William and Simon failed to agree on terms, because that meant the siege would go on, the crusaders would storm the place, and the heretics would meet their fate in the aftermath.

But then William declared he was surrendering Minerve whatever the terms. Forced to accept a peaceful outcome, Arnaud-Amalric allowed the heretics the option of converting in exchange for their lives. Crusade veteran Robert Mauvoisin thought this was setting a bad precedent, but Arnaud-Amalric assured him that very few perfects would do it. As the secular authority responsible for punishing the heretics, Simon remained outside Minerve while the clergymen, including Guy of Vaux-de-Cernay, went in and tried to convert them. Guy was told by a house full of male perfects to stop wasting their time. The female perfects he found in another house were even more dismissive of him. In all, 140 perfects were handed over to Simon, who made his own attempt to convert them, but to no avail. They were marched to a pyre made ready for them outside the town and tossed into the fire, although Peter of Vaux-de-Cernay says some of the Cathars were so rooted in their beliefs that they willingly jumped in. Bouchard of Marly's mother Mathilde had by this point joined the crusade and the combination of her preaching and shrieks from the flames convinced three of the women to convert at the last moment.[16]

The siege of Termes, Simon and King Peter of Aragon, Raymond breaks with the crusade

After Minerve, Alice de Montfort received a message from her husband to join him at a palace in Pennautier, just north of Carcassonne. There, in a room with silk carpeted floors, she sat on the war council Simon held with Robert Mauvoisin and other knights, including Crespi de Rochefort, a Montfortian vassal from the north, and Simon the Saxon, who was actually a Norman. Two newcomers were another Norman, Roger des Essarts, and an Englishman, Hugh de Lacy, the earl of Ulster. Lacy, a political exile from King John's court, joined Simon's inner command likely through Essarts, a long-time friend who was himself a trusted aide of Philip Augustus. The plan was to attack Termes, thirty-four kilometres southeast of their position, but the big issue was who to leave in charge of Carcassonne. The fall of Minerve had led renegade lords like Aimeric de Laurac to seek peace, and although Simon again accepted their oaths, his experience suggested he needed someone he could truly trust to defend his base of operations.

The task was given to a Burgundian, William of Contres. *The Song of the Cathar Wars* provides a nice account of his arrival at Carcassonne. The servants helped William out of his armour. They had the fireplace in the great hall roaring, plenty of beef and pork ready for him and his men to eat and their beds were made up for a good night's sleep. They needed it, because a spy had informed Peter-Roger at Cabaret twenty kilometres to the north that Simon and his men were already on their way to Termes, but the siege engines were still packed up in ox carts outside Carcassonne waiting to be transported there. Peter-Roger led a raiding party to destroy the equipment, but the commotion they raised quickly alerted William and his men. While William flailed away at the insurgents from his Hungarian warhorse, Crespi and Simon the Saxon pounded the others so hard that these men 'never needed a road to walk on again'. Peter-Roger himself had been nabbed, but slipped away after slyly joining in the chants of 'Montfort! Montfort!' coming from the crusader ranks.[17]

The insurgents had been beaten off and the siege engines saved, but Simon needed all his available troops as the siege of Termes began in late July. This allowed Peter-Roger and his men, in a more ferocious mood than ever, to roam about and pick off isolated pockets of crusaders. Some they killed, others were left blinded and mutilated, found wandering the countryside in agony and despair. Simon's diminished force was unable to make any headway against Termes until reinforcements arrived from the north, led by the bishops of Chartres and Beauvais and counts of Dreux and Ponthieu. Archdeacon William of Paris not only brought men and money, but also expertise on how to operate siege engines, although where he acquired it was anyone's guess.

As the siege dragged on into autumn, Simon twice escaped instant death. He was talking to a knight in close quarters when a huge stone launched from the castle struck and killed the knight. The other time an enemy bolt disrupted the mass he was attending and impaled the soldier standing behind him. Added to these dangers was his poverty. He spent so much money on men and material that he had to skip certain meals for fear his troops would see him with nothing to eat.

In the castle, they had plenty of meat, wine and bread, but the crusaders had cut off their water supply. The lord of Termes, another Raymond, came out to negotiate with Simon. He offered to hand over the castle, but was to get it back in the spring. It was at this point that the bishops and counts from the north began packing up to leave, even though they had not reached the forty-day term of service required for crusader indulgences. Simon begged them to stay, otherwise he would be forced to accept Raymond's ridiculous offer. Alice also threw herself at their feet, but they ignored her pleading as well.

Only the bishop of Chartres was moved by their entreaties to delay his departure. He was Renaud de Mouçon, a veteran of the Third Crusade who launched the reconstruction of Chartres Cathedral that turned it into the wonder of the medieval world that it became. It was on Renaud's advice that Bernard-Raymond de Roquefort, the bishop of Carcassonne who marched with the crusaders, was sent in to negotiate. Roquefort came from a family of Cathars and his mother and brother were just then inside the compound. Raymond of Termes was now in a stronger position thanks to seasonal rains replenishing his stocks of water. He refused to let the bishop see his family and reneged on his earlier offer to surrender the castle, even just for the winter.

But Simon too had received replenishment, in the form of German crusaders from Lorraine. Manning the siege engines under Archdeacon William's guidance, their fire made direct hits on the walls, which were undermined at the same time by a group of sappers led by Simon himself. These operations, together with dysentery that broke out inside the castle after the rains came, gripped the defenders with terror. On the night of 22 November 1210, they put the ladies in the keep and slipped out. Raymond was among them, but, having forgotten something, he went back and was spotted. The alarm was raised and he and other members of the garrison were captured and imprisoned. There is no report on what became of the heretics inside. William of Tudela only says that Simon 'behaved very well to the ladies'.[18]

Simon now had a free hand to recover the remaining fortresses and territory that had deserted him the previous year. He went north to reclaim the Albigeois, which had also broken away, and there met Raymond of Toulouse in December. Raymond was again in a bad position. Just before the siege of Termes got underway, a council of prelates had convened at Saint-Gilles under the leadership of Arnaud-Amalric and Thedisius, a priest from Pisa who had been named legate following the death of Milo. They were gathered to consider lifting Raymond's sentence of excommunication. The pope was for it, but as with the Fourth Crusade, the legates on the ground believed they were better informed of the situation. They felt the business of peace and faith had no chance of implementation so long as Raymond was still in the picture.[19]

One look at Simon de Montfort made that clear. With the most meagre of resources, he was able to get things done because he had the will and commitment that Raymond pitifully lacked. The bishop of Toulouse was of similar breed. He was Fulk, the son of an Italian family who had been brought up in Marseille, where he was a troubadour before taking orders and becoming the bishop of Toulouse in 1205. He actively supported the preaching campaign against the heretics and rallied his diocese to the cause of the crusade by setting up a 'white brotherhood' in the city to attack not just heresy, but also usury, which was another ill plaguing the south in the eyes of Church officials. With their connections to heretics and the Jewish community, the merchant families of the suburbs rightly understood that they were the bishop's intended targets and so formed their own 'black brotherhood' in response. Before long, these two brotherhoods were battling it out on the narrow streets of the city.[20]

The energy and determination of Simon and Fulk made Raymond look incompetent and clueless, but it was the mistrust he inspired in the legates, both past and present, that led Arnaud-Amalric and Thedisius to devise a scheme to keep the count side-lined as much as possible. The pope had indicated that Raymond ought to be absolved unless there was proof he was a heretic or had conspired in the murder of Peter of Castelnau. He added, however, that Raymond was to follow the instructions of the legates in the meantime. That was the loophole the legates needed. Thedisius told the council that Raymond had failed to fulfil the instructions imposed on him during his reconciliation, particularly expelling heretics from his lands. He saw no reason for proceeding further and the prelates agreed. The count of Toulouse had come to Saint-Gilles expecting to be purified, instead he was excommunicated for a second time.[21]

Since the pope had final say in the matter, Raymond was given another hearing at a larger, more inclusive conference convened in Narbonne on 22 January 1211. A month before then, he went to meet Simon in the Albigeois, presumably to seek his support, but inexplicably he brought along several men Simon identified as traitors to the crusade. Suspecting he had walked into a trap, Simon demanded to know what they were doing there. Raymond said he had no idea, they were not with him. Whether true or not, he blocked Simon's intention to take the men captive and that broke their meeting up on a note of ill will.[22]

They met up again at the conference in Narbonne. Peter of Aragon was on his way to Montpellier and stopped by to plead on behalf of his brother-in-law Raymond. Arnaud-Amalric and Thedisius, now joined by a new legate, Bishop Raymond of Uzès, were prepared to be generous to the count. Raymond would be given all the property of heretics within

Toulouse and his other lordships and a share, as much as a third, of confiscations elsewhere. All he had to do was commence his long-awaited crackdown on the Cathars. There were other conditions, but they would be revealed at a council of bishops in Montpellier a week later.[23]

The legates hoped the conciliatory stance would move Peter to finally recognise Simon as his vassal, but not even their subsequent begging got the king to budge. The next day they brought Simon with them and again threw themselves at his feet. Not until Simon knelt himself and humbly offered his homage did Peter grudgingly accept it. They all then left for Montpellier. There the king agreed to marry his 3-year-old son and heir James to Simon's daughter Amicia, who was about the same age, and until that time the boy was to be raised in the de Montfort household in Carcassonne, more or less as a hostage for the deal. Since Amicia had been engaged to Raymond's own son and heir, Peter now offered his sister Sanchia to the boy. Raymond VI was already married to Peter's other sister Eleanor, so the marriage of young Raymond (13) and Sanchia (24), which took place in March, made father and son brothers-in-law.[24]

In front of the council of bishops at Montpellier, Arnaud-Amalric handed Raymond the list of conditions he had to fulfil in order to obtain absolution. He was to keep the peace and get rid of his mercenaries by the next day at the latest; he must restore any rights he expropriated from the clergy, who were never again to be bothered by him; all heretics and Jews were no longer to enjoy his protection; neither the count nor anyone in his entourage were to eat meat more than twice a week or wear the rich fabric they were accustomed to–only good, plain russet would do; their castles and strongholds were to be destroyed; the local urban nobility, a common feature in the south which had done much to hinder Simon's progress, was to be displaced to the countryside; usury was to be abolished completely, as well as unjust tolls; the crusaders were to be given free access to his lands; the laws of the king of France should always prevail; and lastly, Raymond was to go to the Holy Land, join one of the knightly orders there, and stay there until further notice.

According to William of Tudela, who provides this list, Raymond and King Peter had waited outside in the cold wind while the conditions were drawn up.[25] Both were scandalised by their undue harshness, but for Raymond it was more a case of dashed hopes than injustice. The conditions were in keeping with his reconciliation, but he figured his collaboration with the crusade had earned him some leniency. His visit to Innocent only reinforced that expectation.[26]

What Raymond failed to understand is that the Church did not expect him or any one man to crush the heretics. That could only be done through the business of peace and faith, by laying the groundwork for a whole new social, political and economic order in the south buttressed by a newfound awakening in the spiritual mission of the Church. Experience with Raymond had shown it would be that much harder to implement while he was around. It was best if he went straight to the Holy Land and let them bring the crusade to a successful conclusion. When he returned, his lands, indeed the entire region, would be cleansed of heresy and mercenaries. He could then proceed into honourable retirement, knowing that his son stood to inherit a lordship at peace with itself, its neighbours, and importantly, with the Church.

If the legates were right in seeing Raymond as too narrowly focused on his own interests, they should have known he was not going to take their hint and simply disappear, although he did initially do that by departing without taking leave of them. He rode headlong towards his lands, where he published the list of conditions and wrote letters to all his friends in high places. He presented himself as a victim of the Church in need of their support. He was not disappointed with the results. Convinced the northerners had come to imprison or enslave them all, the southerners rallied behind Raymond and the other insurgent nobles. They would resist the crusade as an invading army and drive the Frenchmen, led by Simon de Montfort, from their homeland.[27]

Cabaret and Lavaur taken, the first siege of Toulouse fails, the southerners go on the offensive

One insurgent who had already seen the writing on the wall was Peter-Roger. The spring arrival of new crusaders could only mean that his hilltop fortification of Cabaret was next, and his brutal reprisals against the northerners suggested something unpleasant awaited him and the garrison if they fell into Simon's hands. When two of his knights defected to the crusaders, Peter-Roger fell back on the hostage he had been holding for sixteen months. He went into the dungeon of his castle and had Bouchard of Marly freed from his irons, had him bathed, groomed, given a fresh pair of clothes and a horse, and told him that Cabaret was his. 'Never had (Bouchard) known such happiness since the day his mother gave him birth', says William of Tudela, perhaps in reference to the presence of Bouchard's mother with the crusading army.

Like the other southern lords, Peter-Roger knew Simon put great store in oaths, even if they themselves did not, and he expected Simon to honour Bouchard's promise of an amnesty in exchange for Cabaret. After partying all night in Carcassonne, Bouchard led the crusaders into the fortress and there Simon's banner was raised above the tower of the castle. Peter-Roger's peaceful surrender of Cabaret had been more than just about saving his own neck, however. There were also the heretics he was sheltering, who likely left at the same time Bouchard did and fled fifty kilometres northwest to Lavaur, the last major holdout against the crusaders. In mid-March, Simon had his troops on the road heading in that direction.[28]

Lavaur had long been a centre of heresy. Back in 1181, it had been besieged and occupied as part of a more militant preaching mission, with troops supplied by Raymond of Toulouse's father. Only two heretics were reclaimed for the faith then and Catharism continued to thrive there. By the time the crusade arrived, the lordship of the town had passed to Giraude de Laurac, the sister of Aimeric. Like her mother, she became a perfect at the death of her husband. William of Tudela notes the fame of Giraude's hospitality and generosity. It would have been her nature to receive heretics or anyone else fleeing from the crusaders. William of Puylaurens suggests something more mercenary. He says the refugees were welcomed in the hope they would become wounded in the coming struggle and, thinking death was near, ask for the *consolamentum*. That way the Cathar church could claim their property.[29]

Giraude left the defence of Lavaur to her brother Aimeric. He had been unhappy since swearing fealty to Simon for a second time and exchanging his lordships for some low-lying lands far from the action. In doing so, he went from being a rich and well-respected knight to an ordinary farmer. Aimeric knew that, in coming to his sister's aid, he was betraying Simon again, but he had every reason to believe they could hold out in Lavaur, which had strong ramparts, deep ditches and a naturally fortified position overlooking the river.

Even as new regiments poured in from the north and Lavaur was completely invested, the defenders still believed they would prevail once help arrived from Raymond of Toulouse. Raymond, however, preferred to keep a foot in both camps. He sent a handful of knights to assist the garrison, but allowed provisions to flow from Toulouse to the crusaders besieging them. He arrived at Lavaur to plead his case to his cousins from the north, Robert and Peter de Courtenay, who had recently joined the crusade, but they merely implored him to come to his senses before it was too late. Indignant at being lectured to, Raymond glowered at Simon and left. He ordered members of the White Brotherhood who had joined the siege to return to Toulouse, which they did, and cut off all supplies to the crusaders.[30]

Reinforcements were on their way from Carcassonne, many of them Germans and Frisians. Halfway to Lavaur, in the forest of Montgey, they were ambushed by the men and mercenaries of Raymond-Roger, the bellicose count of Foix, and Giraud de Pépieux. The crusaders fought hard, but were outnumbered and wiped out. Local villagers clubbed the survivors to death and despoiled their bodies. Peter of Vaux-de-Cernay reports that Raymond-Roger's son Roger-Bernard caught up with a priest who had fled the slaughter and cleaved a large hole in his tonsure. A nobleman who did make good his escape reached Lavaur with the news. 'When the French heard it', says William of Tudela, 'they almost went out of their minds'. Simon and the Courtenays left with a mounted troop to hunt down the bandits, but they were long gone. The crusaders returned to Lavaur in a vengeful mood.[31]

The bishops and abbots led the rest of the clergy in singing *Veni Creator Spiritus* below the ramparts. On 3 May 1211, Holy Cross Day, the sappers succeeded in breaching a wall and Lavaur fell. The garrison was eighty strong, including Aimeric, his knights, and various townsfolk who mingled in with them in the belief that chivalry would save them. Whether that may or may not have been the case, the massacre of the crusaders at Montgey condemned the lot of them. Simon had Aimeric and his knights hanged, the others were dispatched with knife and sword after the gallows started to collapse. Raymond's knights and the rest of the townsfolk were spared.

The 300 to 400 heretics found inside were taken out to a meadow and tossed onto a burning pyre. According to Robert of Auxerre, an attempt was made to convert them first, probably led by Bishop Peter of Paris and Archdeacon William, both from the reforming schools. Giraude was not among them. On Simon's orders, she was dropped, kicking and screaming, into a well and buried under a hail of stones from above. This bit of Old Testament justice was 'a shame and a sorrow', says William of Tudela, who adds that the other noble ladies of the town were set free 'by a kind and courteous Frenchman, who behaved most honourably'.[32]

William also says that the booty from the siege included warhorses, armour, rich fabrics, and plenty of wheat and wine, all of which went to a merchant named Raymond of Salvanhac. He acted as financier to the crusade, which for that day and age meant he was a usurer. The Church considered moneymen of this sort as disreputable as mercenaries, but his job was also making sure the papacy received its local taxes. His loans and interest were paid out of the revenues of two towns, with the booty taken from the various sieges making up the difference. In the case of Lavaur, it seems unlikely Simon would have deprived his men of a share of the spoils from a hard-fought campaign that had claimed the lives of hundreds of crusaders as well. As overall commander, he was entitled to a one-third share and it was probably this loot that Raymond piled into the back of his wagons.[33]

By the end of the siege, the army would have received notification that Innocent had confirmed Raymond of Toulouse's latest excommunication on 15 April. His lands were now officially open to confiscation and the first of them targeted by Simon was Les Cassés. On the way there, he had Montgey burnt to the ground in reprisal for the massacre of the crusaders in the nearby forest. The villagers had expected it and fled before his arrival. At Les Cassés, the garrison surrendered rather than risk the fate of Lavaur. The bishops were unable to convert any of the sixty-odd heretics discovered hidden in a tower inside and all were consigned to flames.[34]

The army moved on to Montferrand, which was defended by Raymond's brother Baldwin. These two had a difficult relationship. In 1165, their mother Constance was pregnant with Baldwin when she decided she had had enough of their ill-tempered father and went to live at the court of her newly-crowned brother Philip Augustus. There Baldwin grew up to be pious and ambitious, completely unlike his weak, licentious brother. Indeed, when Baldwin came south for the first time after the death of their father in 1194, Raymond demanded he prove his identity. He eventually acknowledged they were kin and took him into his service, but although Baldwin distinguished himself, Raymond refused to endow him with any lands or titles. Baldwin defended Montferrand for his brother, who promised to send help, but none came and he was forced to surrender the fortress. He and his fourteen knights were allowed to go free after swearing to never make war on the crusaders or to support the heretics.[35]

With Simon seemingly unstoppable that spring, Raymond again looked for a way out. His offer to put himself and all his possessions except Toulouse at the mercy of the crusade found some support among the barons, but fell through because they would give him no guarantee about the return of his lands. He then claimed he went to meet the legates under safe-conduct but was assaulted and chased by Simon and a party of knights. A deputation from the consuls of Toulouse went on a separate mission to the legates, only to be warned to get rid of Raymond. If not, the churchmen told them, 'we shall crush you and you shall suffer the fate of the heretics and their protectors'. Given the choice between war on one side and standing by their lord on the other, the consuls chose Raymond. The city was put back under interdict, and Bishop Fulk, who was still with the army, ordered the clergy to leave.[36]

These peace initiatives are only known from a letter written by the consuls to Peter of Aragon to justify their defiance of the crusade and Church. Whatever effort had actually been made, it is unlikely Toulouse would have acted otherwise. The consuls may have felt their count was the victim of an unexplained vendetta by the legates, but he was not entirely blameless. Raymond had dealt with numerous papal officials over a ten-year period, different men from different backgrounds, and all of them came away with the same low opinion of him. There was also no denying that things might not have come this far with a little more sincerity and adroitness on his part and less evasiveness and bungling. His joining the crusade in the first place was a good example. He meant to keep it away from Toulouse, now it was on their doorstep.

Their loyalty to Raymond aside, the deciding factor was what the crusade meant to Toulouse, because they were in the same position as the other southern communities. The lives of their heretical and Jewish populations were at stake. One look around made it obvious how quickly things were apt to change with someone else as their lord. In the lands conquered by Simon, the heretics had mostly vanished, whether burnt alive or forced into hiding. Bring in a man like that, whose drive, purpose and mobility were already legendary, and their people were doomed.

With the fall of Montferrand, the road to Toulouse was open, but Simon's forces were again depleted by the departure of his most recent forty-day crusaders. In June, he marched straight north, secured the rest of the Albigeois and crossed over into Quercy for the first time. Raymond was then at Bruniquel, barely fifteen kilometres distant, and in the face of Simon's advance he and the inhabitants decided to burn the fortress and flee. Just then Baldwin showed up and asked Raymond to give it to him, which he did but not before sacking it first. Convinced his brother only had contempt for him, Baldwin went to Simon to negotiate a switch of allegiance, then rode to Toulouse to hear Raymond refuse one last time to abide by the commands of the Church. Baldwin returned to Bruniquel and came out openly for the crusade. Sometime after that William of Tudela, a clerk from Navarre, joined his household and began composing *The Song of the Cathar Wars* in Occitan.[37]

The army next turned around and went more than 100 kilometres south to meet up with new German troops at Carcassonne under Count Theobald of Bar, a boastful warrior eager to attack Toulouse. On 16 June, their crossing of the River Hers was contested by troops under the counts of Foix and Comminges, the latter another of Raymond's cousins. After a vicious fight that claimed thirty-three peasants in a nearby meadow, the defenders were thrown back with huge losses. Raymond's illegitimate son Bertrand was captured in the retreat and had to surrender his horse, armour and 1,000 pounds to regain his freedom.

The crusaders went straight for an assault on the city but were fiercely repulsed. The counts of Bar and Chalon's insistence that they could take it by siege had to strike Simon as misguided overconfidence. Of the five kilometres of walls surrounding Toulouse, they barely had enough men to cover two gates. He took on an uncharacteristic supporting role while the two counts hammered away. It was a pathetic show of strength that only encouraged the defenders, despite Raymond's protests, to make repeated sorties against them. These attacks forced the besiegers to stay in their armour all the time with their weapons close at hand, and their morale suffered further from having nothing to eat but beans and overpriced bread. They broke camp after two weeks and headed south to Foix to lay waste to Raymond-Roger's county in retaliation for the Montgey massacre. The town of Foix itself they torched.[38]

Unable to take Toulouse, Simon proposed to go north again to isolate the city on all sides. The count of Bar argued against it but found himself isolated when his own men chose to follow Simon. As the army began what ultimately became a 200-kilometre march, the count turned off for Carcassonne amidst a torrent of taunts and jibes. Arriving in Cahors, Simon found Arnaud-Amalric, for no apparent reason, hiding in a cloister, but the local bishop and nobility were ready to stand behind him. Keeping a promise he had made, Simon led the army further north on a pilgrimage to Rocamadour, famous for its cult of the Virgin. There the German contingent, their service at an end, continued their journey home while Simon and his core followers turned back for Carcassonne.[39]

They found the situation grave there. Two of their knights had been encircled by men of the count of Foix while on patrol and told to surrender. One of the knights, Lambert de Thury, received a personal oath that they would be neither killed nor mutilated and Raymond-Roger respected it. He was, however, always glad to inflict misery on his enemies and had the two men chained in a dungeon so small that they could neither stand nor lie outstretched and the only light they had was a candle lit during feeding time. He otherwise kept them in good health for the huge ransom they would bring. The other knight was Walter Langton, the brother of Stephen Langton, who had studied with the pope in Paris and was Innocent's choice to become archbishop of Canterbury. King John's refusal to admit Stephen as the new archbishop earned him excommunication in November 1209.[40]

Simon made it his first priority to win Lambert and Walter's freedom and succeeded in capturing some of Raymond-Roger's knights to make the exchange. But Raymond of Toulouse had been busy putting a coalition together to take advantage of the usual shortage of manpower that plagued the crusaders at the end of summer. His allies now included Gaston de Béarn from Gascony, who was a vassal of King Peter of Aragon, and Savaric de Mauléon from Poitou, whose fealty was to Raymond's brother-in-law, King John of England. In September 1211, as many as 5,000 men marched out of Toulouse, with horses and mules hauling bread and wine while buffaloes and oxen pulled carts laden with catapults. As they covered the whole ground in front of them 'like locusts', the troops brimmed with confidence. They were going to crush the crusade and capture that beast of a warrior Simon de Montfort. Once he was in their hands, they cried, they would 'skin him alive'.[41]

Chapter 5

North versus South
1211–1213

In Carcassonne eighty-five kilometres away, Simon held a war council. Most of his men were in favour of hunkering down for a siege, but Hugh de Lacy declared that momentum had carried them this far. To give it up now would finish them off. His view prevailed, but with just 500 men, they were outnumbered nearly ten to one. Not even their superior cavalry could cope with those odds. In personal terms, the threat could not have come at a worse time for Simon. His family was just then scattered about. Alice was seventy kilometres north of him in Lavaur, having given birth to a daughter, Petronilla, who was under the care of nurses in Montréal, and their 15-year-old son Amaury was seriously ill in the west at Fanjeaux. The southern resurgence was causing more defections and each of these towns could be easily lost.[1]

As the host approached, the crusaders garrisoning Montferrand fled down the road for Castelnaudary. Telling them not to lose heart, Simon left a detachment at Carcassonne and moved to join them there with the rest of his men. They received some unexpected reinforcements when Guy de Lucy and his regiment of fifty knights arrived from Aragon. As a vassal of King Peter, Simon was required to supply him with men in his war against the Moors. The end of their term of service occurred just in time, even though Peter was quite indignant about it and tried to prevent their departure.[2]

The crusaders were at dinner when the first southerners breached the defences of Castelnaudary thanks to treachery on the part of the inhabitants. Although they were driven out, a subsequent full-scale assault would have overwhelmed them. Raymond, however, chose to take up a position on a nearby hill and fortify it. His plan was to lob giant stones at Castelnaudary with his siege engines while the noose around the crusaders tightened with every defection. Simon thought it was a disgraceful way to conduct a war and had to be restrained from leading a foolish charge against the southerners that could only end in disaster.[3]

Needing reinforcements, Simon began recalling as many units as he could afford to without the rest of the region collapsing around him. He sent his marshal, Guy de Lévis, and Matthew II of Marly, Bouchard's brother, to bring in men and supplies from Carcassonne and towns further afield, including Béziers. All but a few of their recruits deserted along the way. At Simon's command, Bouchard set out from Lavaur with a hundred knights. They were joined by men serving under Bishop William of Cahors and Martin Algai, a mercenary commander who had been King John's seneschal in Gascony. Knowing most of the territory was now hostile to them, they took a long, convoluted route and linked up with the supply train coming from Carcassonne. They had less than six kilometres to go when they found their way blocked at St-Martin-La-Lande by Raymond-Roger, the count of Foix. He was simply too belligerent to endure Raymond of Toulouse's passive style of warfare and so broke camp to intercept the relief force.

Simon now took a huge risk and sent half of his men in Castelnaudary, about forty knights, to Bouchard with orders to attack. They included Simon of Neauphle, a recent arrival and an old comrade from the Fourth Crusade, whose family had founded and remained benefactors of the abbey of Vaux-de-Cernay. Before their departure, Simon V addressed the knights who were of southern origin. He told them that if out of fear or affection they felt the urge to cross over, they should stay behind and he would arrange safe-conducts for them to join Raymond's side. One of these men, William Cat, assured him that they would never desert him. Simon must have taken his words to heart. Cat was a native of Montréal and from a heretical background, but he had been knighted by Simon and had risen high in his and Alice's favour. They made him tutor to their son Amaury and one of the godfathers of their newborn daughter.

In the morning Bouchard put his men in formation. With the reinforcements from Simon and the men accompanying Lévis and the supply train, the crusaders had about 700 troops. Opposite them were at least three times that number. As the two sides neared, the French spurred hard and drove into the thick of the southerners amassed in front of them. They broke through their ranks, but then were thrown back in retreat, with Martin Algai and Bishop William leaving the action altogether. Raymond-Roger aimed to pursue them, but a great many of his soldiers were mercenaries who could not resist rifling through the supply train first. By that time Simon, observing the battle from afar, decided on an all-out gamble. Leaving his foot soldiers to defend Castelnaudary, he led his remaining knights on a charge that caught Raymond-Roger off guard. They smashed into his exposed flank and created such panic that some of the southerners tried to save themselves by crying out, 'Montfort!' The count of Foix and his son fought back with everything they had, but they were next hit by Bouchard counterattacking from the other side and driven from the field.

Seeing Simon leave Castelnaudary, Savaric attempted to take the town, but he was repulsed by the foot soldiers and quickly withdrew when he saw the crusaders returning in triumph. Simon was so worked up he wanted to take off after him, but his men were exhausted and knew Raymond still had a much larger force and stronger fortifications. In fact, it may have all been over for the northerners had Raymond sallied forth at the same time Simon did, but he did not have that aggressive spirit in him. Two days later, while Simon set out to recruit men to resume the attack, Raymond ordered his own troops to burn their siege engines and head home.

For Simon, it was a brilliant but costly victory. In addition to losing thirty knights, he learned that Lévis had only barely avoided an ambush after leaving Carcassonne set by none other than William Cat, the one local Simon thought he could trust over all others. Cat had figured it was all over for his patron and decided to switch sides while the battle was in progress, the one thing Simon had implored him and the other southerners not to do. It proved to be a game changer. In the words of William of Puylaurens, it was from that point on that Simon 'began to eschew association with knights who spoke our tongue'.[4]

As the chronicler indicates, this change of attitude towards the southerners was underscored by the myriad of languages confronting the crusaders, who themselves typically spoke some form of French or German. Occitan was the language of the south, but it had a variety of dialects like Gascon, Provençal and Limousin. Messengers had to be skilled in many of these dialects just to get around, not to mention delivering the message itself. We later see Alice de Montfort sending one such multi-lingual messenger to report to her husband. Despite whatever fluency she or Simon might have achieved in Occitan during their years in Languedoc, their French and the languages of their compatriots would always distinguish them as aliens in that region, particularly to southern lords like Raymond-Roger. At the battle outside Castelnaudary, he drove his men forward with commands like, 'Keep at it hard, don't rest until we have killed these foreigners'.[5]

There was also the difference in beliefs that went beyond ordinary religion. To the northerners, it seemed like the southerners were excessively superstitious. At Castelnaudary, Spaniard Martin Algai saw a white falcon flying swiftly overhead from left to right and interpreted it as a good omen. That earned him a rebuke from Frenchman Bouchard of Marly, who told him the battle would be decided on the field, not in the air. A somewhat lighter illustration has Viscount Roger of Couserans, a nephew of Raymond-Roger, coming to Simon at the siege of Lavaur to offer his homage. As Roger commenced the formalities of submission, Simon chanced to sneeze. Roger stopped short, and when no second sneeze was forthcoming, he stepped aside to consult his men. It was their belief that if the person they were dealing with sneezed only once, it was a bad omen for that day. The northerners saw what the fuss was about and started ridiculing Roger, who reluctantly went through with the act of homage for fear of what Simon might think of his fortitude.[6]

By far the most serious divide between the crusaders and their opponents was the southern concept of *paratge*. This untranslatable Occitan word gives the idea that life is all about balance and preserving the natural order of things. *Paratge* makes the world a sunny, kind and joyous place, but take it away and it becomes dark, harsh and lamentable. The crusade had obviously upset that balance, insinuated an alien invader among them. It had undermined their *paratge*, or 'culture' for lack of a better word. No attempt at restoring it was viewed as shameful. Quite the opposite. Smiling at a crusader before sneaking away to ambush him was perfectly legitimate, as was maiming or killing him after he was captured. Raymond-Roger, for one, was not a knight who took defeat honourably. Although soundly beaten at Castelnaudary, he put it out that Simon had been 'flayed alive and hanged' while other rumours spread that he had fled back to France.[7]

To Simon and other men who had grown up assuming the code of knighthood was sacred everywhere, the conduct of the southern lords was baffling and inexcusable. According to the troubadours, Languedoc was the land of chivalry, but it must have been ages ago, before the mercenary spirit had come to define the warrior class there. But however appalling their tactics were, there was no denying their effectiveness. Believing the rumours that the feared crusader had been finally brought low, towns and fortresses deserted in droves, up to fifty in all. The treachery was often made worse by an atrocity, as was the case of Lagrave in the Albigeois. In charge of it for the crusaders was a knight named Pons de Beaumont, who had been with Simon since the beginning. Around this time he asked a local carpenter to repair his wine casks. As Pons peered inside one of the casks to inspect the repair, the carpenter chopped his head off with an axe. It was the signal to the other inhabitants to slaughter the remaining French soldiers stationed there.[8]

For the rest of 1211, Simon continued to lose territory and men. Another ambush by the count of Foix and his son killed among others de Montfort family friend Geoffrey of Neauphle. Normally Simon would have to wait until spring or summer for new crusaders to arrive, but by the end of the year his forces had been replenished with a hundred knights brought from France by Robert Mauvoisin, and before him a smaller contingent under Alan de Roucy. But the biggest boost came from the arrival of his brother Guy, who spent Christmas with him at Castres. For six years Guy had been the acting lord of Sidon in the Holy Land, but in 1210 his stepson Balian reached his majority and assumed the coastal lordship from him. Guy and his wife Helvis had a son Philip, then about 6 years old, and daughter Petronilla. Together they journeyed to Languedoc to stake their fortunes on the crusade.[9]

The mild start to winter allowed Simon to go on the offensive in the Albigeois. They quickly overran Touelles, about ten kilometres northeast of Lavaur, and executed all the defenders except one, Giraud de Pépieux's father Fredolius. He was exchanged for a knight then being held in chains by Raymond-Roger. They next moved on to Cahuzac, where Simon received a message from the counts of Toulouse, Foix and Comminges to say that they were coming after him with their combined strength. When they failed to arrive, Simon gathered up part of his troops and went after them on a chase leading up to Toulouse. The plan of the three counts may have been to scare the crusaders away from any more sieges that winter or draw them into a trap. William of Tudela says Raymond could have easily destroyed them, but he was immobilised by fear again. The ploy ended up costing him two more fortresses and Simon went back to Cahuzac and took it by storm. They found enough food inside to have a regular feast in celebration of Epiphany on 6 January 1212.[10]

The three counts decided that their best strategy was to occupy fortresses and let Simon wear himself down with fruitless assaults. This happened at Saint-Marcel, which was held by Simon's arch-enemy Giraud de Pépieux. In a move called 'stupid' by William of Tudela, Simon tried to take it with barely a hundred knights against five times that number inside. He needed half his men just to guard his supply train. Rations dwindled until a month into the siege his men had no bread at all. On 24 March, the day after Good Friday, he raised the siege and retired to Albi with his men.[11]

There they celebrated Easter with Guy, the abbot of Vaux-de-Cernay, who had left France after receiving word of his election as the bishop of Carcassonne. His predecessor, Bernard-Raymond de Roquefort, was still alive and had been loyal to the crusade, but his position as bishop had long been compromised by the heretics in his family. Guy brought along his nephew Peter, who had accompanied him and the de Montforts on the Fourth Crusade. At that earlier time he was about 12 years old but already able to read Latin thanks to his education at the abbey. Now ten years later, Peter was a monk and says he came south to support his uncle on his journey 'to a foreign land', perhaps also to serve as his secretary. He commenced writing *The History of the Albigensian Crusade* sometime after his arrival because he felt the crusade 'should not be forgotten by generations to come'. Drawing only on the eyewitness accounts of the crusaders up to that point, the young monk's narrative is one-sided and made even more partisan by his personal admiration for Simon and disgust with Raymond of Toulouse and Raymond-Roger. But as far as accuracy and detail are concerned, his work remains matchless among the principal sources of these years.[12]

Another episcopal election had greater consequences for the region. Archbishop Berengar of Narbonne, an uncle of Peter of Aragon, had long faced deposition over corruption and his own use of mercenaries as rent collectors. Having played no part in the crusade, his death now allowed a fiercer, more energetic prelate to succeed him and none fit the bill better than the abbot of Cîteaux, Arnaud-Amalric. In May, he and Guy of Vaux-de-Cernay were consecrated in their new roles in Narbonne. Guy de Montfort and his nephew Amaury attended the ceremonies and sometime during their visit Amaury wandered about the former, decrepit palace of the local viscount. When a window he tried to open fell out, a mob of citizens accused him of vandalism. They marched on the Templar House where Amaury was staying and killed two of Simon's squires in the ensuing riot. Amaury was so certain he was next that he put on his armour and hid out of sight. Even his uncle Guy dared not stray from his residence at the palace of the new archbishop until the mob had dispersed and both de Montforts could leave the city safely. The incident was a sobering reminder of how unpopular the crusade and its leader had become among the people of the south, even in a city like Narbonne, which had only reaped benefits from all the wartime activity.[13]

Arnaud-Amalric did not let the unfortunate uprising interfere with his plans to lead a hundred French knights across the Pyrenees into his homeland of Catalonia, where another crusade was getting underway to push back the Almohad caliphate in Spain. On 16 July 1212, the united forces of the Christian kingdoms of Aragon, Castile and Navarre crushed the Moors at Las Navas de Tolosa. The archbishop was there, but many of the Frankish knights who marched on the crusade had departed before the battle, complaining of the heat and lack of booty. To King Peter of Aragon, who commanded the left wing of the attack, it was the same kind of faithlessness shown by the Montfortian knights in his service the year before. He had not forgotten about that other crusade to the north of him and planned to use the prestige he enjoyed from his triumph to go there and deal with it in person.[14]

Opening a new front, the war grows more savage, the Statute of Pamiers

The crusade in Spain did not deprive Simon of the usual complement of men he expected for the spring campaign season. It had been a bumper year in recruitment thanks to the preaching of Archdeacon William of Paris and an Augustinian canon, Jacques de Vitry, with crusaders pouring in from as far away as Italy and Dalmatia. High-ranking nobles and clergy like Duke Leopold of Austria and Archbishop Aubrey of Reims joined the cause, as did Simon's old comrade and fellow dissenter from the Fourth Crusade, Enguerrand of Boves. Simon had enough troops to create a corps under the command of his brother Guy and Marshal de Lévis and dispatch them to conduct operations in the south while he took the rest of his men north to recover the Albigeois. He took Saint-Marcel, which had thwarted him in the spring, but found the garrison at Saint-Antonin defiant and insulting. The commander called him and the other crusaders 'stick carriers', a pejorative term for pilgrims, and had his men constantly harass them with sorties and arrowshot.

In a scene reminiscent of Béziers almost three years earlier, the poorer crusaders, who were armed with whatever they could find, retaliated after one sortie by bombarding the barbicans with stones. Within an hour, they had stormed the outer walls. The inhabitants and clergy fled to the church, where these actual stick carriers despoiled them of everything they owned, even the clothes on their back. The people were then marched in front of Simon to hear their fate. Seeing how they were simple country folk whom, if put to the sword, would leave the town desolate, he ordered them freed, but the commander and his knights were hauled off in chains.[15]

The Albigeois was again his, but instead of returning south, Simon took his men north and westward into the Agenais. On 3 June, his men arrived at Penne, a strong fortress built by Richard the Lionheart in the 1180s, then under the command of Hugh d'Alfaro, a mercenary captain from Navarre. He was not only Raymond's seneschal for the Agenais, but had married his illegitimate daughter Guillemette. Hugh was determined to put up a fight, and for that he cleared out most of the inhabitants, stockpiled the castle, and brought in 400 fellow mercenaries.

Simon responded by ordering his brother to bring up his corps to aid in the siege. That must have relieved Raymond-Roger down south. He had found there was little he could do to stop Guy and his men from rampaging through Foix with the same lightning speed as his brother.[16]

The extra men came in time, because Simon was again plagued by the problem of crusaders ready to leave after their forty days, even while a siege was in progress. He had nine engines and one monstrous unit built and operated by Archdeacon William of Paris pounding the fortress endlessly. With no help from his father-in-law in sight and food and water running low, Hugh agreed to surrender in return for their lives. Simon, his force dwindling by the day, allowed the mercenaries to walk on 25 July. But he had a score to settle with one of their profession. Twenty-seven kilometres to the north was the fortress of Biron, which belonged to Martin Algai. Remembering how Martin had deserted him in the thick of the battle outside Castelnaudary, Simon marched there and offered the garrison their lives if they would hand him over to him. The legendary mercenary captain was produced, told to confess his sins, and then dragged and hanged from a gibbet.[17]

Simon next awaited the arrival of his wife Alice, Bishop Guy and Peter of Vaux-de-Cernay, who were bringing foot soldiers from Carcassonne. As the men began faltering in the heat, Alice and the bishop let the soldiers take turns riding behind them on saddle or else they dismounted entirely and continued on foot while two men rode on each horse. She took part in the war council held outside Penne, in the tent of Archbishop Aubrey of Reims. As the weather was stifling hot, Lambert de Thury wore a shirt of Phrygian silk to stay cool, but the archbishop was overly conscious of his wealth and status and sat on a brown cushion robed in layers of fur.[18]

They decided to assault Moissac, thirty-eight kilometres to the southwest and defended by a large force of mercenaries and militia from Toulouse. As the siege got underway, they ambushed Simon near a copse, killing his horse and wounding him in the foot with an arrow. William of Contres and another knight fought them off until Guy de Montfort arrived with reinforcements and scattered the attackers. Archbishop Aubrey's nephew, however, was seized and dragged away by four of the militia. Once inside the fortress, they killed him, chopped up his body and tossed his remains over the wall. Far from distancing themselves from this act of savagery, the southerners began to make it a practice to hack away at the corpse of any crusader they brought down.[19]

Simon had another close call when he, his brother Guy and some other men attempted to force a breach from inside a 'cat', a wagon covered in ox hides that provided protection for siege work next to the walls. As the cat was moved into position, the defenders tossed straw, salted meat, fat and oil on top of it and set it alight. The crusaders outside the cat were hampered in their efforts to put out the fire by enemy crossbowmen standing by to pick them off. They eventually managed to pull the contraption back and save the occupants from being burned to death. Peter of Vaux-de-Cernay describes how the men inside it, including the de Montfort brothers, were shaken by the experience. It would have been a singular irony had Simon gone up in flames like the innumerable heretics who had fallen into his hands.[20]

The ferociousness of the siege led nearby towns to sue for peace. They did not want to be next and the wine harvest was approaching. The people of Moissac realised they could no longer count on help from the outside and the battered state of their defences meant it was only a matter of time before the crusaders stormed their city. Not wanting to test their mercy, they asked for terms. They agreed to turn over the garrison, swear not to take up arms against 'Christians' in the future, and pay a ransom of 100 gold marks. The crusaders nevertheless ransacked the monastery and various parts of the town, leading the local abbot, who had fully supported the siege, to write an intemperate letter to Philip Augustus about their hooliganism and ungodliness. On 8 September, 300 mercenaries and militia from Toulouse were taken into captivity. Peter of Vaux-de-Cernay says the crusaders carried out the grim task of executing them 'with great enthusiasm'.[21]

The whole point of opening up this new front in the Agenais was to encircle Toulouse, but the legality of it was called into question. The territory had formed the patrimony of the Angevin kings of England until Richard the Lionheart gave it to Raymond as the dowry for his sister Joanna. At her death in 1199, the land passed to Raymond to keep for his and Joanna's son until he came of age. But the overlord remained the king of England, Raymond's brother-in-law John. Any incursion into the region was an infringement of King John's rights, but Simon could argue that John too was an excommunicate. Under the papal mandate, the crusaders were allowed to seek out and occupy heretical lands under the control of an excommunicated lord, whoever he was. Heresy was probably not as strong in the Agenais as further south, but the first heretics of the crusade had been burnt there in 1209.[22]

John was in no position to contest Simon in any case. In August 1212, while the siege of Moissac was underway, the king was in Nottingham preparing to invade Wales. There, word reached him that a cabal of his barons had deposed him and elected Simon as their new king. Most of these barons had probably never met Simon, but would have known that John stripped him of the earldom of Leicester five years before without due process. Simon had as much grievance against the king as they did, and his capable leadership of the crusade made him just the candidate to rattle John with rumours that his ouster was imminent. Simon could have heard of his 'election' from English crusaders Hugh de Lacy and Walter Langton, whose families had also been wronged by John, but there is no evidence he was aware of these events. The one baron who might have been expected to keep him informed was his cousin Amaury VI, the earl of Gloucester, but he and Simon seemed to have had no personal relationship, either in England or France. Amaury died the next year in 1213, leaving behind a widow but no children, and the senior branch of the de Montfort line was extinguished with him.[23]

From Moissac, the army moved southeast towards Montauban, where William of Tudela had lived for many years before joining Baldwin's household. It too had a tough militia, bolstered by a hundred mounted troops brought in by Roger-Bernard of Foix. Simon decided to bypass it when he received word that Pamiers was being blockaded. This allowed Roger-Bernard to leave the fortress and resume his guerrilla activities. In one notorious case, he took his haul of knights and pilgrims from one ambush to his castle, where he set up a torture chamber for them. According to Peter of Vaux-de-Cernay, who says he heard about it from one of the knights who survived the ordeal, ropes were used to suspend the priests in the air or else tied around their genitals and pulled with agonising effect.[24]

With the help of Enguerrand of Boves and his German crusaders, Simon easily relieved Pamiers and together they chased Raymond and Raymond-Roger around until they came to Muret, about twenty kilometres southwest of Toulouse. To get to the town, they had to cross the River Garonne, but the enemy had set fire to the bridge during their retreat. Simon and some of his knights swam across to put out the fire at the other end, but heavy rains and flash flooding still rendered the bridge unsafe. Those unable to swim or who were too weak were forced to pitch camp on the east bank of the river while the main army was in Muret. They were mostly poor pilgrims and camp-followers, and Simon despaired to think that they were exposed to an attack by the Toulousains. Much to Marshal Lévis's disbelief, he and a few other knights swam back across to be on guard with them for however long it took to repair the bridge.[25]

From Muret, they moved into the county of Comminges. Simon was on shakier ground there than in the Agenais, because heresy was not especially known there, and because Count Bernard IV, whose only offence was being an active supporter of his kinsman Raymond of Toulouse, was a vassal of King Peter of Aragon. But the bishops of Comminges and Couserans had already arranged for the local nobility to swear homage to Simon. Their neighbours in Gascony had done so earlier, when they came in person during the siege of Penne, but their lord, Gaston de Béarn, remained evasive. Simon took control of Comminges in a few days with practically no resistance. The only destruction he wrought was on the lands of Roger, the viscount of Couserans. He was the same Roger who was spooked when Simon sneezed during his formal submission at Lavaur. Like so many other southern lords, Roger eventually turned his back on Simon, although what if any part the sneeze had to do with it went unrecorded.[26]

Save for Toulouse and Montauban, the conquest of Languedoc looked to be complete. It took more than three years of bitter fighting, but the heretics and mercenaries had been suppressed, their supporters either driven out or bottled up. It was time to give the business of peace and faith constitutional character by promulgating uniform laws and customs for the conquered territories. Simon summoned a parliament to meet in Pamiers in November for this purpose. A committee of twelve comprising four churchmen, four crusaders and four local officials were charged with drafting the articles of enactment, which they then submitted to Simon.

After taking them under advisement with seven bishops and various laymen, he issued them on 1 December 1212 as the Statute of Pamiers.[27]

Not surprisingly, the first articles deal with religion. The liberties and privileges of churches and ecclesiastical institutions were affirmed. All tithes were to be paid, no taxes imposed by secular rulers, no clergy detained by them. Households failing to attend Sunday services or celebrating feast days without a good excuse risked being fined. Jews and former heretics were banned from holding positions of authority. Heretical communities were to provide their best Cathar houses as churches and homes for priests and to banish any converted perfect who had preached there. Anyone found succouring heretics in the future, for whatever reason, stood to be disinherited. Only the Church had the authority to judge who was a heretic, but since no punishment was decreed or recommended, it was assumed the current process of immolation would continue.

The prospects of a just and moral society reflected in the statute were meant to reconcile the local population to the new order. Taxes were to be restricted by charter and exempted entirely for poor widows. Only tolls that had been in place for the last thirty-four years were to be retained. The Church had long campaigned against lords like Raymond of Toulouse imposing unjust tolls as a scurrilous form of raising revenue. Justice was to be administered free of charge. The poor were to be given court-appointed counsel and the accused the option of bail. Acts of personal revenge and vendetta were no longer permitted. Bread was to be baked and sold according to weights and standards, prostitutes escorted to the city gates.

Freedom of movement was guaranteed, even for serfs, but like other articles, it was a concession, not an innovation. The lax feudalism of the south had always been seen as one of the reasons for all the violence and disorder, but bringing it into line with the north in one fell swoop would only engender further hostility and alienation. On the other hand, the southern custom of dividing up estates within the family was to cease. Introducing primogeniture would rid the region of that irksome class of petty lord for whom grievance and daily strife were a way of life.

Judging by these laws, Simon was looking at decades to recast Languedoc as part of a faithful, peaceful Christian commonwealth.

Wealthy widows and heiresses with lordships were allowed to marry Frenchmen, but had to wait ten years before marrying an indigenous lord without permission. Newly enfeoffed Frenchmen had to provide the service of French knights for twenty years. After that, local knights could be used. Simon's followers also needed his permission to go to France, and lingering there beyond the agreed timeframe was discouraged. He had always been hampered by the lack of dependable manpower and wanted to ensure he had loyal troops at his beck and call throughout the year, not just during that absurd anomaly known as the crusade season. But the most telling sign that the war-footing was there to stay came from what was missing in the statute. None of the forty-seven articles proscribed mercenaries or even mentioned them. Simon was committed to eradicating them, but he remained a realist about what it might ultimately take to win the struggle.[28]

The pope flip-flops, Amaury becomes a knight, the armies of north and south gather

Even while the Statute of Pamiers was being discussed and approved, the pope heard a different story of the situation in Languedoc. Far from bringing peace and faith to the region, the crusade had brought only death and apocalypse. Truth be told, he might have feared as much. From the start Innocent had wanted no repeat of the Fourth Crusade, where his officials ignored his instructions, but apparently he had lost control of this one as well. It was mostly because of Raymond of Toulouse. Since confirming his excommunication in April 1211, Innocent was nagged by doubts that the process had been rigged against him. Once again, his legates were doing everything their way, not his. In May 1212, he ordered them to reopen the matter of Raymond's purification, but no action had been taken. Thedisius later claimed they had been forced to put it off because of illness and 'the general bad state of the air'.[29] The more likely reason is the prelates were holding out for Simon to consolidate his position and underpin it with a wholesome Christian constitution.

Privately they could ask themselves what would be the point of visiting the Raymond issue again. For ten years they had gone in nothing but circles with him. His recent humiliations certainly made him more desperate than ever for reconciliation. Unable to pay his allies, he was forced to go to Bordeaux for his son, who had been kidnapped for ransom by Savaric de Mauléon. Toulouse was still loyal to him, but it too was in a wretched state, with trade disrupted by the encirclement and heretics and refugees pouring in from the countryside with their livestock.[30] Since the legates refused to budge on their own accord, Raymond went to Aragon in September 1212 to ask his brother-in-law to intervene for him. Peter's victory over the Moorish host had not only given him the clout to win papal sympathy for the southern cause, but it showed that he had what it took to beat someone like Simon in the field.

By the end of November, two Spanish envoys were in Rome lobbying against the crusade. Inasmuch as the legates were seemingly defying him, Innocent was prepared to believe the worst. On 15 January 1213, he wrote to Arnaud-Amalric to announce that he was suspending the crusade. From what he had heard, it had been a success and Christian troops were needed elsewhere. He kept the tone hopeful and polite, both of which were missing in another letter he sent, this one to Simon:

> Envoys of King Peter, the illustrious King of Aragon, our dearest son in Christ, have informed us on his behalf that you have turned your hands against Catholics, when they should have been directed against heretics, and used the army of the crusaders, which you have induced to spill the blood of the just and injure the innocent, to occupy the territories of the king's vassals ... in so doing greatly wronging the king himself; this even though no heretics live in those territories and no ill report of contamination by the evil of heresy has involved the people living there.

He further denounced Simon for underhandedly appropriating Peter's lands while the king was busy fighting the infidels. He ordered him to return them immediately or else 'by retaining them illegally you appear to have worked for your own personal advantage rather than the general advantage of the Catholic faith'.

The next day Innocent sent a third letter. Addressed to all three legates, he accused them and Simon of stretching out their 'greedy hands' to obtain lands where there was no heresy. He also had assurances from

Peter that Raymond was truly sorry and ready to place his son under the king's protection while he went on crusade to whatever land the Church decreed. The pope ordered the legates to discuss Peter's proposal and get back to him. It would then be up to him to decide who made the most suitable ruler of the region.[31]

On 13 January 1213, two days before the first of the papal missives was drafted, the long-awaited council of bishops was convened by Thedisius in Lavaur. By then the prelates were aware of Peter's complaints and agreed to meet him the next day between Lavaur and Toulouse. Twenty archbishops and bishops heard him out, then went back to Lavaur to discuss his demands. The king also met Simon and Guy de Montfort to arrange a truce. Peter of Vaux-de-Cernay, who was present at these events, says the king praised the brothers and also Simon's sons, and although he does not mention which sons, it could be the first written reference to the young Simon VI de Montfort, who would have been about 5 years old at this time. Interestingly, no mention is made of Peter's own son James, who was also the same age and then being raised by the de Montforts in anticipation of his marriage to their daughter Amicia.[32]

The substance of the king's demands was the restoration of the lands seized from Raymond-Roger of Foix, Bernard of Comminges and Gaston de Béarn. They were his vassals and he had a duty to protect them, especially from other vassals like Simon. He denied they were heretics or had done anything wrong, but agreed they should make amends for whatever could be proved against them. Peter was told that the three southern counts had wilfully supported heretics and attacked the Church, but they would not be denied absolution if they sought it. The prelates remained unmoved about Raymond, however. They insisted he had 'piled iniquity on iniquity, crime on crime, evil on evil and in alliance with heretics, mercenaries and other evil men he attacked and subverted the Church of God and Christianity, the faith, and peace, so violently as to render himself unworthy of any consideration or favour'.[33]

On 21 January, they reported the outcome of their council to the pope. It was thanks to Simon de Montfort, 'that intrepid athlete of Christ', that progress was being made, but Toulouse still remained a 'bilge-hold' of heresy and Raymond was more pernicious than ever. Other letters were drafted by various abbots, bishops and archbishops, all attesting to

Raymond's faithlessness and demanding a continuation of the crusade. They were bundled up and handed to legates Thedisius and Hugh of Riez, who set off to see the pope at the head of a delegation of clerics.[34]

Aware that his own efforts in Rome had paid off, Peter dismissed a warning from fellow Catalan Arnaud-Amalric not to interfere and on 27 January took oaths of fealty from Raymond, Raymond's 15-year-old namesake son and the three counts. He left behind a contingent of household knights in Toulouse and returned to Aragon in February. From there he sent Simon a letter repudiating him as his vassal. A few days later Lambert de Thury arrived to tell Peter that Simon was ready to settle everything peacefully or to renounce his allegiance, it was up to the king. Some members of the Aragonese court wanted to hold the messenger accountable for what they saw as Simon's insolence and disloyalty, but none of them were prepared to back up their words in knightly combat with Lambert.[35]

In accepting the count of Toulouse as his vassal, Peter had brushed aside Philip Augustus as Raymond's nominal overlord. Peter proposed to overcome that snag by both kings joining forces to oppose a crusade neither of them had liked from the beginning, and they would underscore their alliance with a marriage between Peter and Philip's daughter Marie. This created another snag, because Peter was already married, to a woman named Marie no less. Although she was the mother of his heir James, he had only married her to gain possession of her rights to Montpellier. He longed to get rid of her and instructed his envoys in Rome that, in addition to bringing the crusade to an end, they were to secure him an annulment from the pope.[36]

In terms of moral rectitude, Innocent might have wished Peter and Raymond were more like Simon. Both men were notorious womanisers, whereas Simon and Alice had been inseparable since she joined the crusade and she was an indispensable helpmate during his campaigns. The public devotion of the de Montforts to each other inspired loyalty in their followers and perhaps recognition in their foes that Simon took his own vows seriously and therefore expected everyone else to do the same. Peter's condemnation of Simon's integrity might have carried more weight had he treated his own wife with equal respect. On 19 January 1213, the pope followed up his scathing letter to Simon by refusing

Peter's request for the annulment. Marie, who was in Rome at the time, died a few months later.[37]

Peter's envoys in Paris had also brought along documents confirming the pope's suspension of the crusade, but they were too late. The firebrand bishops of Toulouse and Carcassonne had persuaded crown prince Louis, the 25-year-old heir to the French throne, to take the cross and lead a host of knights to Languedoc. Philip Augustus was none too happy about it but convened a parliament to make arrangements for his son's departure, which was set for 21 April. Suddenly it was called off. Philip had decided to conquer England and wanted Louis to lead the invasion force there. The pope had encouraged this move because King John had defied him for the past five years by refusing to accept Stephen Langton as the archbishop of Canterbury. Clearly something more than excommunication and interdict was needed to break his will.

John capitulated in May. As part of his reconciliation, he made his kingdom a papal fief. Since John was now his vassal, Innocent told Philip to stand down, but the king of France had spent too much money putting everything together. He moreover saw John's submission as rank cynicism, akin to Raymond of Toulouse joining the Albigensian Crusade on the eve of invasion. Indeed, John was still prepared to ignore the pope as he saw fit. With his new power as John's overlord, Innocent ordered him to return the earldom of Leicester to Simon, perhaps hoping it might temper the crusader's roving eye for new territory. It was not until two years later, in 1215, that John got around to acting, but only then to commit Leicester to the custodianship of Simon's cousin Ranulf, the earl of Chester. John was facing another baronial revolt and needed Ranulf's support.[38]

Intending to go through with the invasion, Philip sent his fleet, commanded by Savaric de Mauléon, to Flanders. The English fleet chanced upon it at Damme and destroyed most it. Philip was forced to call off the expedition, but he refused to allow his son to go south and assist the crusade.[39] By this time the papal legates Thedisius and Hugh had arrived in Rome and were telling their side of the story in Languedoc. Innocent gradually became convinced that Peter of Aragon was the one telling the lies. On 21 May 1213, he sent him a sharp rebuke: 'We are amazed and disturbed that, by using your envoys to suppress the truth and give a false account of matters, you have extorted from us a papal letter ordering the restitution of their territories to the counts of Comminges and Foix and Gaston de Béarn.' He could not believe a good Catholic king would take heretics and their protectors under his protection in so openly a fashion. He ordered him to cut them adrift immediately and repair his relations with Simon.

The pope would not, however, resume the crusade, not at least until he could bring it fully back under his control.[40] In the meantime, he appointed another English friend of his from the Paris schools, Robert Courçon of Derbyshire, as legate to France for the purpose of redirecting Christian firepower back to the Holy Land. That left Guy of Vaux-de-Cernay practically alone among preachers still recruiting for the Albigensian Crusade. Simon would have been bereft of any spring campaigning were it not for brothers Manasses and William de Seignelay, one the bishop of Orleans, the other the bishop of Auxerre, who brought a small force of crusaders to Fanjeaux. Some of the men were employed by Simon in destroying abandoned castles or laying waste to cropland, others followed Guy de Montfort to besiege Puycelci. The fortress had still not fallen when the new crusaders went home after their forty days. Three of Simon's core knights, Peter de Sissy, Simon the Saxon and Roger des Essarts volunteered to garrison Pujol, a small castle close to Toulouse, to keep up the harassment as the harvest approached. Simon had misgivings but consented.[41]

The region was relatively quiet enough for many crusaders and clergy to gather in Castelnaudary on 24 June 1213 to witness the knighting of Amaury de Montfort. Due to the destruction of the town, Simon had pavilions and a makeshift altar erected in a nearby meadow for the occasion. He naturally wanted the ceremony imbued with religious overtones, a reminder that they were engaged in a holy war, but since his ordinary coterie of churchmen were elsewhere, he asked the two episcopal brothers to perform the rite of passage. The bishop of Orleans demurred, however, averring that knights were dubbed by other knights, not priests. He could understand Simon's wish to make the young man a 'knight of Christ', but did not want to do it on his own authority. When he was at last persuaded and mass had been celebrated, Amaury was escorted to the altar by his parents, with Alice holding his left hand, Simon his right. The two bishops girded the youth, who was then about 18 years old, and led the rest of the clergy in an eruption of *Veni Creator Spiritus*. (It is tempting to think that at the moment Amaury became a knight by being dubbed on his shoulders with the blade of a sword, a female Cathar initiate became a perfect by the laying of hands on her shoulders in a *consolamentum* ceremony.) Afterward Simon took his son to Gascony, where he enfeoffed him with certain lands and pointed out the others that were still holding out against them.[42]

With Simon far away and the bishops on their way home, Raymond saw his chance to strike. Together with the other counts, he set out in early July to capture Pujol, which was only thirteen kilometres from the city. It had been occupied by the crusaders solely to disrupt the harvest, which was fast approaching. The garrison dropped fire, rock and boiling water on the attackers, but the southerners pressed home their siege. Roger des Essarts was hit in the head by an arrow and killed. Word that Guy de Montfort was on his way with a relief force prompted Raymond and the consuls of Toulouse to put a quick end to it by offering the crusaders their lives in return for their surrender. Roger-Bernard took the survivors into captivity, but the militia, in contempt of the oaths sworn by their leaders, slew Simon the Saxon once they had him in their hands. Peter de Sissy and the other prisoners were hauled away to Toulouse. One of them managed to escape to a church, but he was found, dragged out, and killed. A frenzied mob then descended on the prison and butchered Peter and the other crusaders in their cells before dragging their bodies through the city streets and disposing of them 'like carrion'.[43]

There was little Simon could do by way of reprisal. King Peter was gathering an army in Aragon to invade Languedoc and barely any new crusaders had arrived that summer. He had the pope to thank for that. His suspension of indulgences for the crusade he himself had launched was the work of the man who now aimed to destroy it completely. Simon and the legates sent two abbots to Peter to remind him of Innocent's about-face and his order to him to desist from his warmongering. In fact, Innocent had reminded Peter of it himself in a second letter, but blundered by also confirming that the kings of Aragon enjoyed the privilege of being immune from excommunication by anyone other than the pope. Since the king had nothing to fear from the legates, he figured he would annihilate the northerners and deal with the pope about it afterwards. It was the same attitude that Innocent had deplored so much about the Fourth Crusade.[44]

In late August, Peter began moving his host northwards and was outside Muret by 8 September. Two days later the forces of the southern nobility and militia of Toulouse joined them. The militia began the assault on Muret, but were advised by Peter to keep their progress in check. While the town was strategically important, the whole point of the attack was to lure Simon there and destroy him. He was then sixty-five kilometres southeast in Fanjeaux. Baited as expected, he was making ready to leave when Alice confided in him that she had had a dream the night before that her arms were haemorrhaging. Surely it was an evil portent. Her fears made him snap that she had been in the south too long. He told her that if he had dreamt he was going to be killed in the battle to come, it would make no difference. He was going anyway, 'gladly and confidently' if only to refute such superstitious nonsense.[45]

He headed northwest while she went northeast for Carcassonne. On the way he received a report from the thirty knights defending Muret that the situation was becoming critical. He recalled Amaury from Gascony and dispatched a messenger to Alice to send as many knights as she could muster. She persuaded the viscount of Corbeil, who was getting ready to go back to France after his forty days of service, to ride the opposite way to her husband. Simon and his men stopped at the Cistercian abbey of Boulbonne to pray, and while there he was warned that the coalition's army was larger than anything he could put in the field and that he was facing a remarkable warrior in King Peter.

Unfazed, he showed the doomsayer a letter his men had intercepted, which was written by Peter to the wife of a nobleman of Toulouse. In it, he tells her that he has gone to all this trouble of driving the French out of Languedoc out of love for her. Simon did not see how he could lose to a man who engaged in such mush, acting like a silly troubadour on the eve of battle. The king's letter throws the characters of the two opposing generals into sharp relief: Where Peter is relaxed and smitten, wooing a married woman from afar with praises of love, Simon is tense and prayerful, speaking curtly to his wife in what may be the last time they ever see each other.[46]

Chapter 6

Supremacy
1213–1216

Simon gathered his troops in Saverdun, about thirty kilometres southeast of Muret. As he later told Peter of Vaux-de-Cernay, he was eager to get started to save the garrison, but his men advised him to halt in order to rest and feed the horses. There was also a chance they might have to fight their way there. He reluctantly agreed but was up early the next morning, 11 September, to make his confession to Master Clarin, his chaplain, and to draw up his will. He sent the will to the abbey of Boulbonne with instructions that it go to Rome for confirmation by the pope in the event he fell in battle.[1]

He continued to receive reinforcements. One of them, a new arrival from France, was his half-brother William IV des Barres. Three weeks earlier, on 20 August, Simon had granted two pecks of salt to the monastery of Grandchamp, which was founded by their mother Amicia, in memory of his father Simon IV. Throughout his time in the south, now more than four years, Simon had continued to support Amicia in her role as the lord of Montfort l'Amaury and this particular salt was to come from Alice's dowry at Conflans. The messenger who delivered the copy of the grant likely informed his family of the grave developments in Languedoc. As the son of one of the most famous warriors in all Europe, who had bested both Richard the Lionheart and William Marshal, the younger William had much to prove in riding to his brother's aid.[2]

Also moving with the army were seven bishops and three abbots. Arnaud-Amalric had intended for them to constitute a small host, although he himself was absent due to illness. Peter was not overawed by them in any case and rejected all their peace proposals. When Bishop Fulk of Toulouse asked him for safe-conduct to go directly to him and the Toulousains to negotiate, the king quipped that a man travelling with an army needed no safe-conduct. By nightfall the crusaders had reached the River Garonne and entered Muret over the bridge, with no resistance at all from the coalition. Simon's top commanders wanted to mount an immediate attack, not least because there was just one day's provisions left in the fortress, but he reasoned that they had been on the march the entire day and the prelates were insistent on having one more opportunity to bring Peter around.[3]

The next day, 12 September 1213, a priest left Muret to inform the king that the bishops were prepared to come to him barefoot and talk. Peter had already decided to attack that day, confident that if Simon had ten times the number he appeared to have, they would flee before his might. Raymond of Toulouse thought it was foolhardy and advised him to set up a strong defensive position. Let Simon and his men wear themselves down in useless charges, then spring forth and rout them. Peter and his Aragonese knights considered that kind of talk cowardly. In a jab that had to hurt, Michael of Luesia, one of the heroes of Las Navas de Tolosa, implied that the southern Raymonds would not be in their predicament had they shown more bravery in defending their lands.

In respect of peace talks, Simon left the gate open after the priestly messenger left, but the Toulousains took advantage of it to attack. They were beaten back, but Simon lost his patience and told the bishops they were getting nowhere. It was time to offer battle. He went in for one more prayer, but as he knelt at the altar, the leather strap holding up his metal leggings snapped. He took it in stride, ordering a new strap brought to him. He and his men confessed their sins, finished the service, and fortified themselves with a 'modest meal'. Outside, as he mounted his horse, Simon's stirrup broke off. The saddle was fixed and he tried again, but this time the horse flinched and knocked him to the side, stunning him for a moment. Since they were in the upper part of the fortress, the Toulousains below could see it all and had a good laugh at his difficulties. They could mock him all they wanted, he insisted, they would rue the day before it was over. Before setting off, he told his own troops there was more at stake in the fight ahead than religion and politics. In a speech attributed to him by William the Breton, Simon evoked Charlemagne and Roland as their ancestors and exhorted his men to prove themselves worthy of such noble lineage.[4]

Simon's impatience for the battle to be joined was matched by Peter's. The king was informed that two more battalions of Catalan cavalry were on their way, but he refused to wait for them. He even allowed Simon to march out of Muret with his men and get into formation unmolested, almost as if by invitation. It was either extreme chivalry or Peter just wanted to get it over with. In behaviour that would have made Simon smirk 'typical', the king had passed the night in the embraces of a mistress, whether the noble lady of Toulouse or another object of his affections. He had woken up so exhausted he had to sit down during morning mass. How far his personal urges and preoccupations clouded his judgement is arguable, but one look at the men amassing opposite him suggests his confidence in victory was not misplaced. Altogether the coalition had anywhere from 2,000–4,000 knights and horse sergeants, with the same estimate of foot soldiers and militia. Simon had 800–1,000 mounted men and a similar number of foot soldiers, whom he ordered to stay behind and guard the fortress. Taking a median total of 6,000 coalition troops, the crusaders were outnumbered outside the walls of Muret by at least six to one.[5]

Simon drew up his men in three lines in honour of the Trinity. His brother William des Barres would lead the attack, while Bouchard of Marly commanded the second line and he himself took the third, to be used in reserve after the initial onslaught. The coalition was also deployed in three ranks, with the first line formed by Catalans and the count of Foix and his men. This arrangement was probably at Raymond-Roger's own initiative. He not only wanted to refute the Aragonese jibe about a lack of courage among the southerners, but also redeem himself for his defeat by the crusaders at St-Martin-La-Lande two years earlier. Peter placed himself in the second line, also likely in response to the acrid comments of his war council. It would not do to call Raymond of Toulouse a coward and then hold back in the rear as the clash got underway. He did, however, don ordinary armour so as not to call attention to himself and risk being captured. He had already mortgaged much of his kingdom for this expedition; paying a ransom for his freedom would break it completely.[6]

Not quite two kilometres separated the armies. The first line of crusaders set off, making their way across a marshy area until they got their bearings on the centre of the coalition line. Spurring their horses on, they slammed into it with incredible violence, pummelling Raymond-Roger and his men backwards 'as the wind drives dust from the ground'.

The second line of crusaders followed up with an impact that drove a wedge even deeper into the coalition forces. Noticing the king's standard, the French began cutting their way to it with such tumult that young Raymond VII of Toulouse, watching from a nearby hill, remembered how it sounded like a whole forest being felled at once. Peter was somewhere in the thickest part of the fighting, and as the men around him began to fall, he cried out, 'I am the king!' in an attempt to save his life. Either he was not heard or not believed. He was struck down and killed alongside Michael of Luesia and many other Spanish noblemen.[7]

Seeing both his lines swallowed up in the fighting, Simon led his reserve on a sweep in order to hit the coalition in the flank. His stirrup broke again as he engaged the enemy, so he fixed his spur in the saddle blanket to keep his balance. Then the spur snapped. Forced to fight from a sitting position, he clobbered one opponent off his horse after the man struck him hard on the head. By this point, the Aragonese had learned that their king was dead and ran for it. The first two crusader lines took off in pursuit, but Simon, knowing how vastly outnumbered they still were, regrouped his own men in the event the coalition managed a counterattack. But they were soundly thrashed that day, Raymond-Roger for a second time in open combat with the crusaders. He and the other southern counts took flight to avoid capture.[8]

While the battle raged in the field, the militia of Toulouse launched another full-scale assault on Muret. Their bishop pleaded with them to come to their senses. As a sign of his sincerity and charity, Fulk sent them a monk's cowl. That only made them laugh. They grabbed the cowl and beat the messenger who brought it. They were sure their side had won and in the distance they could see horsemen approaching under the standards of the coalition army. It could only mean the king of Aragon had vanquished the French and was coming to help them take Muret. When they realised that the standards were in fact trophies, that it was the crusaders riding towards them, they were overcome with terror. It was fresh in everyone's mind how the Toulousains had murdered the prisoners from Pujol and dumped their bodies outside the city gates to be picked apart by birds and wild animals. The friends and comrades of these unfortunate men were now bearing down hard on them to exact a terrible revenge.[9]

In their panic, the Toulousains forgot all about their possessions in the camp and fled to the river. Some managed to get on the boats and escape, but the mass of them were cut down with sword and mace or drowned. The number of men slain in this gratuitous manner was staggering, but some were taken captive for ransom. William of Puylaurens says it was 'pitiful to see and hear the laments of the people of Toulouse as they wept for their dead; indeed there was hardly a single house that did not have someone dead to mourn'. He adds that the ones who made it safely back were reproached by the citizenry for visiting them with this horrible fate on account of their treatment of the prisoners.[10]

The casualties on the crusader side were ridiculously small: one knight and several horse sergeants were killed. Simon asked to be led to the body of the king. It had already been stripped naked by the foot soldiers who came out of Muret to loot the battlefield. The victor walked barefoot from there to the church to offer thanks and give his horse and armour as alms for the poor. Having gone to church at least seven times in the past couple of days, Simon believed he owed his victory to God.[11] Earthly devices certainly played their part, but the battle of Muret ultimately came down to a contest of generalship and it was not even close. Peter had presumed Languedoc was his for the taking if he just showed up. He did not bother with negotiations, leadership or the disposition of troops. His love life was of greater concern to him than his faith, his men, even his own son, who was in the hands of his enemies. His recklessness in the face of an army forged on loyalty, discipline and determination allowed Simon to deliver the punch needed to knock out an opponent six times bigger in less than twenty minutes. The southerners had hoped Peter would free them from the grip of the accursed crusade. Instead, he made it look more invincible than ever.

New legates, new settlements, Baldwin is executed, a doubtful pope, Toulouse surrenders

Muret may have vindicated Raymond of Toulouse's advice on how to beat Simon de Montfort, but it was still another inglorious defeat for him to shoulder. In his bitterness and sorrow, he privately told the consuls of Toulouse to cut whatever deal they could with the legates. In December

1213, he went to England to seek support and took his son with him. With Peter of Aragon now dead and Philip Augustus still a non-entity in his troubles, Raymond switched his homage to King John in return for 1,000 marks. John got that money from a tax he imposed on the Cistercian order as their punishment for supporting the crusade. Stephen Langton, at last the archbishop of Canterbury, objected to Raymond being in England, and after Christmas both father and son were ejected by the legate there, Nicholas of Tusculum.[12]

The inexplicable defeat sent shockwaves throughout the region. Rabastens, another fortified settlement in the Albigeois that had defected, was quickly abandoned. Simon gave it to his brother Guy, who sent his men there to occupy it. Fear of this sort was the exception, however, for what the crusaders mostly encountered in the aftermath of Muret was anger, especially in the east. The house of Provence, which was related to Aragon, tried to prevent the passage of recruits coming from France. Simon headed that way to deal with their resistance, but found all the major cities on his route hostile and unwilling to receive him and his men. At Narbonne and Montpellier, they were forced to camp overnight in the orchards and woods outside the walls. Nîmes also barred them entry, but relented when they noticed the swell of indignation in the armed force before their gates.[13]

Raids by Aragonese mercenaries fuelled much of the unrest. It was not only revenge for their king they were after, but also their new king. Six-year old James of Aragon was still at Carcassonne and Simon had shown no signs of handing him over. If he was intent on the marriage of the young king going forward to his daughter, the pope disabused him of that and other ideas. Innocent was then in a state of disbelief. In 1208, he had declared war on Raymond of Toulouse after a legate named Peter was murdered. Now, not quite six years later, it had come to this, a crusader king dead at the hands of another crusader, all of Languedoc in an uproar, heresy there practically forgotten. In January 1214, he sent a new legate named Peter, a cardinal from Benevento, to go there and take charge. He wanted Peter to take custody of James and to reconcile the city of Toulouse and the southern counts. Simon was not to molest any of them. The papal plan was to dump the entire mess on the Fourth Lateran

Council meeting in Rome next year. The senior prelates of the Christian world would decide what to do next.[14]

Neither side had any intention of waiting that long for an outcome they might not like. On 17 February, Baldwin was nabbed in his sleep by turncoats and taken to Montauban. There, Raymond of Toulouse discussed his fate with Raymond-Roger, Roger-Bernard and a Catalan knight who was tagging along. All three insisted he should be hanged, if for no other reason than to avenge Peter of Aragon, and they carried out the deed at a nearby walnut tree. Raymond probably did not lose any sleep denying his brother mercy or a less ignoble form of execution. He had never been close to him, and Baldwin's steadfast support for Simon must have rankled deeply.[15]

Losing a good, loyal lieutenant was a huge blow to Simon, but he could not imagine how big it would be for his future reputation. Since joining Baldwin's household, William of Tudela had been hard at work on *The Song of the Cathar Wars*. His poem had reached the events right before the battle of Muret when suddenly it broke off and no more was heard of William. In all likelihood, he had fallen victim to the killing that surrounded the kidnapping and execution of his patron. His work was discovered, taken to Toulouse, and there, years later, a poet who chose to remain anonymous continued it, only in a completely different vein. Where William was an eyewitness who strove for balanced coverage, the Anonymous despises the crusade, the French and Simon de Montfort in particular. His portrayal of him as an evil, pestilent man out to destroy their culture is a caricature designed to work up and enthral local audiences, but over time it became the fixture of many interpretations.[16]

In March 1214, Narbonne broke completely with the crusade and became the base for the Aragonese insurgency. Simon was able to respond with a large force of men brought south by his stepfather William III des Barres. In one assault led by Simon, his saddle broke under the thrust of enemy lances, causing him to fall off his horse. A vicious fight hovered over him as his men fought off the mercenaries trying to kill or capture him. Barres, the legendary warrior who beat Saladin's men in action, charged with the last line of troops and drove the enemy back inside the gate.[17]

Cardinal Peter arranged a truce between the city and crusaders, but there was no respite. Simon had to hurry 185 kilometres northwest after learning that Raymond of Toulouse had commenced a siege of Moissac. After chasing Raymond back to Toulouse, he set off for the Agenais, where King John had arrived as part of his plan to reclaim the Continental patrimony he lost to Philip Augustus a decade earlier. John and Simon had not seen each other for more than seven years, not since the king stripped him of the earldom of Leicester. Simon was now intent on, if not stripping John of the Agenais, then neutralising his authority there. Before the two could square off, however, Simon was recalled south by the new legate.

Throughout April, Peter of Benevento had been fulfilling the pope's instructions. At Narbonne he reconciled the southerners to the Church. He took oaths from the counts of Foix and Comminges, each surrendering a castle or hostages as a sign of their good faith. Toulouse also gave up 120 hostages, who were detained in Provence, and Raymond avowed that all that was his, including his son, was in the hands of the pope, from whom he would personally seek mercy. Simon followed orders and handed over young King James to the legate at Capestang, a fortress near Narbonne. Peter then took the boy to Aragon himself.[18]

For Simon and Alice, the loss of the king as their future son-in-law was somewhat offset by the daughter-in-law they gained. While in Provence earlier that year, Simon met up with his long-standing friend Odo of Burgundy, whom he had not seen since the duke left the crusade in 1209. Through the mediation of Arnaud-Amalric, a match was arranged between Amaury de Montfort and Beatrice, the daughter of the dauphin de Vienne, Odo's brother. The young lady was brought to Carcassonne for their wedding in June. Another family friend, Dominic de Guzman, was on hand to bless the wedding.[19]

Innocent would have been pleased by these events. Finally, a legate doing as he was told. But there were five other legates and a host of prelates who thought he was pursuing a wrongheaded policy. The whole business of peace and faith had been his idea, but having suffered a little shellshock from developments that were, after all, the Lord's intentions, he was prepared to abandon it. If he wondered why his officials in the field failed to carry out his orders, he had only himself to blame. He lacked the steel and resolve for the punishing work of the true mission. The pontiff was a lawyer who spent all his time in Rome making big pronouncements and threats, but when push came to shove, as it did in Languedoc, he buckled. His deputies believed that it was for his own good, and the good of the Church, that they took matters into their own hands.

This was the case of Guy of Vaux-de-Cernay, Archdeacon William of Paris and Jacques de Vitry, who continued to recruit despite the suspension of indulgences. Guy and William led a new batch of crusaders to Carcassonne in the spring. Peter of Vaux-de-Cernay, who accompanied his uncle, believed it was the presence of these fresh troops that convinced the southerners to make their peace with Peter of Benevento. Since there was an unofficial truce below Toulouse, Simon sent these men north under his brother Guy to avenge the murder of Baldwin. Guy de Montfort was soon joined by Robert Courçon, the legate for France. Robert was supposed to be recruiting for the Holy Land but decided the situation in the south was more urgent. The crusaders took Morlhorn, where they found seven Waldensians. After rejecting Courçon's offer of conversion, they were burnt at the stake, the last heretics of any sort mentioned for the rest of the crusade.[20]

By the time Simon joined them in the middle of June, the new crusaders had finished their forty days and gone home. Since he was unable to garrison all the strongholds there, he razed them in an attempt to create a demilitarised zone. The only major siege conducted was at Casseneuil, 115 kilometres northwest of Toulouse. The lord was Hugh of Revignan, another turncoat whose men included many who had betrayed Baldwin. In a pre-dawn raid, members of their garrison almost nabbed Amaury from his tent while he was sleeping. The greatest difficulty facing the crusaders was replacing the bridge that had been destroyed by the defenders. Two contraptions were built, but the first sank under its own weight and the second proved too short to span the twenty-five metres to the opposite bank. The defenders had a good laugh out of each failure. Simon gave his engineers a pep talk and at last they constructed a protective tower, manned by crossbowmen, that rolled with the causeway being built beneath it. Casseneuil was finally taken on 18 August 1214. Those put to the sword did not include the mercenaries, who had managed to slip away.[21]

The fortress was destroyed and the town given to Dominic de Guzman, who had returned to preach in Languedoc in 1211 during the siege of

Toulouse. His success in converting ladies perfect led him to found a convent for them at Prouille outside Fanjeaux. Lambert de Thury, Alan de Roucy and Robert Mauvoisin became benefactors, and in May 1213 Simon, Alice and Amaury confirmed a donation made to the convent by Hugh de Lacy. The new source of revenue from Casseneuil was intended to support Dominic's intention to move his base of operations to Toulouse.[22]

The garrison at Casseneuil had expected King John to come to their rescue, but he was in Poitou retreating before the forces of Prince Louis. Worse for him, on 27 July his allies in the north, led by his nephew Otto, the Holy Roman Emperor, were defeated by Philip Augustus at the battle of Bouvines in Flanders. Philip's commanders included Alice's brother Matthew Montmorency, Simon's half-brother William des Barres and his brother-in-law Bartholomew of Roye. It finished any hope of John recovering Normandy or other English lordships that had been confiscated by Philip. Prepared to cut his losses and go home to face a baronial crisis, John paid Simon 20,000 shillings (£1,000) through the archbishop of Bordeaux to leave his lands in the Agenais in peace.[23]

Simon moved northeast from Casseneuil into the Périgord region, where they destroyed all the fortresses that had been abandoned. One they found particularly hard to pull down was a stronghold named, ironically enough, Montfort. At nearby Sarlat they made a gruesome discovery. The lord and lady of the place, Bernard de Cazenac and his wife Alice, were notorious for their cruel treatment of widows and the poor. Before fleeing, the depraved couple had 150 peasants mutilated in an orgy of terror at the local abbey. Peter of Vaux-de-Cernay apparently heard the horrific tale from his uncle Guy, who was with the army at the time, but the anonymous poet of the *Song* calls Bernard a fine specimen of a knight, full of 'staunch courage, good sense and generosity'.[24]

With the northern territories seemingly secure, Simon went to Figeac in Quercy to sit in judgement on cases before the king's court. In essence, this was Philip's tacit recognition of him as the count of Toulouse. Robert Courçon added weight to Simon's new stature by confirming him and his heirs in possession of Agen, Cahors, Rodez and Albi. The cardinal based his decree on 'liability of seizure', the justification for the confiscation of an excommunicate's lands. It was the doctrine Innocent had devised to propel the crusade forward but which he had clearly come to regret.[25] Courçon was the latest in a long line of legates who, having seen the situation for himself, knew they were on the right track. Southern noblemen had helped give rise to heresy through their attacks and despoliation of Church property. The way the prelates saw it, the depredations would always continue as long as Raymond of Toulouse was the count. They were convinced that would change with Simon in his place.

The churchmen took another step towards making that happen by convening a council of five archbishops and twenty-eight bishops in Montpellier in January 1215. Peter of Benevento had returned from Aragon, where he helped set up a minority regency for King James I, and found all his work of reconciliation undone by the intentions of Courçon and the other legates. By unanimous decision, they urged him to grant Toulouse and Raymond's other lands to Simon so that he should be the 'sole ruler'. Peter said he had no authority to make the grant, but did not object to Archbishop Bernard of Embrun going to Rome to get it. Raymond was just then there, pleading before Innocent, who was again moved by his submission. The pope was at the same time overawed by the phalanx of churchmen demanding that he accept the *fait accompli* presented before him and finish the crusade. Unwilling to offend either party, he deferred the decision to the Lateran Council meeting later that year. He nevertheless sent Simon a remarkable letter, full of praise and duplicity, asking him to accept the mandate of temporary ruler but with an admonishment from II Timothy 2:5.[26]

> Do not think to wipe away the sweat of battle until you have won the palm of victory. Rather, since you have started so well, see to it that this good beginning (and the subsequent progress you have so commendably worked to achieve) will lead on to the desired conclusion. Put your faith in patience and the perseverance which deservedly brings the crown of success, and remember always that, in the words of the apostle, no one is crowned except he strive lawfully.

Since the inhabitants of Montpellier 'nourished a deep hatred' of Simon and the French, they awaited the outcome of the council at the hospice of the Knights Templar outside the city walls. They ventured in once, at the invitation of the legate and several prelates, but certain townsmen stationed themselves at different points within the city, even in the church of the Blessed Mary, to assassinate Simon as he strolled about with his brother and two sons. The plot was revealed in time and the de Montforts avoided the ambush.[27]

After the council, Peter of Benevento sent Bishop Fulk to Toulouse to make the arrangements of the new owners. It was the bishop's first visit to the city in nearly four years. He took possession of Narbonnais Palace, garrisoning it with knights and sergeants, in effect setting himself up as the local potentate. The Raymonds, father and son, went to live with their wives in the home of a leading citizen before both left to wander from place to place in search of help, much like other members of the dispossessed southern nobility. Guy de Montfort later came to take oaths of fealty from the municipal population and supervise the destruction of their walls.[28]

Just when it seemed the crusade was winding down, the French Crown, which had resisted involvement for seven years, finally showed up. Prince Louis, eager to fulfil his vow, arrived in the spring of 1215 in the company of Bishop Guy and Matthew Montmorency among others. At first wary of his intentions, Simon and the legate found Louis quite useful in getting the city-states to tear down their walls. They encountered opposition from the various consuls naturally, but were quite surprised to find Arnaud-Amalric vehement about blocking any interference in Narbonne's sovereignty. He was not only the archbishop of Narbonne, he claimed, but the duke of Narbonne as well.[29]

It was not a new claim. Since becoming archbishop in 1212, Arnaud-Amalric had been calling himself the duke of Narbonne despite the fact that the counts of Toulouse were entitled to that mostly honorific title. It was perhaps hoped that the title would help him overcome the reluctance of the city leaders to support the crusade, but their insults after the victory over Peter of Aragon made it clear to Simon that Narbonne needed a firmer hand. He asserted that if anyone was the rightful duke of Narbonne, it was he as the new de facto count of Toulouse and he wanted the walls down.[30] Acrimony grew from then on between these two former partners, Arnaud-Amalric and Simon de Montfort, who together had made the crusade what it was. Their feud became so bitter and unseemly that in July, three months after sending Simon his letter of congratulations, Innocent was writing to him again, this time warning him to back off:

> You have tried to usurp the duchy of Narbonne from the man to whom you owe everything, sullying your reputation with the stain of ingratitude. Take care that you do not give him just cause for complaint at our ecumenical council, for if he does, we shall punish you in whatever manner we shall think fit.[30]

Simon ignored him. Arnaud-Amalric could go to the council all he wanted. Like the pope, he too was a spent force. The crusade was now under the direction of a new league of papal officials and churchmen and they were all marching in step with his conquest of the south.

Lateran IV, Simon becomes the count of Toulouse, the feud with Arnaud-Amalric grows worse, young Raymond comes to the fore, clampdown on Toulouse, Guy II gets married

The Albigensian Crusade was just one of many talking points at the Fourth Lateran Council that met in November of 1215. Mindful that the previous gathering in 1179 had condemned the heretics and mercenaries flourishing in Languedoc, Innocent III could report to assorted Christendom that the crusade he had wrought to wipe both off the map had achieved the impossible. But the proceedings described by the Anonymous show he was still a troubled man. He informed the 400 bishops, 800 abbots, and as many priors, priests and accredited lords and officials as could fit in the old basilica that he did not believe Raymond of Toulouse was guilty of anything that justified seizing his land and titles. That said, he opened the floor to debate.

Both sides were well represented in Rome. Raymond was there and so was his son, who had made a difficult journey from England. Bishop Fulk, Guy of Vaux-de-Cernay and Guy de Montfort were among the delegates representing Simon and the crusaders. The most interesting speech devised by the Anonymous was given to the count of Foix, 'a fine figure of a man, with a fresh complexion'. Raymond-Roger denied being a friend of heretics. He admitted that his sister was a Cathar perfect, but she had just as much right to live on the lands of their father as he did. He seemed unconcerned telling Innocent that the men who came to drive her and all other heretics away deserved mutilation and death. Neither the sign of the cross nor an indulgence from the pope made a thug a crusader in his book. 'I rejoice to think of those I have killed and regret the escape of those who got away', he reflected. He was seconding an observation that had been made by another southern lord, who crowed that he would have gouged out more eyes and lopped off more noses had he known it was open for discussion at the council.

The free admission of torturing and murdering crusaders did not move Innocent to outrage, rather a plea for all of them to 'walk in the light, bringing good peace on earth'. That was the crux of his problem with Simon. His sword had a broad sweep. 'He destroys Catholics just as much as heretics', the pope lamented. In his mind, the rightful settlement was to give the Raymonds their possessions back, make sure the widows and orphans received their inheritances, and Simon could keep whatever was left. Bishop Fulk was raised to anger by it. What that meant was to dispossess Simon, if that was even possible at this stage, and all because of some misplaced sympathy for heretical supporters. He warned the pope that if he pursued this track, the southern bishops were 'as good as dead'. Languedoc would go back to the state it was in before the crusade, only the attacks against the Church would take on an extra personal agenda. But Innocent could not bring himself to finish what he had started and deferred judgement to the assembly, which did it for him. On 14 December 1215, he was forced to declare that Simon was in and Raymond was out:[31]

> Since the count of Toulouse has been found culpable on both charges (of harbouring heretics and mercenaries) and his territory will never be able to be kept safe in the true faith under his rule (as has long been clear from sure indications), he is to be excluded forever from his rights of dominion, which he exercised badly.

Raymond was told to go live somewhere else, with a pension of 400 marks to be paid annually if he showed the proper obedience. Raymond-

Roger and the other counts would get their lands back in time and young Raymond was to receive certain lordships like the marquisate of Provence. According to the Anonymous, Innocent consoled the losers by telling them not to worry. 'If your claim is valid, God will help and support you.' He was even more encouraging to young Raymond. 'Allow mercy to defeat and conquer you. But against any who try to disinherit or bring you down, defend yourself well and maintain your right.' It was an extraordinary thing to say. Whether out of petulance or still wanting to have it both ways, the pope basically gave him his blessing to undermine the Church and continue the war.[32] His unscrupulous behaviour confirms why he had lost control of the two crusades he launched. Beneath the veneer of piety and legality lay a weak man who should have never been in that business in the first place.

His complete opposite in terms of resolve and conviction was Arnaud-Amalric, who never once doubted that Raymond of Toulouse was guilty of all the crimes attributed to him. A ruler more unfit than Raymond to deal with heretics and mercenaries he could not imagine, nor one fitter for the iron will of governing than Simon de Montfort. Indeed, no one, not even Simon, was more assured of the righteousness of the crusade than Arnaud-Amalric. It therefore had to be galling to the southern bishops to hear their senior prelate taking the middle ground at Lateran IV. It was tantamount to him backing Raymond. Of course, his opinion about the former count had not changed in the least, but in his eyes Simon had become the bigger threat. He was desperate to keep him at bay like so many other southern lords before him. It would seem that the crusade, now that it was no longer his show, had put the fear of God in Arnaud-Amalric.

The inevitable clash occurred on 4 February 1216. When the archbishop tried to stop Simon and his crusaders from entering Narbonne, he was grabbed and tossed aside. He responded by excommunicating them and placing the city under interdict, but Simon had come prepared. Waving a papal privilege that permitted divine services whatever the sanction, he ordered mass to go ahead in the ducal chapel and to ring the bells as usual, louder if possible. He stayed a whole month in the city, forcing Arnaud-Amalric to stand by helplessly as the French did whatever they wanted, even pelting his residence with stones.[33]

It was only after Simon went to Toulouse to take oaths of obedience on 8 March that he started calling himself the duke of Narbonne and count of Toulouse. Doubtless the ceremony was accompanied by very few cheers from the citizens. Their fear and loathing of him was more than about heretics or loyalty to the house of Saint-Gilles. Toulouse had enjoyed a large measure of independence precisely because Raymond was so weak. Their new count made no secret of his intention to impose his will on the city. Simon ordered the destruction of more fortifications while at the same time converting his new residence, Narbonnais Palace, into a citadel where he could come and go without the locals knowing it. He wanted them to feel his presence at all times. He nevertheless promised to be a good lord to them and as a gesture of conciliation permitted the hostages taken by Peter of Benevento two years ago to come home from Provence.[34]

All that remained was for Simon to go north and do homage to Philip Augustus for his new territories. After years of scorning the crusade, the king was happy it turned out as well as it did. Simon not only brought Toulouse under the closer hegemony of the Crown, but also the lands lost by Aragon. He may have intimated to Simon that the earldom of Leicester could soon be his again as well. Prince Louis was then preparing to invade England at the invitation of the rebellious barons there, the same ones that elected Simon their king in 1212. They had already given their oath of fealty to Louis and were now waiting for him to land with his army so they could depose John and put a Capetian on the throne.[35]

According to Peter of Vaux-de-Cernay, Simon was feted everywhere he went like a conquering hero, the man who had finally destroyed heresy. People rushed to get close to him, believing they were blessed simply by touching the hem of his tabard. The honour had to be overwhelming. A decade earlier he had returned from the Fourth Crusade in obscurity, with none of the glory that had been bestowed on the men who had won the Latin Kingdom. By comparison, Toulouse and the surrounding territories only amounted to a principality, but unlike his original crusading companions, he had won them within the letter of his mandate, or so he could claim following Lateran IV.

His mother Amicia having died the previous year, Simon paid a visit to Montfort l'Amaury to settle her estate and renew her grants to religious houses.[36] He was probably eager to get back. He had not been to France in seven years, not since a chance flip through a holy book at the little church in Rochefort led him to taking the cross, but it was more than the simple belief that his place was now and forever in the south. His massive new lordship was still a work in progress and could become unglued without the kind of vigilance and speed that had always kept him ahead of the game. He found that out soon enough.

Back in February 1216, while Simon was humbling Arnaud-Amalric, Raymond of Toulouse and his son left Genoa and landed in Marseille. They were given a rapturous welcome throughout Provence, with pledges of men and aid should they seek to regain what had been, in their minds, unlawfully taken from them. It was decided that young Raymond, who was 19 years old, would lead an assault in the east while his 60-year-old father went to Spain to drum up support for an attempt to retake Toulouse. The target was Beaucaire, which Simon held of the archbishop of Arles as Raymond VI had done before him. Since Raymond VII had been born there, and it was hundreds of kilometres from any immediate help, it was both a symbolic and safe start to their campaign.[37]

Guy de Montfort was at Lavaur on 1 June when he received word that the garrison at Beaucaire, commanded by Lambert de Thury, had come under siege. Together with his nephew Amaury and Bishop Guy and Peter of Vaux-de-Cernay, he led a relief force to Nîmes more than 200 kilometres away in just three days. By 7 June, Simon had arrived from France with paid volunteers, but their combined forces at Beaucaire were outnumbered. Their only option was to besiege the besiegers, but it had little effect. Raymond was easily supplied from across the River Rhône from all of Provence, while the crusaders had to undertake guarded convoys coming from Nîmes twenty-two kilometres away.[38]

The garrison put up a sturdy defence. The Provençals built an iron-shod battering ram to weaken the walls of the keep, but the defenders managed to lasso it with a rope from above and keep it suspended out of reach of the crew. The attackers next built a 'weasel', which was a smaller version of the cat siege engine, and used it to get next to the walls to drive home a spike. Seeing it from above, Lambert's chief engineer scored a bull's-eye when he dumped a pot of burning tar on top of it, causing the weasel to burst into flames. The situation in the keep had nevertheless grown desperate, with the men reduced to eating their mules and horses, and they let their comrades know by waving a black flag.[39]

The crusaders launched four attacks against the entrenched besiegers, each one repelled. The Anonymous represents Simon as 'dark with rage and grief', if not deranged. Peter of Vaux-de-Cernay admits he was stumped. 'He was unable to rescue the garrison, but totally against leaving them exposed to certain death.' Difficult sieges were nothing new for him. Termes lasted a lot longer and Moissac had been particularly brutal, but this one was the first where the object was to save his men trapped inside. The lesson of Pujol had not been lost on him, and the Provençals had proved in this fight that they were equally ruthless when it came to crusaders who fell into their grasps. A knight named William of Berlit had been captured in a skirmish. After hanging him from an olive tree, his captors chopped off his hands and feet and launched them into the keep, where cannibalism was being discussed by the increasingly frantic garrison.[40]

As the end of summer approached, one of them slipped out and informed the crusaders that they had been without bread, water and wine for three weeks. Urged on by his brother Guy, Simon began negotiations. After several days of going back and forth, it was agreed to swap the garrison for the castle. It was a surprising concession by Raymond VII. He was on the verge of storming the keep and there was nothing Simon could do to stop him. The young man did not have to give him anything. But he was probably worried by the news that the pope had died six weeks earlier on 16 July 2016. Innocent had been sympathetic to his cause and even included Beaucaire in his settlement for him at Lateran IV. Whoever was elected the new pope might not look so favourably on him if his first foray into the field ended in a massacre of crusaders.[41]

Had negotiations failed, Simon may have had no choice anyway but to abandon the counter-siege, which he did on 24 August. He had received at least twenty reports that Toulouse was conspiring to betray him. Raymond VI was in fact on his way to reclaim the city when Simon's approach sent him back to Aragon. The delegation of citizens that went out to meet Simon only made matters worse by denying any treachery. According to the Anonymous, they told him he could put his sword away, he would be welcomed if he came among them 'singing, garlanded and wearing a gold-embroidered tunic'. Simon had the lot of them locked up before sending a squad of soldiers under his brother to shake down the city. This way he could pay his men under the guise of penalising the inhabitants for their disloyalty. The people saw it for the pillage that it was and rioted. Some soldiers they captured, others were driven out of the city. Working himself into a fury, Simon ordered part of Toulouse set on fire, both in retaliation and to get past the barricades erected everywhere. Still denied entrance, he stormed off to Narbonnais Palace and threatened to kill the hostages there unless his men were handed over and the barricades came down.

The next day Bishop Fulk persuaded the city to seek Simon's mercy and all would be forgiven. The Anonymous, who finds Fulk equally repugnant, says the captive crusaders were returned, but then Simon reneged on his end, even against the advice of his brother, just so he could have his revenge. His men went up and down the streets armed with clubs, seizing more hostages amidst the cries of women and children. The city was also slapped with a fine of 30,000 marks to regain his goodwill. Simon was broke after France and Beaucaire and was told that it was an amount the city could afford, despite the recent destruction. 'Blinded by money', says William of Puylaurens, Simon put harsh measures in place for collecting it, including marking those houses in default of payment with crosses. Together with other actions undertaken to curtail the liberties of the city, Simon had the people 'groaning under the yoke of servitude'.[42]

In November, he travelled 120 kilometres southwest to Tarbes in Gascony. Gaston de Béarn had died in 1214, leaving behind a widow, Perronelle, who was the heiress of Bigorre. Her next marriage was to Nunyo-Sanchez, a cousin of Peter II of Aragon and regent for James I, but Simon wanted Perronelle for his second son Guy and had her second union nullified by the Gascon bishops. Guy II was about 18, Perronelle 32. Although the marriage made young Guy the count of Bigorre, father and son were unable to take Lourdes and other possessions of the county due to resistance from the jettisoned husband and his allies. But Simon had essentially accomplished what he set out to do with his older sons. He set them both up with lordships on the fringes of his own principality, each at opposite ends. The de Montforts had become a family enterprise and were digging in to stay.[43]

Chapter 7

Twilight of the Albigensian Crusade
1217–1229

As Simon was adding Bigorre to the family holdings, the new pope, Honorius III, decided that Raymond-Roger could have his county of Foix back. He had been declared orthodox by the papal commission dispatched earlier by Innocent, who had already ordered Simon to hand over the county to the Church with a view to the count regaining it. Simon had been stalling and Innocent's death effectively allowed him to ignore the order. To get around the new pope's intervention, he declared that Raymond-Roger was in breach of his promise to keep the peace by building a new castle. On 6 February 1217, he led his men to invest the isolated fortress. It was winter and Montgrenier stood at the top of a steep hill, but he probably felt he had a lot to prove after his failure at Beaucaire. The garrison was commanded by Roger-Bernard, Roger of Comminges and Peter-Roger, who had not been heard from since he surrendered Cabaret in 1211. They were an able lot, but starvation forced them to surrender after six weeks. They were allowed to go free on their word to keep the peace for a year.[1]

Honorius could not have been happy about Simon flouting his orders, but he welcomed less the southern resurgence. His priority was a new crusade to the Holy Land, not more quagmire in Languedoc. But he refused to wash his hands of it as his predecessor had done, and in January, in addition to calling for more recruiting, he appointed yet another legate, Cardinal Bertrand. Since Provence was the new flashpoint, Bertrand set himself up at Orange on the River Rhône, but the consuls of various towns just laughed at him when he demanded they return Church property. In late spring, as crusaders began arriving, Simon went to the other side of the river to subdue strongholds around Nîmes. He hanged many of the inhabitants of Bernis. Peter of Vaux-de-Cernay gives no reason for his condemning them other than to say they 'richly deserved it'. It did inspire terror in the region and so cleared the way to the river just as the forty-day crusaders were leaving.[2]

In July, Simon met Bertrand at Pont-Saint-Saturnin. One of their first councils dealt with news from Toulouse that Alice had set out to forcibly convert the local Jewish community. Their children were seized and baptised, with those under the age of six placed in Christian families, while the adults were imprisoned and told to convert or face death. Simon was indignant that she should have usurped his authority in this fashion and ordered her to release those holding out (57 men had converted) and return their property. It was too late for the children, however. According to Bertrand, they were now Christians and so could not be reunited with their families. The Jews of Toulouse, he continued, were to start wearing distinctive badges on their outer garments as decreed by the recent Lateran Council.

Turning to military matters, the legate encouraged Simon to take the fight to the east side of the river. He made the crossing with a hundred knights sent to him by Philip Augustus, but found his presence alone caused many of the 'reprobates' to abandon their towns. His toughest fight was at Crest, which was defended by long-standing opponent Adhémar of Poitiers. Instead of slugging it out to the end, the two sides agreed to a settlement that called for Adhémar's son William to marry Simon's daughter Amicia, now her third engagement (after young Raymond and James). Putting his daughter here, next to his son Amaury in his future lordship of Vienne, would secure that area and provide a base of operations against Raymond VII and his Provençal supporters in the south.[3]

According to the Anonymous, Simon was compelled to seek the settlement because messengers had arrived from his wife warning him of a new rebellion in Toulouse. Learning that Simon was over 300 kilometres away in the east, Raymond VI gathered troops in Aragon and proceeded north to join up with Roger-Bernard and Roger of Comminges. After brushing aside a patrol, they used a thick fog to cover the rest of their approach. They further avoided detection by fording the river to the north and slipping into Toulouse on 13 September.

Their reception was mixed. William of Puylaurens says some people were afraid of being held accountable for Raymond's reappearance and fled, while the Anonymous claims all fell before his feet, kissing his legs, arms and fingers. Ecstatic to have their old count back again, they grabbed clubs, stones or sharp objects and beat or stabbed to death all the French and their sympathisers they could find. The victims did not include Dominic or his converts, however. The preacher had had a vision of Simon's downfall earlier that year and decided, much to his patron's annoyance, to evacuate Toulouse.[4]

Alice was then in Narbonnais Palace with the womenfolk and children of her family. There were her and Simon's children Amicia, Simon, Petronilla and another son, Robert. Guy's children Philip and Petronilla were there (their mother Helvis of Ibelin had died the previous year), as were Alice's two daughters-in-law Beatrice and Perronelle (the latter had given birth to a daughter named after Alice, her and Simon's first grandchild). Both Guys, uncle and nephew, were near Carcassonne when they received her message of the infiltration and massacre. Gathering up what men they could, they reached Toulouse on 22 September and immediately attacked. They forced their way past the barricades manned by civilians and militia, but were then repulsed by a counter-attack under Roger-Bernard. The older Guy tried a second time to smash through the defences but was driven back. As a reminder of what captured crusaders could expect, his men who did not make it out were dragged through the streets and hanged.[5]

Guy I retreated to Narbonnais Palace and set up a defensive perimeter. Simon and the legate rode hard from the east and reached Toulouse in early October. By then Raymond had been reinforced by neighbouring lords and the wandering dispossessed (*faidits*) while the crusaders had no extra troops they could call on. It being the end of the normal campaign season, the southerners had chosen their moment to strike well. Simon nevertheless launched an immediate attack. It too was thrown back and he nearly lost his son Guy when he was hit by a bolt that went through his chest. They fell back to Narbonnais Palace, where Simon held a war council.[6]

Many were veterans who had been with him since the beginning–Hugh de Lacy, Lambert de Thury, and his marshal Guy de Lévis. Evrard of Villepreux was still with the crusade after many years. He was the brother-in-law of Robert Mauvoisin, who had died in 1214. There were also brothers Foucaud and John de Berzy, who had joined up in 1212, serving initially with Guy de Montfort. Foucaud now proposed that they begin constructing a whole new town next to Narbonnais Palace. This 'New Toulouse', which would have lodgings and markets for incoming crusaders, would give them a strong defensive position while allowing them to sortie out into the countryside, destroying cropland and upsetting the economic activity of the city. Old Toulouse would eventually wither under the stranglehold and surrender. It was just the kind of boldness to reinvigorate Simon. He personally led a force to occupy Saint-Cyprien, a suburb that lay all the way across Toulouse, on the west bank of the river, while the rest of them, under Amaury, commenced building the new town.[7]

To get across the river, Simon took his detachment seventeen kilometres south to Muret over the bridge that was newly constructed there. They had no problem getting into Saint-Cyprien, but the towers protecting the two bridges across the Garonne into Toulouse were well defended. The weakness of their numbers was further evident by their inability to stop Raymond-Roger from using the bridges to bring in fresh troops. Fed up with reinforcements pouring into the city, Simon wanted to launch another attack, but his men shuddered at the reputation of the count of Foix. They refused to budge. The Anonymous says Simon fell back on astrology to persuade them. The alignment of the planets at his birth did not allow him to fight alone, he told them. Still they refused. Getting nowhere, he abandoned Saint-Cyprien and led his men to the river and to the boats that would ferry them back to camp.

While embarking himself, Simon's horse tumbled and both fell into a deep part of the river. Fully armoured, he disappeared from view and was presumed lost. Peter of Vaux-de-Cernay says his men started howling with grief, thinking all was lost. Somehow Simon managed to surface, his arms outstretched in prayer, and they fished him out. The account of the Anonymous for this episode is surprisingly subdued, saying only that Simon was quickly saved by one man but that his horse drowned.[8]

By this time the Toulousains were lobbing stones at Narbonnais Palace with their own siege engines. The continuous bombardment made a nervous wreck of Bertrand and his retinue. The legate appealed to the pope, urging him to resume the preaching campaign, and he sent Bishop Fulk and Master Clarin, who was now Simon's chancellor, north to get started on it. Alice went with them, along with Foucaud de Berzy and other knights, but they stuck to the woods for fear of encountering southern patrols. In January 1218, Honorius furiously wrote to cities and people alike to whip up support for the crusaders and to warn those who opposed them of his displeasure. Raymond-Roger received such letter of admonishment and did in fact leave Toulouse, but only because Simon could no longer stop him from recovering his county of Foix as the pope had ordered. His son Roger-Bernard stayed behind to help Toulouse carry on the fight.[9]

Fearing the arrival of new crusaders that spring, a squad of Toulousain knights ventured to attack and destroy New Toulouse. They were led by Hugh d'Alfaro, Raymond VI's son-in-law, and they caught Simon and his men unawares. Only a single knight, Peter des Voisins, and his squire were armed and ready to fend them off. Simon instantly armed himself to save Peter from the fray. It was his normal response for any of his men in trouble, but Peter's case was that much different because he was a knight from Montfort l'Amaury. Together with Lambert de Thury, Hugh de Lacy, Guy the Marshal and other knights, Simon beat off the Toulousains, but they regrouped and charged again, this time with the militia coming up from behind to support them. Simon was assaulted on all sides. He had managed to pound two men to the ground when his saddlebow suddenly broke. He slid off his horse but kept his footing, kept fighting and remounted. The Toulousains were again beaten off and this time rode for their bulwarks. Although Peter des Voisins had been saved, Simon suffered a grievous loss. Sevin Gorloin, the son of the seneschal of Carcassonne, was another knight from Montfort l'Amaury. Shouting 'Montfort! Montfort!' he struck down a host of sergeants and militia before he was surrounded and left 'in pieces'.[10]

In May 1218, Alice and Bishop Fulk led new crusaders into New Toulouse. Their leaders included Michael of Harnes, one of the heroes of Bouvines, and Amaury of Craon. Walter Langton, the brother of the archbishop of Canterbury, was back seven years after his rough treatment at the hands of Raymond-Roger. Simon's plan was to use these reinforcements to retake Saint-Cyprien and make another play for the two bridges, but the Toulousains had dug ditches around the suburb and otherwise fortified it since the crusaders briefly occupied it six months earlier. Harnes and Langton led the charge, but they were overwhelmed in the trench warfare and thrown back. With the militia in pursuit, some of them were forced to swim across an arm of the Garonne for the safety of one of the river islands. Simon managed to keep it from becoming a rout, but it was a humiliating defeat, probably the worst of his combat career.[11]

The crusaders set up camp on the riverbank at a safe distance from Saint-Cyprien. The atmosphere was bleak, and just when they thought it could not get any worse it started to rain. But the rain kept coming, and as the water began to rise, so did their mood, for the river quickly burst its bank. The defensive network of trenches were flooded with all manner of debris, some of it coming from the two bridges, which were swept away in the torrent. To Peter of Vaux–de–Cernay, it seemed as if the Almighty had answered their prayers for assistance. Simon immediately attacked and occupied the shore opposite Toulouse, isolating the defenders in the bridge towers. By boat and rope, the Toulousains made a brave attempt to keep their men in the towers supplied, but Simon battered the battlements ceaselessly with stones until they were forced to abandon their position. All of Saint-Cyprien belonged to the crusaders and Simon could commence his plan to choke off the city.[12]

The flood had ravaged mills and destroyed much of the perishable food in Toulouse. Simon made use of this head start on starving the Toulousains into submission by leading his men into the surrounding countryside to destroy orchards and vineyards. Realising the danger, the Toulousains sent knights, mercenaries and militiamen under Roger-Bernard to contest them in the fields. It was a fierce struggle, but the militia fled and were chased all the way back to the barricades by new-arrivals from Brittany and Flanders. These initiates did not appreciate the risk they were running in getting too close to enemy lines. Crusaders who fell into the hands of the militia were subjected to ever more degrading and lethal forms of torture. They were paraded around town with coin collection bags suspended from their necks. They were deprived of their eyes and tongues or chopped up and flung with a trebuchet towards the besieging lines. In one case described by Peter of Vaux-de-Cernay, an acolyte, possibly related to a member of the legate's party, was buried up to his shoulders, his head sticking out above ground to be used for target practice.[13]

This brutality was sure to continue with the 500 mercenaries brought to the city by Bernard of Cazenac, the sadistic lord from Quercy who took delight in mutilating his peasants. He and his men were joyously received. But it was the arrival of young Raymond that brought out the greatest joy among the Toulousains. The Anonymous says, 'not a girl stayed at home upstairs or downstairs, but every soul in the town, great and small, ran to gaze at him as at a flowering rose'. The vibe in the city rejuvenated, the Toulousains launched an amphibious assault to retake Saint-Cyprien. It failed, but it had to make the new crusaders who had arrived under the count of Soissons wonder who was besieging whom. Simon suggested they make another attempt to storm the city, promising them plenty of plunder, but the count and his men were there to do their forty days, not to undertake suicide missions.[14]

In hindsight, Simon might have better employed them to carry out further reductions in the cropland around Toulouse. But the city had become his obsession, the nut he had to crack. Desperate to break through their defences, he had his engineers build an enormous cat. It was several stories tall, designed to hold hundreds of men for one concentrated assault. Because of its size, the siege engine was easy to hit with catapults and the crew dragging it about came under regular fire from crossbowmen. The first two attempts to get close to the walls ended in failure, but the presence of the menacing colossus was beginning to work on the nerves of the city. The leadership decided to assemble all the men they could for one all-out attack on New Toulouse and burn the cat. It was set for Monday, 25 June 1218.[15]

Simon was now in his mid-forties, with a fifth of his life dedicated to this one crusade. Since taking command of it, he had suppressed the heretics and mercenaries, implemented the business of peace and faith, and acquired a sprawling principality for himself in the bargain. If his new subjects hated him for it, seeing him only as a scourge who destroyed their land and people, all conquerors had to deal with that. But it had been going on for too long. He was under constant strain from the toil and drain on his resources. From the legate he had no encouragement at all, only criticism for not bringing the siege to a successful conclusion. He was so dispirited and exhausted, says William of Puylaurens, that he prayed for death as a relief. (It was precisely at this time that the Fifth

Crusade had established a beachhead in Egypt, the long-awaited assault Simon had campaigned for fifteen years earlier. His English cousin Ranulf, the earl of Chester, was on his way there, as was Robert Courçon and other notables. Although Europe would not learn of the crusade's progress for several months, just the thought of it might have left Simon yearning to join them. Better to die for holy Jerusalem than *Tolosa dolosa* – treacherous Toulouse).[16]

On that morning, Simon was at prayer service when a messenger ran in to inform him that the Toulousains were gathering in strength. He put on his armour but first stopped by the chapel in Narbonnais Palace to hear mass. The messages grew more alarming. There was a two-prong attack underway, against the cat and the camp, and his men were having a hard time of it. Simon refused, however, to leave until the priest had lifted the chalice revealing his redeemer. His spirit fortified, he mounted and rode into the fray. The air was thick with arrows and flying masonry as he joined his men by the siege engines. He moved them into formation and drove off the attackers, but they came back again behind a new volley overhead. Simon was said to have taken five arrows, but it was a stone, hurled from the battlements, that knocked him off his horse. This time he did not get up. It had hit him square on the head, crushing his skull and killing him instantly.[17]

He may have gone out with a smile on his face, however. Just before the stone landed (where it was needed, says the Anonymous), Guy de Montfort had been hit by an arrow near his groin. Despite the pain, he told Simon that the wound, should it leave him impotent, would qualify him to become a celibate knight like the Hospitallers. It was perhaps fitting that the two brothers from Montfort l'Amaury should share their final moment together with a bit of dark humour.[18]

The siege of Toulouse ends, assessment of Simon, Amaury's difficulties, Alice and her son Guy die

Simon's body was quickly covered with a blue cape and borne away, but the Toulousains learned of his death immediately. Seeing the cat abandoned, they rode out and torched it, a nice bonfire to accompany the celebrations that erupted in the city. Trumpets, chimes and bells rang out as the people poured into the streets, holding lit candles and rejoicing. Panic overtook the crusaders occupying Saint-Cyprien. They deserted the suburb so fast that they left most of their equipment and animals behind for the Toulousains. A heavy gloom naturally fell on Narbonnais Palace. The next day, as Alice and her four sons renewed a donation that had been made by her 'late husband of happy memory', Bertrand convened a war council to decide their next course of action.[19]

All were in favour of Amaury succeeding his father as the count of Toulouse. He was then in his early twenties and in many ways well prepared for the burden that lay ahead. He had spent his formative years in the south, learning the business from the master himself. But he also faced the same disadvantages of perennial poverty and temporary or half-hearted crusaders. With the count of Soissons and his company close to departure, the council decided to attempt one more all-out assault on the city. It was a ferocious fight that went well past nightfall, but the militia repulsed them in the end. Guy I then pressed for an end to the siege, which Amaury was loath to do for the effect it would have on his reputation, but others like Alan de Roucy convinced him to cut his losses. On 25 July, they packed up what they could, set fire to New Toulouse and Narbonnais Palace, and left. The Toulousains followed in quickly and were able to put out the fires before much damage was done.[20]

The crusaders went eighty-five kilometres southeast to Carcassonne. There in the cathedral of Saint-Nazaire they interred Simon's body. The Anonymous claims an epitaph was engraved on his tomb hailing him as a 'saint and martyr who would rise again and enter his inheritance and flourish in wondrous joy, wearing the crown and sitting in the kingdom of heaven'. Since the epitaph has never been found, it was probably the poet's own invention. The pretence that one existed in this overwrought form allowed him to use irony and undisguised sarcasm to get in the last word on Simon de Montfort. 'And I have heard it said that this should be so – if by killing men and shedding blood, by damning souls and causing deaths, by trusting evil counsels, by setting fires, destroying men, dishonouring *paratge*, seizing lands and encouraging pride, by kindling evil and quenching good, by killing women and slaughtering children – if by all this a man can in this world win Jesus Christ, then certainly this man wears a crown and shines in heaven above.'[21]

For Peter of Vaux-de-Cernay, Simon's death was a personal loss. He had known him since he was a boy, never doubted his integrity or the righteousness of the crusade. Simon was always 'the athlete of Christ' who worked tirelessly for the faith and whose reward now was to lie in 'sublime peace' next to his Saviour. 'He was the comforter of those beset by grief, a tower of strength for the weak, balm for the afflicted, a refuge for the wretched.' William of Puylaurens was more circumspect with his assessment. He believed Simon was a good man, but he 'inspired terror from the Mediterranean to the British sea' and lost his way by giving up the fight against heresy in favour of trying to 'govern unwilling subjects'. He added that Raymond VI himself praised his adversary for his 'fidelity, foresight, energy and all the qualities which befit a leader'. In being this candidly honest, Raymond was acknowledging a certain grudging admiration that Simon must have enjoyed among his enemies.[22]

Just as Amaury could never hope to compete with his father's legend, so Raymond VII could only do better where his own father left off. His victory at Beaucaire had revived southern fortunes and it could not have been a mere coincidence that Simon was killed within a month of his appearance in Toulouse. In July 1218, he turned 21, the legal age of inheritance, and his father promptly relinquished his domains and titles, such as they were, to him.[23] The struggle over Toulouse would continue between Raymond VII and Amaury VII, each about the same age, one the dispossessed count contesting the legitimacy of the count now recognised by the Church and king of France.

In truth, it was not much of a contest. Both young men were competent enough leaders, commanding the respect they might expect for their age and experience. Neither had excessive baggage, not Simon's prestige or charisma nor the older Raymond's slipperiness and indecisiveness. They were brave, determined and resourceful, and in another era they might have made great friends and companions. But this was the land of Raymond's family and ancestors. Amaury and his kin had no roots in Languedoc. There was only one reason why the de Montforts were still there and he was gone. Simon's death was inevitably followed not just by mass defections throughout the region, but by heretics who had been in hiding or on the run during his rule returning to their former enclaves. Southern churchmen made little attempt to stop them because their own positions had suddenly become precarious. Worried they might now become targets of a vengeful population, they made overtures to the southern nobility to let bygones be bygones, in some cases helping them reclaim certain towns and lordships from Amaury. Not even Arnaud-Amalric, who had never forgiven Simon for their dispute over the duchy of Narbonne, offered his son any help or support.[24]

Amaury did have an important benefactor in the pope. Learning of Simon's death in August, Honorius immediately confirmed the young count in his possessions and implored the king of France to throw his weight behind him. His letter was received around the same time that Alice, Fulk and two other bishops arrived at court to make their own plea. Philip Augustus remained unmoved over the affairs in the south until Honorius, in a follow-up letter, tempted him with part of the proceeds of the clerical tax being collected for the Fifth Crusade. Since the Church was willing to finance the expedition, Philip agreed to send his son again.[25]

Louis was in the mood for such a fight. Back in May 1216, the French invasion of England had finally got underway. English barons had succeeded in imposing a charter of liberties on John, but when he repudiated it, they invited Louis to be their king instead. He landed with more than a thousand knights, including William IV des Barres, and quickly overran half the realm, but John's unexpected death on 18 October revived loyalist fortunes. They crowned his 9-year-old heir Henry in a makeshift ceremony in Gloucester and sought to win over many disaffected barons by re-issuing the charter of liberties, soon to be called Magna Carta. Louis managed to avoid capture and ransoming, but it proved a bitter, humiliating experience for the 30-year-old prince. On 20 November 1218, he took the cross again for Languedoc.[26]

In December, Alice returned with sixty knights and her cousin Bouchard of Marly. This allowed Amaury to undertake sieges and patrols as his father had constantly done. After scoring success in Comminges, he moved north into the Agenais to retake Marmande, which was commanded by Centule of Astarac, a turncoat and son-in-law of the count of Comminges. The crusaders were beaten off after trying to storm the fortifications and they settled in for a siege. Meanwhile at Baziège, south of Toulouse, Raymond VII and Raymond-Roger routed a smaller force of crusaders led by Foucaud de Berzy, making prisoners of him and the other commanders but not of the wounded on the field. When Amaury received the news, says the Anonymous, he 'did not feel like laughing, you can be sure of that'.[27]

Amaury was still labouring away at Marmande when Louis arrived there on 2 June 1219 with an army of twenty bishops, thirty-three counts, 600 knights and thousands of foot soldiers. Resistance was quickly overcome and Centule offered to surrender the town in return for their lives. The bishop of Saintes wanted to burn the lot of them, but nobles like Peter of Dreux, who was the duke of Brittany, argued it would be a disgrace for Louis to execute Centule, who was no heretic. It was decided to spare Centule and four of his lords to exchange them for Foucaud and his men, but the rest of the inhabitants were put to the sword. By one estimate, 5,000 men, women and children were slain and the town torched. Unlike Béziers a decade earlier, this massacre was carried out with extreme malice against a civilian population with no overt ties to heresy. If the intention was to frighten Toulouse into submission, Louis found the Toulousains fully prepared to resist him when he arrived outside the city. Although he had far more men and machinery on hand than Simon ever did, his siege got nowhere and his men reached the end of their forty-day service. On 1 August, he called it off and returned to Paris with his second military defeat in as many years.[28]

For Amaury, Louis's intervention had been an unqualified disaster. The massacre at Marmande increased local hatred for the French while the latest failure before Toulouse proved the southerners could withstand the might of the monarchy. Not even the 300 knights left behind by Louis for a year could help Amaury slow the momentum that was now all Raymond VII's. Towns and strongholds defected to him, others he retook with relative ease. William of Puylaurens says the crusaders had only themselves to blame for his success. They had fallen away from their true state by looking after themselves and not fighting heresy. He gives the example of the Berzy brothers, who had adopted a debauched lifestyle of concubines and married mistresses. After they were exchanged for Centule, the Berzys formed a band of outlaws to raid the countryside, rustling sheep and torturing their captives. Raymond VII's stature grew after he hunted them down, hauled them to Toulouse, and had them publicly beheaded and displayed.[29]

The House of Montfort

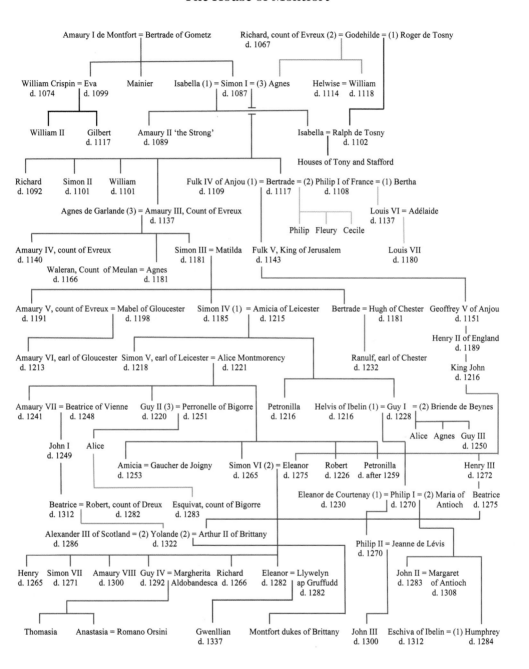

The De Montforts of Montfort l'Amaury

The ruins of Montfort l'Amaury as they stand above the modern town today. It was here, in the early eleventh century, that Amaury I, who came from a line of foresters, built a fortress on the 'strong mount', thus giving the family its surname of Montfort.

The most notorious member of the family at that time was Amaury's granddaughter Bertrade (d. 1117), who left her husband Fulk IV of Anjou for Philip I, king of France. This image shows Bertrade and Philip together while Bertha, the discarded queen, woefully observes them from above. Their union was considered scandalous enough, but Bertrade overplayed her hand when she tried to fast-track her children to the throne over the better claims of Bertha's children. After Philip's death, Bertrade retired to the nunnery she founded at Haute-Bruyères, which later became the family mausoleum.

The Fourth Crusade (1202–1204)

In 1198, the newly elected Pope Innocent III called for a crusade to reclaim Jerusalem for Christianity. Simon V and Guy I de Montfort joined other nobles in taking the cross at a tournament in Ècry. When the crusaders were unable to pay the Venetians the costs of building and maintaining the fleet, they agreed to help them recoup their costs by conquering Zara, a Christian city on the Dalmatian coast. Both de Montforts opposed the diversion and refused to participate in the attack (left). They left the crusade altogether when it was next diverted to conquer Constantinople (below). The brothers and their party made their way overland to Italy and found passage to the Holy Land, where in 1204 Guy married into the local nobility. He returned to France in 1211 to help his brother with a new crusade, against the Albigensian heretics.

The Albigensian Crusade (1208–1229)

In 1208, Pope Innocent called for a new crusade, this time against the Albigensians, whose dualistic Christianity threatened the supremacy of Catholicism in Languedoc. After the initial success, most of the crusaders went home. Simon V took over command and found himself confronted by a coalition of southern lords who were sympathetic to the heretics and saw the crusaders as foreign conquerors. Carcassonne (below) became Simon's base of operations for what turned out to be a war of attrition. The heretics, known as Cathars, had been mostly forgotten by the time Simon was killed outside Toulouse in 1218. Six years later his son Amaury VII surrendered the de Montfort family claims to the French monarchy and returned to Montfort l'Amaury. His uncle Guy I remained in the south and was killed one year before the crusade came to an end in 1229.

On 12 September 1213, Simon V defied the odds and defeated King Peter II of Aragon at Muret (left) close to Toulouse, establishing him as one of the greatest medieval generals. For the religious side of the struggle, Simon was aided by his good friend Dominic de Guzman, the founder of the Dominican order. They are seen together below left in a 17th century painting by Daniel van den Dyck. Both preacher and soldier preferred conversion to immolation. Fewer than a thousand Cathars went to the stake during Simon's decade in the south and they made a remarkable comeback after his death.

ue point queile feſtoue
ques ſy plainear ue ſy

The De Montforts in England

In 1230, Simon VI de Montfort (upper right) went to England to ask King Henry III (upper left) to grant him the earldom of Leicester, which Simon's English grandmother Amicia had inherited in 1204. His appeal was successful and he quickly rose to become one of Henry's closest friends, marrying his sister Eleanor in 1238. He was disgraced only a year later after taking advantage of the king's goodwill. Their relationship never recovered and Simon's rebellion in the 1260s was as much personal as anything else. His victory at Lewes in 1264 (image above) allowed him to install a constitutional monarchy, one of the most radical governments of the Middle Ages.

The six children of Simon and Eleanor de Montfort loyally stood by their parents' quest for wealth and power. The eldest Henry should have become the earl of Chester and Leicester, but he fell with his father on the battlefield of Evesham in 1265. The second and fourth sons Simon VII and Guy IV found promising careers in Italy, but threw them away when they had the chance to avenge their father. The third son Amaury VIII was the family priest, doctor and lawyer in one. He was also the last to survive, dying in 1300. The youngest son Richard disappeared from view after he went to the court of Navarre in 1266 aged just 14, and the only daughter Eleanor II married Llywelyn to become the princess of Wales until her untimely death in childbirth in 1282.

The De Montforts in Italy and Sicily

The thirteenth century was dominated by the papacy's obsession with wresting back control of the Kingdom of Sicily from the Hohenstaufen dynasty. After the death of Emperor Frederick II in 1250, Henry III of England wanted Sicily for his second son Edmund but could not get his barons or clergy interested in the rich Mediterranean kingdom. With Henry engulfed in civil war at home, Charles of Anjou, the brother of King Louis IX of France, moved in and took the prize, with Philip II de Montfort leading his army into Sicily. Charles was crowned king (above) but he needed one more victory at Taglicozza (below left) in 1268 to consolidate his power. Philip's cousin Guy IV de Montfort distinguished himself in the battle and was rewarded with rule of Tuscany and a wealthy heiress. In 1271, he sacrificed everything to avenge his father's death. He found his Plantagenet cousin Henry of Almain at worship in a church in Viterbo (below right) and hacked him to death in front of the terrified congregation. Such had been the horror of the dismemberment of Simon VI at Evesham in 1265 that Guy escaped punishment, but he was captured by the Aragonese in battle in 1287 and died four years after that without obtaining his freedom.

The De Montforts in the crusader states

In 1239, a crusade led by members of the French nobility arrived in the Holy Land. Amaury VII and his cousin Philip I were among them, and Amaury's brother Simon VI landed at Acre the next year. By then Amaury was waiting to be ransomed from an Egyptian prison, where he spent eighteen months following the crusader defeat at Gaza. The brothers left after his release, with Amaury dying en route homeward, but Philip remained behind. He had been born in the Holy Land and it was through his Ibelin cousins on his mother's side that he quickly attained a lucrative lordship. Within a few years he was leading the Christian army (albeit in another defeat) and by 1247 he was the lord of Tyre (below left, under assault from the Venetians in 1122). Philip issued his own coins, which his son John II continued, but his feud with Acre (below right, under siege in 1190) severely weakened the crusader states against encroachment by the Mameluks. He was assassinated by agents of the sultan in 1270. Neither of his sons lived to see the fall of Tyre in 1291.

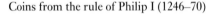

Coins from the rule of Philip I (1246–70)   Coins from the rule of John II (1270–83)

At that time Foucaud de Berzy was the lord of Puylaurens. In the spring of 1220, his widow Ermengarde surrendered the town on guarantee that none of the occupants would be harmed. She, her children and the garrison were allowed to walk free. No mercy, however, was shown to the next garrison put under siege, which was none other than Lavaur. When it was taken, all were executed except a few who had managed to swim across the river. In the summer Raymond's men seized Castelnaudary from Hugh de Lacy. Amaury gathered up all the men he could to lay siege to it, but received another blow when his brother Guy was wounded in the assault and died in the hands of his captors on 20 July 1220. Guy II was then about 23 years old and left behind two daughters with his wife Perronelle. Raymond VII made sure to have him covered in purple and brought out on a litter to Amaury, who had his brother buried next to their father in Carcassonne.[30]

The siege dragged on for the rest of the year. There was now a new legate, Conrad of Urach, who like Arnaud-Amalric had been the head of the Cistercian order. Amaury's essential problem, he could see, was the same one his father had constantly faced, a lack of manpower. Conrad set about establishing a military order similar to the Templars and Hospitallers to attract recruits to serve in Languedoc on a permanent basis. By early 1221, the Militia of the Order of the Faith of Jesus Christ had been set up under the command of Peter Savaric. Calling himself a 'humble and poor master', Peter declared that he and his Knights of the Faith would aid 'Amaury de Montfort and his heirs, for the defence of his person and domains; and to discover and destroy heretics and rebels against the Church, and all others, Christians or infidels, who shall make war against the count'.[31]

It was all too little too late. Broke and bereft of troops, Amaury raised the siege of Castelnaudary. In that same month, on 25 February 1221, his mother Alice died, probably by then in her late forties. Given the dangers of her son's deteriorating position, she had returned to the north with her four underage children. Shortly before her death she committed her 10-year-old daughter Petronilla to the care of the nuns of Saint-Antoine-des-Champs in Paris. It was a Cistercian abbey founded by Fulk of Neuilly and the final resting place of family friend Robert Mauvoisin.

Robert's sister Agnes would oversee the young girl's upbringing with a view to her taking the veil someday if she desired.[32]

Alice de Montfort was buried at the mausoleum of her husband's ancestors in Hautes-Bruyères. Like Simon, she had made a lasting impression on her contemporaries with her courage, fortitude and devotion to her family and the crusade. According to Peter of Vaux-de-Cernay, she was pious, wise and caring, with each of these attributes enhancing the other, and William of Tudela finds her simply incomparable. 'No wiser woman, so God and the faith help me, has anyone ever met in the length and breadth of the world.'[33]

The two counts duel for control, renewal and end of the crusade, Guy I de Montfort dies

The loss of his lordship of Castelnaudary gave veteran Hugh de Lacy no reason to remain in Languedoc and he went back to England under safe-conduct. Amaury's uncle Guy and Marshal Guy de Lévis had so far managed to hold on to their fiefs, but the southerners mounted an attack against Montréal and killed its lord, Alan de Roucy, who had joined the crusade ten years earlier.[34] In Rome, Honorius was alarmed by these developments but had done little more than threaten Raymond VII with the same fate as his father if he continued his aggression.

Of greater concern to the pope was the faltering Fifth Crusade. After an eighteen-month siege, Damietta was finally taken. As hoped, the sultan offered to swap it for Jerusalem, but the more warlike crusaders, led by the legate Pelagius, aimed to march on Cairo despite opposition from the titular king of Jerusalem, John of Brienne. The army lay dormant for well over a year by the time they began their Nile campaign in July 1221. Ill-equipped and advised, they were trapped within a month. Pelagius was forced to swap Damietta for the remnants of his army and prisoners. Occitanian troubadours quickly seized on the ignoble defeat to blame everything on the Church. Jerusalem would be free were it not for the 'false crusade' ravaging their homeland, their Christian homeland, they sang.[35]

The Church, however, was convinced that heresy had been revived in Languedoc and was flourishing again. With supreme effort, Honorius now resolved to persuade the French monarchy to become involved by offering Philip Augustus not only a crusade subsidy, but Languedoc as well. Amaury had, in fact, already tried to unload his inheritance on Philip, but the king was unresponsive. After more than forty years on the throne, Philip was worn out and his son did not inspire hope for the success of such a huge undertaking. Acting on an appeal from Raymond VII, Philip proposed that the two claimants to the county of Toulouse divide it up and live peacefully alongside each other.[36]

They would not have to bother with what Raymond VI might think. In August 1222, he died, still excommunicated. Because he was unable to speak at the time of his death, and therefore made no confession, the Church refused him a Christian burial. It was, as everyone knew, just a pretext to continue hounding the man who, as everybody also knew, was largely responsible for the miseries inflicted on his people. His bellicose ally Raymond-Roger soon departed as well. He was still at it, trying to take Mirepoix from Guy de Lévis, when an ulcer killed him.[37]

Amaury and Raymond tried negotiating a settlement. At one point there was a suggestion that Raymond marry Amaury's sister Amicia. These two had been betrothed as children shortly after Simon V took command of the crusade, but when relations between their fathers broke down, Raymond was married to Sanchia, the sister of Peter of Aragon. In 1220, Sanchia, then in her mid-thirties, gave birth to a daughter Joan, but Raymond was intent on repudiating her as his wife. The proposed second betrothal between Raymond and Amicia came to nothing and she eventually married French nobleman and widower Gaucher de Joigny during these years. But for all the war weariness, the two counts still showed they had a sense of humour. Under the cover of a truce, Raymond visited Amaury at Carcassonne, but they had word sent to Raymond's men outside that Amaury had taken him prisoner. Fearing they were next, they prepared to take flight when the two counts, having enjoyed the joke, appeared together and put them at ease.[38]

A peace conference was held at Saint-Flour under the auspices of Conrad, but the talks broke down and Raymond left to complete his sweep of the Agenais by besieging Penne. Amaury and the legate gathered up all the men they could and chased him off. A new conference was then planned for Sens in Burgundy, but the death of Philip Augustus on 14 July 1223 rendered it pointless. The new king Louis VIII was much more receptive to the offer of adding Languedoc to French royal domains. Except for military talent, Louis was in many ways like Simon. He was very pious, very ambitious, and his wife Blanche of Castile had qualities similar to Alice de Montfort. Having just been crowned, Louis told Conrad that he could not attend to matters in the south immediately, but agreed to send Amaury 10,000 marks from his father's treasury to secure the strongholds he still held there.[39]

Amaury used the money to relocate his family north and, while there, hire a new force of knights. They helped him beat off a siege of Carcassonne launched by Raymond and Roger-Bernard, who had succeeded his father as the count of Foix. When his money ran out, the knights, about sixty in number, asked Raymond for a safe-conduct to leave, but he more or less considered them his prisoners and refused. In the battle that followed, he received the worst of it, even losing his standard bearer, but Amaury was unable to take advantage of this setback for the southerners. The only way he could save Carcassonne was by raising new funds. Understanding the need to retain Carcassonne as a base of operations until Louis could arrive in the spring, Arnaud-Amalric and other prelates mortgaged their estates for the money. Amaury did likewise, offering Montfort l'Amaury as security to the garrison for their wages. Only his uncle Guy, Guy de Lévis, Lambert de Thury and twenty others accepted. The rest wanted out.[40]

On 14 January 1224, Amaury agreed to surrender Carcassonne, Minerve and Penne to Raymond in return for a two-month truce at other strongholds to allow their occupants to evacuate them in peace. Amaury would withdraw to France, where he promised to work for reconciliation between Raymond and the Church. Should he succeed by the summer, Raymond would give him 10,000 marks. The next day Amaury left Carcassonne, which had been his family's home for more than fourteen years. The bodies of his father and brother were exhumed from the cathedral of Saint-Nazaire and taken north for reburial, although this may have already happened earlier, in the autumn of 1222, when Amaury spent several months at Hautes-Bruyères. The church and tombs at Hautes-Bruyères were destroyed during the French Revolution, but surviving records show that Simon was interred under an effigy at the right of the altar, with Alice lying on his left and Guy II placed at his feet.[41]

Amaury's last known act before leaving Carcassonne was to cede, 'for the salvation of his father Simon and brother Guy', the ownership of Cazouls to the bishop of Béziers. Back in 1210, Simon had confiscated the castle of Cazouls from a heretical family and allotted it to the diocese. The revenues from it and other restored property were meant to help Béziers recover from the catastrophic fire that still blackened the legacy of the crusade. Amaury may have considered his grant to be a symbolic act of closure for his family. The next month, in Paris, he offered to cede all of his father's conquests to Louis outright. The king began making plans for his third intervention in Languedoc when, in April 1224, he received a letter from Honorius. He was to call off his crusade.[42]

It seemed as if the pope had adopted all the bad habits of his predecessor, pushing for action, then pulling back from the brink. Here Honorius was stung by the failure of the Fifth Crusade. Since his former pupil Frederick II of the Holy Roman Empire had missed it despite his vow and promises, Honorius wanted him to lead a Sixth Crusade, but in March, Frederick complained about poor recruitment. Forced to choose one crusade or the other, the pope decided to work for peace in Languedoc. He told Louis that Raymond was sincere in wanting reconciliation with the Church and he ordered it done. Twice at Montpellier, Raymond worked out arrangements with a council of prelates under Arnaud-Amalric, his father's old nemesis. He was to make restitution, crush the heretics and provide for Amaury's honour. Prior to the second meeting of the council on 16 August, Amaury wrote to them from the north to remind them not to do anything prejudicial to his rights. He added his belief that Louis would ultimately become involved in the struggle.[43]

Louis was already then involved in an unexpected act of aggression. In May, he reacted to the pope's about-face with a superbly angry letter declaring he was done with the business of peace and faith in Languedoc once and for all. In that same month, the five-year truce between France and England came to an end. Still humiliated by his defeat across the Channel in 1217, Louis decided to use the men and resources collected for the crusade to instead conquer Poitou, the lordship of which belonged to the underage English king Henry III. Internal divisions kept Henry and his regents from responding in time, and in July the last holdout La Rochelle surrendered to Louis thanks to the treachery of none other than

Savaric de Mauléon. It was an embarrassing episode for Honorius. Not only was Henry III his ward and vassal, but the war between England and France ruined any hope of launching the Sixth Crusade anytime soon. Honorius was already then in his mid-seventies.[44]

The council at Montpellier was satisfied with the arrangements made with Raymond, including his promise to deal with heretics and give back Church property. He also agreed to pay an indemnity of 20,000 marks, out of which Amaury's honour could be satisfied as the pope saw fit. Discussions on approval started in October and lasted well into the next year. Despite claiming to have washed his hands of the business, Louis was very much working behind the scenes to make a crusade happen. It would give him papal protection from an English counterattack, which might well be undertaken in an alliance between Henry III and Raymond VII, who were cousins, and the absorption of Toulouse would put Louis in a good position to wrest Gascony from England as well. To oppose reconciliation for Raymond, he sent Guy de Montfort to Rome in early December. Few crusaders had more esteemed credentials than Guy, but his presence carried special weight because Honorius was keen to ensure that Guy's nephew Amaury received an honourable settlement. In the end, Honorius did what medieval popes did best: he put off a decision pending the arrival of a new legate.[45]

He was an Italian cardinal named Romanus. Although officially open to a peaceful settlement with Raymond, Romanus was intent on re-launching the crusade. He had no connections to Louis or the French royal family, rather he believed, as the Church had all along, that heresy in Languedoc would never go away under the southern princes. Raymond did himself no favours in any case by continuing to squabble over certain rights, which made Honorius question his sincerity. In November 1225, Romanus convened a grand council of over 1,000 churchmen at Bourges (minus Arnaud-Amalric, who had died in September) to discuss the issues of the day. The two counts of Toulouse were invited to make their cases before the assembly. Amaury told the prelates that the pope and king of France had conferred the county on him and on his father before him and he presented the charters confirming their grant. Raymond's reply was that he had lost his inheritance through war and defeat but he had justly recovered it. He was nevertheless ready, for the sake of peace, to pay Amaury 3,000 marks in compensation.[46]

Not until the council was over was Raymond informed that the prelates had voted not to absolve him. On 28 January 1226, he was excommunicated by Romanus together with a group of bishops. Two days later Louis took the cross. The renewed crusade also started out from Lyon, with an army twice the size of the one that set out in 1209. With Guy and Amaury in their ranks, they met their first and only resistance at Avignon. After three months, the well-fortified city surrendered, but no massacre took place. As the army moved westward, Raymond was deserted by all his allies. The army marched through Castelnaudary, Puylaurens, Lavaur and the Albigeois, a nostalgic homecoming for the de Montforts. The plan was then to go back to France and deal with Toulouse the next year, but Louis caught dysentery from the unsanitary camp conditions. Bouchard of Marly and thousands of others succumbed to it, as did the king on 8 November at Montpensier. Five day before his death, Louis summoned his leading men, Amaury de Montfort and William IV des Barres among them, to swear fealty to his 12-year-old son and heir. Cardinal Romanus led the army back to France, where young King Louis IX was crowned under the watchful eye of his mother Blanche of Castile and the twelve peers of France, one of whom was Amaury, now just the count of Montfort.[47]

A strong force under Humbert de Beaujeu was left behind and for the next two years sieges and running warfare returned to Languedoc. Humbert gradually gained the upper hand by continuously destroying crops and vines in the hinterland of Toulouse. Raymond VII sought terms and in April 1229 was reconciled to the Church. He had to pay a huge indemnity, forfeit some land, and marry his daughter Joan to the new king's younger brother Alphonse, who would inherit the rest of Raymond's lands if he had no other heirs. Toulouse itself would go to the Crown after his death. Narbonnais Palace and other strongholds were to be garrisoned by royal troops at Raymond's expense and he was to go on crusade for five years. As for heresy, an inquisition would be established to deal with that. After twenty years, the crusade was over.[48]

One of the final casualties of the conflict was Guy de Montfort. Still fighting in the south, he was killed on 31 January 1228 by an arrow during an attack on Varilhes, just south of Pamiers. He was about fifty years old. His burial site is unknown, but the anniversary of his death was remembered every year at Hautes-Bruyères. He was succeeded as the lord of La Ferté-Alais by his son Philip, who would have been in his early twenties by this time. Philip had likely accompanied his father during the crusade and received his fief of Rabastens after his death. He was also enfeoffed with Castres and settled down to become a southern lord. During these years Philip married Eleanor, the daughter of Peter de Courtenay, the count of Auxerre, who was present at the siege of Lavaur in 1211. By 1230, Philip was a widower with one son, also named Philip.

Guy's daughter with Helvis, Petronilla, became a nun at the Cistercian house of Port Royal, which was founded by Alice's uncle Matthew of Marly. On 16 June 1224, Guy married Briende de Beynes, the widow of Lambert de Thury, in Joyenval and together they had three children. The first two, Alice and Agnes, joined their half-sister Petronilla as nuns of Port Royal. Guy's son with Briende, Guy III, inherited the lordship of Lombers near Albi, which he obtained from his mother's first husband.[49]

Chapter 8

New Lords in the Family
1230–1241

In addition to his wife Beatrice and children John, Margaret, Laure, Adele and Perronelle, Amaury's household at Montfort l'Amaury included his brother Simon VI. Born around the start of the crusade, absolutely nothing is known about Simon's youth. His mother probably took him north following the death of his father in 1218, perhaps even placed him with the monks at Vaux-de-Cernay for his education. Many years later an English chronicler wrote that Simon had been 'commendably endowed with a knowledge of letters', meaning fairly well educated.[1]

Latin was a standard subject of the day and among the works available to young Simon to read at the abbey, although not likely on the curriculum, would have been *The History of the Albigensian Crusade*. It comes to an abrupt end in 1218, suggesting that Peter of Vaux-de-Cernay died before completing it, not quite 30 years of age.[2] While Simon entered adulthood with memories of his father, how he looked, talked and carried himself, the *History* introduced him to the legend, the heroic crusade commander who was everywhere at once, whose faith and skill won him great victories, who dealt personally with popes and kings and had taken the radical step of devising a constitutionally-ordained government for his conquered territories. It was hard enough for an ordinary reader not to be inspired by his courage, knightly feats, and devotion to his family and men, let alone a son named after him. Like Amaury, he knew he had a lot to live up to.

In 1226, Simon was 18 and in all likelihood part of his brother's retinue when the crusade reignited that year. The other brother Robert may have joined them and died during the course of the crusade. Robert appears for the last time in a charter issued by Amaury in May of that year. Three years later, in 1229, Simon reached the legal age of inheritance. His best prospects were to go to England and put in a claim for the earldom of Leicester as his father had done more than twenty years earlier. Although King John had dispossessed Simon V of Leicester almost as soon as he granted it to him, the grant itself confirmed that the de Montforts were by law entitled to the confiscated earldom. As his father's successor, Amaury styled himself the count of Montfort and earl of Leicester and revived the claim with John's successor, King Henry III.[3]

Henry, however, had soured on cross-Channel lordships thanks to the example of the Marshal family. Back in 1217, Henry's regent William Marshal had the future Louis VIII, then attempting to take the English throne from the 9-year-old king, trapped in London. Had Marshal taken him prisoner, he could have forced Louis's father Philip to surrender at least some of the lands seized from John. But Marshal let Louis go, with an indemnity of 10,000 marks no less, because he had his own lands in France and was afraid Philip would seize them in retaliation. Henry, who was almost obsessed with getting Normandy back, later considered Marshal's action a betrayal.[4]

In any event, Henry was in no position to grant Leicester to anyone. By this point the earldom had passed to the custodianship of Ranulf, the earl of Chester. In 1227, the king had declared himself of age and, needing Ranulf's support, granted him the earldom for life. But Ranulf was an old man, well into his fifties, and he had no children. By right, the earldom should revert to the de Montforts, the family that had been unjustly deprived of it. Henry had no reason to raise an objection to Simon becoming an English earl because, unlike Amaury, he held no land or title of the king of France. The brothers themselves reached an agreement with each other. Amaury ceded his rights in England to Simon and in return Simon ceded his rights in France to Amaury together with an unspecified amount of money. In February 1230, Simon VI left for England.[5]

According to a contemporary, he was a 'strenuous, handsome knight', but there the description ends. At best his appearance can be gleaned from his seal, which took after his father's in showing a forester on horseback ready for the chase. The figure is tall, beardless, and sports a fine crop of hair. The timing of his arrival could not have been more fortuitous. Peter of Dreux, the duke of Brittany, had switched his allegiance to England as part of a wider revolt among French barons against the regency of Blanche of Castile. Henry was planning to take an army to Brittany in the hope of winning back other Continental lands lost by his father. Having the son of the famous warrior Simon de Montfort might somehow fit into that scheme. An agreement was worked out with Ranulf that Simon might come into possession of Leicester at a later time. In April, the knight who had accompanied Simon to England, Amaury de Misternun, approached Henry at Reading with an offer from Simon to enter the king's service. Henry accepted and put him on retainer at £267 per year on the expectation that Leicester would eventually be his.[6]

Henry's expedition fell far short of his hopes. Blanche let him roll through the countryside while she put down the revolt. She knew everything with England would come down to a bidding war over Poitou. The two most powerful lords in that region were Henry's mother Isabella, the countess of Angoulême, and her husband Hugh Lusignan, the count of La Marche. They already had a good deal with Blanche, including a pension and respectable amount of autonomy, and so they decided not to risk either for Henry. The king returned in October 1230 with a few more allegiances, but at a cost of more subsidies. Ranulf stayed behind at his castle of Saint-James-de-Beuvron in Brittany, and it was there that Simon, whose whereabouts during the expedition are unknown, approached him.[7]

According to Simon's later account, he asked Ranulf to release Leicester to him. Recognising the strength of his younger cousin's claim, the old earl agreed, but in return for £200. Like Amaury, Ranulf wanted to benefit if Simon's quest turned out successful. In February 1231, Amaury attempted to speed up the process by beseeching Henry in a letter. If the king would not restore the earldom to him, Amaury, then 'I send to your lordship's feet my brother Simon who holds nothing of the French king. If you restore him my property, I shall hold myself well satisfied'. Amaury certainly had no hope of ever inheriting Leicester himself. In November 1230, he was named the constable of France at the death of the previous holder, his uncle Matthew Montmorency. For Henry, it would not do having the first officer of the French Crown sitting in on his counsels while he plotted his next move against France.[8]

In August 1231, Ranulf and Simon journeyed to Wales, where Henry was building a castle. There on the thirteenth of the month the king received Simon's homage for Leicester. It was not all the newly ennobled English baron might have wanted. He did not obtain the title of earl, and of the earldom itself he only received half. His great-aunt Margaret was still in possession of the other half granted to her and Saher de Quincy (who had joined the Fifth Crusade and died during it). The estates, he also found, had been much exploited in the intervening quarter of a century. The woodland Simon was counting on selling in order to pay off his debts had been much depleted.[9]

Simon had no sooner joined the ranks of the English nobility than he became involved in his first political squabble. The justiciar at the time was Hubert de Burgh, the man who had guided Henry through most of his minority. Like Simon, he had come out of nowhere (Norfolk to be exact), but his attempts to gain respectability by marrying a Scottish princess and having Henry name him the earl of Kent was met with contempt from Ranulf and the ancestral nobility. They resented his grip on power and accumulation of wealth and castles. When Simon learned that Hubert had made two grants of patronage that fell under the gift of the earl of Leicester, he protested at Ranulf's urging and left court. With so few supporters among the barons, Hubert was anxious not to alienate the newcomer early on and worked out a compromise with Simon on the grant. Hubert, however, soon lost the confidence of the king and was disgraced in August 1232.[10]

Ranulf died two months after that. By then, Simon had found a different mentor. He was Robert Grosseteste, the archdeacon of Leicester, who like Ranulf was about 60 years old (the age Simon's father would have been at this time). An intemperate intellectual and zealot in equal measure, Grosseteste was among the senior churchmen of the day eager to keep Christians and Jews from intermingling. The Jews should go out into the world, he felt, and earn a living with their hands instead of lending money to Christians at usurious interest rates. It was perhaps under his influence that Simon, in one of his first acts as the lord of Leicester, ordered the Jews living in his half to leave. When they moved to the half controlled by Margaret de Quincy, Grosseteste justified the action and gently advised her not to interfere.[11]

For the next two years, Simon seems to have kept his head down, wisely in view of the events that shook the realm in that time. After Hubert de Burgh was driven from power, a regime under his archenemy Peter des Roches, the bishop of Winchester and Henry's own first mentor, began encouraging the king to take a high-handed approach to kingship. Disaffected barons took this amiss and looked to Richard Marshal, the earl of Pembroke, for leadership. Henry and Marshal had clashed before. At the death of Marshal's brother William II in April 1231, Henry had hedged whether to allow Richard to inherit Pembroke because he was then living in Normandy and, unlike Simon, Richard held land of the king of France. Henry eventually admitted him, but new difficulties arose because the widow of William II was Henry's youngest sister Eleanor. Richard was not inclined to part with one-third of the Marshal estate that was due Eleanor as her rightful dower. They worked out an agreement that gave Eleanor £400 for her dower lands in Ireland and Wales. Although acceptable at the time, it was far short of what she was entitled to and would become a millstone around her and Henry's necks for decades to come.[12]

The insurrection launched by Marshal in 1233 struck mostly at his opponents, but its effects engulfed the entire realm. He was backed by the Welsh and nearly all the bishops, who had their own grievances against the king and their fellow bishop Peter des Roches. Because Roches and many of his followers came from France, Marshal raised the rallying cry that he was fighting to rid foreign influence over the Crown. Given he was a foreigner himself who had only recently come to England, it was a brazen attitude to take, but it worked. Marshal's inadvertent death in Ireland in April 1234 made him a martyr and forced the king to sack Roches and his associates.[13]

Simon was a foreigner and former protégé of Ranulf, who had long been a firm ally of Roches, but he emerged from the conflict unscathed because he had no noticeable links to the regime himself. Another close friend of Ranulf he got to know in these years was his father's old comrade-in-arms Hugh de Lacy. Upon returning to England in 1221, Lacy had had to fight to regain his lordship in Ireland and it took several years before he was fully restored to favour. Simon might have seen or encountered Lacy as a boy, especially during the siege of Toulouse. Now he was witnessing charters for the veteran crusader, then in his sixties, and perhaps beseeching him to tell him again about Muret and all the other feats of his parents that he was too young to remember.

In October of 1234, Simon can be found at his first known council meeting and by the following year he was a leading councillor. Henry was eager to cultivate his rise. Personally there was much that brought the two men together. They were both sons of very capable, energetic parents, but had lost them by the time they reached adolescence. They were about the same age, were pious and ambitious, and each was persuasive in argument. Simon was described as having a 'courteous and pleasant way of speaking' and the speeches attributed to Henry show that few of his contemporaries were quicker or sharper in debate. Importantly, neither man was married nor had been with any woman as far as the record shows.[14]

For himself, Henry wanted a wife who could score him an alliance against France. In April 1235, he married by proxy Joan, the heiress of Ponthieu, because that county was located next to Normandy. Since he and Joan were related within the prohibitive degrees, he needed a papal dispensation to make the marriage binding. Blanche of Castile, who was still very much in charge in Paris despite her son Louis IX coming of age, made sure the dispensation was not forthcoming. Louis himself recently married Margaret of Provence, whose father Count Raymond Berenger V had no sons to succeed him. To try and thwart the French from getting their hands on Provence, Henry began negotiations to marry Margaret's sister Eleanor.[15]

Simon also set out to find a wife. Sometime during 1235, he crossed the Channel to ask Mahaut, the countess of Boulogne, for her hand. She was several years older and a widow with two children. It came to nothing, as did Simon's pursuit of another older widow, Joanna of Flanders, who inherited her county at the death of her father Baldwin, the first Latin emperor of Constantinople. Blanche was not amused by Simon's suits. He received word of her disapproval and fled back to England. Suspicious of what may have unfolded, Blanche had Joanna brought before her court to swear that she had not contracted any marriage, future or otherwise, to Simon. The queen dowager was rightly angry because both counties were strategically important and she may have suspected that Henry had put

Simon up to it. If one of his barons came into possession of Boulogne or Flanders by right of his wife, it would strengthen England's hand against France. Simon had agreed to make the mercenary bids for the countesses in the expectation that if he failed, as was likely, Henry would find him a suitably rich bride at home. He certainly would have wanted to marry well, preferably to a widow or heiress with enough wealth behind her to help alleviate his debts.[16]

In January 1236, 12-year-old Eleanor of Provence arrived in Canterbury to become Henry's wife and queen of England. At her coronation banquet held in Westminster Hall, Simon served as the steward of England, a ceremonial office attached to the earldom of Leicester. His duties largely consisted of him assisting Henry in washing his hands during the feast. It was a great honour being seen standing next to the king, and Roger Bigod, the earl of Norfolk, had tried to claim it on account of a dispute between their earldoms over the office going back to the previous reign. Another officer at the queen's coronation was John de Lacy, the earl of Lincoln. A distant relative of Hugh de Lacy, John was another former member of Ranulf's affinity and inherited his earldom by marrying the earl of Chester's niece Margaret. She was a granddaughter of Saher and Margaret de Quincy and therefore Simon's second cousin.

Following the wedding, Simon grew close to John de Lacy and William of Savoy, an uncle of the queen who had joined the council. William's family were powerbrokers in European politics and Henry saw their support as key in maintaining pressure on France.[17] Like John de Lacy, William of Savoy was about 15 years older than Simon. Together these three came to dominate the king's counsels. In October 1236, Simon styled himself the earl of Leicester for the first time in a charter, even though Henry had not conferred the title on him. Presumption like this undoubtedly drew unfavourable comment, nor was it the best time to enjoy such supremacy. Henry's wedding and that of his sister Isabella to Emperor Frederick the year before had left him massively in debt. In the old days, the king simply manipulated his rights as feudal overlord to get the money. Magna Carta put a stop to that. Henry and the monarchs who followed him now had to summon large assemblies of barons and clergy and ask them for a tax. These assemblies had taken on the name 'parliament', meaning to discuss, because any mention of taxation generated a lot of discussion. In January 1237, Henry secured a tax from parliament, but it proved as unpopular as the reforms then underway by the council to find other sources of revenue.

Simon also took sides in the feuds left over from Marshal's rebellion. He joined Peter de Rivallis, a top official of the Roches regime, in denouncing Richard Siward, one of the insurrectionists, to the king. To achieve peace between these baronial factions, Henry had a legate dispatched to England to serve as mediator. The cardinal appointed to the post was Otto of Montferrat, a grandson of Boniface of the Fourth Crusade. Otto accomplished that task straightaway, then travelled with the king, Simon and the rest of the court to York to work out a peace treaty with Henry's brother-in-law King Alexander II of Scotland. The legate nevertheless aroused indignation among the clergy for attempting to reform their squalid state of affairs. Such were the concerns for his safety that three earls, two of them Simon and John de Lacy, gave him a personal escort. Matthew Paris, a monk at St Albans, bemoaned Otto's presence and the 'great desolation' of the kingdom in general. He blames these ills on certain 'infamous and mistrusted' councillors and names Simon among them.[18]

Amaury goes to England, he leaves on crusade, the battle of Gaza

In late 1235, Amaury visited England in the company of nine of his knights. As the constable of France, he would have been received in state by Henry, although details are lacking. The de Montfort brothers probably met then and paid a visit to their great-aunt Loretta, the widow of Robert IV de Beaumont. For the last fifteen years she had been a recluse in Hackington, not far from Canterbury. Their visit to her can be surmised from another visitor she received years later. He was Theobald, the son of Bouchard of Marly and therefore a cousin of the de Montforts on their mother's side. As a younger son, Theobald had been destined for a career in the Church and had risen to become the abbot of Vaux-de-Cernay in the year of Amaury's visit to England. It seems that Amaury, who was still a benefactor of the abbey, encouraged Theobald to undertake his later journey to see Loretta because, as it turned out, she had a miracle story to tell about the Virgin Mary.[19]

A preaching campaign for a new crusade had begun the year before, and Amaury's visit to England can be seen in connection to his intention to join it. His stated destination was the shrine of St Thomas Becket in Canterbury. Pilgrimages of this sort were common to crusaders seeking spiritual support for their expeditions. For material support, the money Simon owed him for the successful acquisition of Leicester likely came up during the visit. What arrangements they made are unknown, just that Amaury was 'pacified so that he might not raise any dispute in the matter'. Simon also took the cross at this time, probably in the summer of 1236, along with other English nobles. In July, Henry decreed that if Simon died 'either beyond or on this side of the seas', the income from his estates was to be used to pay off his debts for four years after his death. With his income hovering around £500 a year, it suggests his indebtedness stood at three or four times that figure.[20]

His brother was in worse straights. Amaury had left the south with debts of around £10,000, and Montfort l'Amaury generated about the same income as Leicester. Taking the cross was the only sure-fire way out of this dilemma. The constable would lend his prestige to a crusade still in the planning stage and in return receive substantial backing from the king and pope. In October 1237, Pope Gregory IX, who had succeeded Honorius in 1227, ordered the archbishop of Sens to give Amaury £2,000 worth of crusade legacies and redemptions collected in his lands, and the bishops of southern France were asked to provide another £2,000 towards paying off his debts. Louis IX and the Crown, mindful of how much they owed the de Montforts for their acquisitions in Languedoc, gave Amaury just over £10,000 and the signal honour of bearing the arms of France in the Holy Land.[21]

The crusade itself would not set out for some time due to developments in the east. To begin with, there was Emperor Frederick II, who had vowed to go on crusade back in 1215. He kept putting off his commitment, even as the Fifth Crusade struggled towards defeat in Egypt. In 1225, he was given the hand of Isabella of Brienne, the heiress to the kingdom of Jerusalem, as incentive for him to embark on his crusade. But two years later and he was still stalling. Pope Gregory finally excommunicated him. The emperor eventually reached the Holy Land and took advantage of divisions among the rival sultanates to win back Jerusalem through diplomacy, along with a ten-year truce. Gregory found his victory distasteful but was reconciled to it. With the truce set to end in 1239, the pope wanted to have a contingent of crusaders ready to defend Jerusalem in the expectation of renewed hostilities.

Frederick, however, had not contented himself with the achievement that had eluded the Third and Fifth Crusades. He tried to impose his authority on the crusader states through his wife and after her death through their infant son Conrad, now the titular king of Jerusalem. The local barons resented his presumption and fought the imperial officials he had imported to take control. The barons had their own rivalries among themselves, as did the communities of the seafaring cities of Pisa, Genoa and Venice. Quarrels between the knightly orders had, moreover, led the Templars to favour the Syrian sultanate while the Hospitallers were inclined to the Egyptians. Any crusader from the west who landed in this atmosphere was more likely to find himself caught up in a civil war than holy war.

Then there was the situation in the Latin Empire. Baldwin had been succeeded in 1206 by his brother Henry, who proved an effective ruler until his sudden death ten years later. Henry's brother-in-law Peter de Courtenay, the count of Auxerre, was elected emperor, but he was captured before he reached Constantinople and died in prison, just like Baldwin before him. Since Peter's son, another Baldwin, was still a minor, the Latins sought to consolidate his position by marrying him to Mary, John of Brienne's daughter from his third marriage. John had been the titular king of Jerusalem by right of his older daughter Isabella (Mary's half-sister) until Frederick, Isabella's husband, took the title from him. Now John became the titular emperor of the Latins by right of his new son-in-law Baldwin II. In 1237, while young Baldwin was in the west trying to raise money for troops, John of Brienne died and Constantinople came under assault from a Greek-Bulgarian alliance.

For this new crusade, Gregory decided one group should set out for Constantinople and the other for Jerusalem. Frederick hindered both expeditions, mostly on account of his ego and his wars in northern Italy. No relief force made it to Constantinople, which was only saved by the Venetian fleet, and by the time the crusaders bound for the Holy Land gathered in Lyon in July 1239, the pope had excommunicated the emperor again. It was in this atmosphere of acrimony and disunity in the Christian world that the crusade left the following month.[22]

At the head of it was Theobald IV of Champagne. He had been an infant in May 1201 when his namesake father died in the midst of organising the Fourth Crusade. The death of his mother in 1234 made Theobald the king of tiny Navarre and it was that title that earned him the nominal leadership of the crusade. After him came Hugh IV, duke of Burgundy, whose family and the de Montforts had been friends for more than four decades. Also making the crusade were two of Amaury's cousins, Philip de Montfort and Matthew II of Marly, the latter being the brother of Theobald the abbot. Philip had been born in the Holy Land and was going back there to stay. He left his lordships of La Ferté-Alais, Rabastens and Castres to his son Philip II, who was probably still a minor at the time. As the younger Philip later married the granddaughter of Guy de Lévis, the former marshal who fought alongside Guy de Montfort in Languedoc, he may have come of age in the Lévis household centred around Mirepoix.[23]

Some of the crusaders went overland to Brindisi and took ships from there. Amaury was in the group that left from Marseille. They were almost there when a storm drove several ships all the way back to Sicily. Amaury was in one of them, for Frederick ordered his officials on the island to give the constable an honourable welcome. The dating of Frederick's letter suggests Amaury and his men arrived in the Holy Land long after the main body under Theobald reached Acre on 1 September 1239. The king of Navarre summoned a council of the barons, prelates and military orders of the crusader states to determine their strategy. As expected, Jerusalem had come under attack once the truce ended, but there was no desire among the locals to strengthen its defences. The city was the emperor's problem, not theirs. That was all they could agree on. Some wanted to march on the sultanate in the north, some on the sultanate in the south. When the army of 4,000 knights left on 1 November, it headed south, but only to build a castle at Ascalon. That would be their demonstration against the Egyptians. They would then march north for something similar against the Syrians.[24]

Keeping the army supplied en route was a major problem. Peter of Dreux, who had left Brittany to his son John, somehow learned of a large enemy convoy not too far in the distance. Without consulting the others, he stole away at night, ambushed and routed the escort troops and returned with the booty. The success of his raid was offset by the maverick nature of it and the inevitable jealousy it incited in the other commanders, who felt they now had to prove themselves. Perhaps none more so than the son of the legendary Simon de Montfort the crusader.

Together with Duke Hugh of Burgundy and Count Henry of Bar, Amaury proposed that they ride on ahead with a detachment to do some foraging in Gaza and rejoin the army afterwards at Ascalon. Theobald, Peter of Dreux and the military orders thought it was insanity. They should stay together until they reached Ascalon and then, maybe, confront the Egyptians, who were on alert after Peter's bushwhacking foray. Amaury knew better than all of them that crusading was a dangerous business which demanded bold action. He and the others gathered up their men and, ignoring Theobald's order for them to desist, set off on the coastal road on the night of 12 November 1239.

In the morning they crossed the brook that marked the frontier and settled down for a breakfast of poultry, capons, cheese and fruit. They could not have chosen a worse spot, a sandy basin with high dunes on both sides. In leading the crossing, Walter of Brienne, the lord of Jaffa and nephew of John of Brienne, had not thought to secure the dunes or send out scouts ahead. The Egyptian commander, Rukn al-Din al-Hijawi, knew from his own scouts that they were coming and had mustered far more men than the force of 600 knights and indeterminate number of foot soldiers and crossbowmen who had entered his territory. His men now seized the dunes and blocked the pass in front of the crusaders. Walter and Hugh advised a retreat, but Amaury and Henry of Bar, whose father had been ridiculed for his inept siege of Toulouse in 1211, argued that it would doom the infantry. It would have been unthinkable for Amaury, knowing the example of his father, to leave any of his men behind. Walter, Hugh and several other lords were less motivated by chivalric ideals and raced for Ascalon.

The battle began with Egyptian archers and slingers pummelling the crusaders below. The crossbowmen returned the fire and might have swept the dunes clear of the enemy had their ammunition held out. The fierce engagement that followed allowed the crusaders to occupy a narrow passage that gave them shelter from the bombardment above. Rukn al-Din did not want to risk an attack on the wall of heavily-armoured knights in front of the passage, so he pretended to flee in order to draw the defenders out of their well-guarded position. It was the oldest trick in the book and the crusaders did emerge from the passage, but only in a vain attempt to escape. They quickly found themselves surrounded in the open plain. In the subsequent battle, Amaury and eighty knights were captured and marched off into captivity. The rest were killed, with Henry of Bar never accounted for.

Theobald was informed of the plight of the raiding party as he reached Ascalon. He responded with an immediate thrust into Gaza, but he was talked out of pursuing the retreating Egyptians for fear they might kill their captives. The military orders seem to have been behind this decision, earning them the scorn of one of the prisoners who happened to be a poet. Theobald, who was also a poet, led his men back to Acre without building the intended castle at Ascalon. He evidently believed it would impede negotiations to free the prisoners.

The chronicler known as the Rothelin Continuator says Ayyub, the sultan, had no intentions of freeing them. When dispatching his troops, he ordered Rukn al-Din to bring back only the most valiant among the enemy, whom he would keep imprisoned for the rest of their lives. Chronicler Matthew Paris says Ayyub was impressed to find the constable of France one of those captured. He had Amaury brought before him and ordered him to point out other nobles of high rank. Amaury told him he was the only one, figuring this would make it easier to obtain his freedom. When the sultan learned otherwise, he flew into a rage and put the constable under closer confinement.[25]

The king's sister, Simon gets married, gets ousted and goes on crusade, Amaury dies

On the night the French set out on their ill-fated incursion into Gaza, a group of English nobles met at Northampton to swear an oath to fulfil their crusader vows. They would go to the Holy Land and only the Holy Land, meaning they refused to be diverted to Constantinople or for some other purpose the pope had in mind.[26] Their nominal leader was Richard, the earl of Cornwall and brother of the king. Just fifteen months younger than Henry, he owed his title and lands to him and resented him for it. That resentment grew as others came to dominate Henry's counsels, especially foreigners like William of Savoy and Simon de Montfort. By the time of the meeting at Northampton, however, William was dead and Simon was nowhere to be found. He had disappeared.

He had, in fact, fled the country following a scandal that nobody saw coming. It went back to his search for a wife that saw him being chased out of France. If Henry had promised Simon an English bride of wealth and status, they may have both known then that it was going to be the king's youngest sister Eleanor. She was born around 1215, the year before her father King John died, and raised in the household of Peter des Roches after her mother Isabella went back to Angoulême and started a new family there. As a princess, Eleanor might have been destined for a foreign court like her older sister Joan, married to King Alexander II of Scotland, and Isabella, married to Frederick II. But in 1224, when Eleanor was 9 years old, she was married to William Marshal II, who was a widower in his thirties. Henry wanted to draw the rich and powerful baron into a closer relationship with the Crown. The marriage was not consummated until Eleanor was 14 and it proved to be a happy union.

William's sudden death and his brother Richard's subsequent rebellion left Eleanor exposed to the machinations of the peace deal. In 1234, she took an oath of chastity before Edmund, the archbishop of Canterbury, which seems to have been a concession to the Marshals. By never remarrying and having children, Eleanor's dower lands in England, which netted her £530 a year on top of the £400 she received for Ireland and Wales, would revert back to their family without the potential for lawsuits. Eleanor probably undertook the oath willingly because she had a very pious nature and had spent the last three years managing her estates with drive and enthusiasm. Marrying again might mean surrendering her independence and lordship to her husband.

What Eleanor may not have counted on was the desire to become a mother that overcame her during the years of Simon's rise at court.[27] When and where these two met is unknown. They would have crossed paths several times, for Eleanor, although a chaste widow, had not shunned life at court. She and Simon had several manors in the neighbouring counties of Wiltshire and Berkshire, and her Wexcombe was just a couple of kilometres from his Collingbourne. They may have struck up a relationship, completely platonic but had confided in Henry their wish that it could be more. The king was deeply attached to his sister, but they were asking him the impossible. The archbishop of Canterbury would lead the Church in an uproar over her discarded vow and the nobles would follow suit because Eleanor was a princess. If she were to marry anyone, it should be to a foreign ruler and not a foreign adventurer.

This is all conjecture in the absence of diaries and records, but it would explain why Simon undertook two marriage proposals that were doomed from the outset. Henry was going to make him earn Eleanor's hand. The marriage itself would have to be performed in secret, at a time when the court was quiet. On 7 January 1238, the day after the Christmas season ended, Henry had the two of them married by his chaplain in a little chapel next to his bed chamber. When word of it got out, the reaction from the Church was muted. The archbishop was in Rome and Otto the legate was seemingly on board. The nobles, however, were up in arms, mainly under the direction of Richard of Cornwall. Henry had disposed of a state matter on a whim, without consulting the council, and all for the benefit of a smooth-talking Frenchman. Richard, however, had also married on his own initiative (to Isabel, daughter of William Marshal) and was using his outrage to wring benefits for himself. In the end, he received presents from Simon and £4,000 from Henry as a subsidy for his crusade.[28]

Knowing the stakes, and not wanting to risk the king's disfavour, Eleanor and Simon probably waited until after their wedding to consummate their relationship. She was pregnant by the time Simon left for Italy at the end of March. He was out to obtain a dispensation for her vow of chastity from the pope, with money provided to him by Henry, and to meet his new brother-in-law Emperor Frederick. He was back in October, and at the end of the following month a son was born to the de Montforts, named Henry after the king. On 2 February 1239, Henry formally invested Simon as earl of Leicester at a ceremony in Winchester. Then in April, Amaury arrived at Westminster to make a full renunciation of his rights to Leicester. Richard of Cornwall led the witness list on behalf of his brother-in-law Simon. In late June, Simon was chosen as one of the godfathers of Edward, the king and queen's first child and heir to the throne. He had truly arrived.[29]

And like that, it was over. The ceremony of the queen's churching was held on 31 July, but Simon and Eleanor were barred from attending. When they demanded to know why, he accused them of conspiring to break her vow of chastity so as to force him to allow them to marry. Why it should have bothered him long after the fact became apparent when Henry arrived at the real source of his anger. He had learned that Simon owed £1,900 to Peter of Dreux, who had brought suit against him at the papal court in Rome. The pope ordered the bishop of Soissons to investigate the matter and if necessary excommunicate Simon. A settlement was then reached where Peter sold more than two-thirds of the debt, probably at a discount, to Thomas of Savoy, an uncle of the queen. Simon gave assurances that his brother-in-law, the king of England, was good for the money.

Two years earlier, in 1237, Thomas of Savoy had married Joanna of Flanders and so became the count that Simon had aspired to be. Thomas had come to England on a state visit around the time of the queen's churching and asked the king to pay up for Simon. Henry flew into a rage because he knew nothing at all of being named security for the debt. Simon had counted on the royal goodwill to acquire an earldom and princess for a wife and apparently assumed that it had become his prerogative. What was particularly galling was that Henry had been paying Peter of Dreux subsidies for a time as his vassal for Brittany. If Peter took that money and lent it to Simon, it meant that Henry was expected to cover that old money with new money. The king felt so defrauded that he did not care that it was his wife's special day or that he offended his beloved sister in the process. He ordered Simon thrown in the Tower. At this point Richard of Cornwall, wanting to spare his sister further anguish, intervened, but the danger persisted. The de Montforts caught the quickest boat they could find and fled to the Continent, leaving their 10-month old son behind.[30]

In all likelihood they went to Montfort l'Amaury to stay but just missed Amaury, who had left the month before to muster with the crusading army in Lyon. In April 1240, Simon returned alone to England, both to fetch his son and raise money for his own crusade. He acquired £1,000 from selling his woods to the Hospitallers and gave 320 acres of land to the Augustinian canons of Leicester in what was officially a grant but may have been a concealed sale. He was received by the king and queen, who seemed generally happy to see him, but Simon nevertheless continued to nurse a grudge. Henry had not only humiliated him in front of everybody, but, having paid off Thomas of Savoy for him, the king sent his officials to Leicester to recoup the money.[31]

On 10 June, Richard of Cornwall, whose wife Isabel had died in January, left Dover and headed for Paris, where he was entertained by King Louis and his mother Blanche of Castile. It seems that Richard also met Beatrice, Amaury's wife, who showed him a letter said to be from her husband but which had more likely been sent on his behalf. It probably came from Hugh, the duke of Burgundy, who was Beatrice's cousin. The letter contained information which Amaury, locked up in Cairo, could not have known about, like the king of France's anger towards the military orders for not being of more assistance to the crusaders.

Simon may have seen the letter and met Richard, but he did not accompany him to Marseille and the ships hired for passage to the Holy Land. He made his journey overland in order to visit Frederick. This could have been Henry's idea, who wished to show his brother-in-law the emperor his support in the ongoing struggle between the empire and papacy. Henry also dispatched a couple of his household knights to serve with Simon on his crusade. Since they were going through Italy, it was decided that Eleanor, who had given birth to a second son that spring, should join them. That way she could see her sister Isabella the empress. Frederick set the family up in a grand palace in Brindisi. Eleanor was pregnant again when Simon and his retinue sailed for the Holy Land.[32]

Their arrival cannot be pinpointed the same as Richard of Cornwall's, who landed at Acre on 8 October 1240. Richard found that Theobald and Peter of Dreux had already gone home. Following the defeat at Gaza, Theobald had accomplished nothing more than marching back and forth and was unable to keep Jerusalem from falling into enemy hands. The growing tensions between the rival sultanates, however, allowed him to negotiate separate truces with Damascus and Cairo that came with concessions. He chose the one with the Egyptians because it returned Jerusalem and other land to the crusader states, more than what Frederick had achieved, and provided for a prisoner exchange. That made it a successful crusade all things considered, but Theobald was fed up with the bickering between the Christian parties and sailed for home before the truce was ratified or the prisoners released.[33]

As the new nominal leader of the crusade, Richard of Cornwall came under intense pressure from the military orders to back their respective sultans. The Hospitallers argued that the Egyptians offered the better deal, the Templars that Syria was the closer threat. In late November, he sent envoys to Cairo with an offer to ratify their agreement. In the meantime he devoted his energies to repatriating the bones of the fallen at Gaza and to helping the duke of Burgundy finish the building works at Ascalon. He had lots of time for it, because his envoys did not return until February with the ratified truce, but no prisoners. The pope by then had grown anxious about Amaury and ordered his representative in England to raise 5,000 marks (£3,333) from the sale of redemptions to obtain his release. The prisoner swap finally took place on 13 April 1241. Amaury and the other captives walked free after nearly seventeen months. It was incidentally thirty years ago that spring that Amaury's cousin Bouchard of Marly was also freed after sixteen months of imprisonment at the hands of the Albigensians.[34]

Perhaps his brother was there to welcome him. There is no way of knowing because Simon's presence in the Holy Land is not mentioned in a single source. The only proof he was there is a letter that was sent to Frederick by the baronial faction of the crusader states who were the most at odds with imperial officials. They proposed to end the conflict by having Frederick name Simon as his *bailie*, or regent, for his underage son Conrad, who was the titular king of Jerusalem. The move seems to have been the work of Philip de Montfort, Simon's cousin, who was related to the Ibelins, a powerful baronial family that had been at war with the emperor since he first rode roughshod over their rights. Given Simon's connections to Frederick, he seemed the one candidate who could be expected to act fairly for both sides. He certainly jumped at the opportunity, both on account of his ambition and uncertainty of his position in England.

The letter was dated 7 June 1241. Richard of Cornwall had already left for Sicily in May and would spend the next four months as a guest of Frederick's court.[35] Later that summer, the de Montfort brothers and Duke Hugh returned to the Italian mainland. It can be presumed that Simon intended to take the letter to Frederick in person, but whether that happened or not, no action was taken on the request to appoint him regent. He had a greater concern in any case when the ship pulled into Otranto, about eighty kilometres south of Brindisi. Amaury had fallen ill, which may have been brought on by the rigors of his confinement, and died there on 28 August, six days after Pope Gregory's death. He was in his mid-forties, about the same age as his father had been when he fell before Toulouse. Gregory was nearly 100.

Amaury was taken to Rome and interred at the Basilica of St Peter's. The nuns of Hautes-Bruyères had his heart brought back for burial in the family mausoleum. The bishop of Chartres officiated and an effigy was erected in his honour at the right of the altar. Blanche of Castile, who valued Amaury's loyalty during the uncertain days of her regency, sent his daughter Adele condolences in the form of a fine golden belt.

Historians would mostly remember Amaury VII de Montfort for failing to live up to the legend that his father was. As the story will soon show, Simon VI proved that it was not an impossible task, but then the circumstances faced by both of them were completely different. Unlike Simon, Amaury had had to fight for his patrimony, and his ability to hold it together for as long as he did and rise to the top of the French nobility suggests he had the same courage, determination and leadership skills that made his younger brother the more famous of the two.[36]

Chapter 9

More Crusades and Political Undertakings
1242–1254

As Simon VI de Montfort's rise in England began with making a good impression on his baronial cousin Ranulf of Chester, so it was with Philip I de Montfort in the Holy Land, and he had a lot of cousins. Philip's mother Helvis had two brothers, John and Philip of Ibelin, both of them powerful lords of the crusader states, who first came into conflict with Emperor Frederick on Cyprus. The Ibelins emerged victorious in the civil war that raged on the island for five years, ending in 1233. The struggle continued on the mainland as a new generation of Ibelins took on the imperialists. There was Helvis's oldest son Balian of Sidon and his cousins Balian of Beirut, John of Jaffa and John of Arsuf, while Baldwin and Guy of Ibelin remained in authority on Cyprus. During the ill-fated expedition to Gaza, Philip adhered more to his newfound eastern relations than to his de Montfort cousin Amaury. When his half-brother Balian of Sidon and cousin John of Arsuf opted for retreat, he went with them.[1]

In 1240, Philip married Maria of Antioch, the heiress of Toron, a rich lordship close to the major seaport of Tyre. The match was clearly the work of the Ibelins. Tyre was then in the hands of the chief imperial officer Richard Filangieri, and the cousins now had one of their own to keep an eye on him. Philip discovered soon enough that Filangieri had a plot underway to seize Acre, the largest city of the kingdom of Jerusalem. With help from the Venetian and Genoese communities, who also disliked the imperialists, Philip arrested the local ringleaders and sent word to Balian of Beirut. Filangieri, who had taken cover among the Hospitallers, slipped out during the night before Balian arrived with troops.[2]

The people of Tyre now appealed to the Ibelins to expel the imperialists. To accomplish it legally, they waited until the absent King Conrad turned 15 on 23 April 1243, marking the end of Frederick's regency.

Conrad's nearest royal relative in the Holy Land was his great-aunt Alice of Champagne, another cousin of the Ibelins. She and her new husband Ralph of Nesle were installed as the regents and the imperialists were driven out of Tyre on 10 July. Alice and Ralph expected to rule from the city, but the Ibelins refused to hand Tyre over to them. They informed the regents that the barons and high court held sway in the kingdom of Jerusalem. That had been the source of all the trouble with Frederick and they did not want a repeat of it. Alice and Ralph rather saw it as the Ibelins wanting all power for themselves. Duped and disgusted, they left for Europe, probably as the cousins had intended.[3]

The Ibelins were supreme in the crusader states, but the infighting between the military orders and between the Italian seafaring communities intensified. It was the same in the Muslim world, and in 1244 war erupted between the rival sultanates. The Templars had lately become allies of the Syrians and convinced the Ibelins to join forces with them against Cairo. They promised them a share of Egypt once they defeated Ayyub. They were supposed to muster for action in the summer, but just then a 10,000 strong force of horsemen swept down from the north. They were the Khorezmians, a Turkic people who had been driven from their homeland by the Mongols. Ayyub had hired them to ravage his enemies and nothing, it seemed, could stop them. They devastated everything 'like a swarm of locusts' and on 11 July 1244 they stormed Jerusalem. They pillaged and burned much of it, killing anybody who had stayed behind after the surrender. The holy city was a wasteland when they continued south to join the Egyptians.

In early October, the Christians marched south of Acre with an army of 5,000 infantry and 1,000 cavalry. Philip de Montfort was placed in command along with Walter of Brienne and the masters of the Templars, Hospitallers and Teutonic Knights. Their Syrian allies provided more men, but they were lightly armoured. At the village of Hiribya (La Forbie) northeast of Gaza, they confronted an Egyptian army of 5,000 infantry under the command of a young emir Rukn ad-Din Baybars and the Khorezmian horsemen. The Syrians advised fortifying their position in the belief that the Khorezmians would grow restless and disperse. Walter of Brienne wanted to destroy them and figured this was their best opportunity. On 17 October 1244, the order to attack was given and the

Frankish knights charged the Egyptians. They were making no headway when the next day the Khorezmians, who had chased off the Syrians, slammed into their exposed flank. The Christian army was destroyed in a matter of hours. Only 800 were taken captive, including Walter of Brienne, who was later killed in a Cairo prison. Philip and sixty-three knights of the orders managed to escape to Ascalon.[4]

The kingdom of Jerusalem was weakened by the debacle, but Ayyub was unable to follow up his victory. He still had to impose his authority over the Syrians and to get rid of the Khorezmians, who, having served their purpose, had grown troublesome. In 1246, Alice of Champagne died and her regency passed to her son King Henry I of Cyprus. Eager to court the support of the Ibelins, he made various grants to them, including giving Tyre to Philip de Montfort. Since the port city belonged to the royal domain, the grant was questionable, but Philip started calling himself the lord of Tyre and all but merged it with nearby Toron to form one large and lucrative lordship under his control.[5]

The loss of Jerusalem led Louis IX of France to take the cross. In August 1248, he launched the Seventh Crusade and reached Cyprus with a force of 15,000 men on 17 September. Amaury's son John, now the count of Montfort, and Philip's half-brother Guy III, the lord of Lombors, were among the troops. John had recently married Jeanne of Chateaudun, and together, for the salvation of his soul and those of his ancestors, they made a donation of land (240 acres) to the abbey of Port Royal, where three of Guy's sisters were nuns. Jeanne, who was pregnant when John left, was the daughter of Geoffrey, the viscount of Chateaudun. He and his men arrived on Cyprus well over a month after the others and the delay may have been the cause of a dispute between them and the Genoese crew that ended in the death of two of the sailors.[6]

It was one of many quarrels the king had to resolve while they prepared to winter on Cyprus, which turned out to be a costly mistake. At the time, Ayyub was preoccupied with a siege of Homs, far to the north of the crusader states. A landing in Egypt and march on Cairo might have finished him. Many of the crusaders, moreover, went broke during the wait on Cyprus and had to borrow from Italian bankers or enter the king's service. The worst, however, was the plague that broke out in the encampments. It claimed the lives of William IV des Barres, now well into his fifties, and John I de Montfort. A letter dated 31 March 1249 lists them among the nobles who had gone 'the way of all flesh'. That was not exactly the case of the count of Montfort, however. It seems that his body did not decompose after his burial in Nicosia. The Cypriots took this to mean that John was a saint and so they had a gilded tomb built for him. It later became a popular place of pilgrimage and legend has it that a descendant of his stripped off a bit of the withered flesh to take back with her as a relic. The shrine was still in Nicosia at the time of the Turkish occupation in the sixteenth century but disappeared sometime afterwards.[7]

Jeanne gave birth to a daughter she called Beatrice, probably after John's mother. It is possible that the news of her husband's death was brought to her in person by no less a figure than Mary of Brienne, the Latin empress. During the sojourn on Cyprus, she and her brother John II of Brienne arrived to ask Louis for aid for her husband Emperor Baldwin, who was still under siege in Constantinople. When the army left for Egypt, Mary and her brother went to Europe. Sometime later John of Brienne married Jeanne. She died on 19 September 1254, by which time John was calling himself the count of Montfort by right of his stepdaughter Beatrice.[8]

The army that left for Egypt had been reinforced with 700 knights from Cyprus and the crusader states, including Philip de Montfort and his Ibelin cousins. It was John of Jaffa who led the landing outside Damietta on 5 June 1249. They brushed aside the defenders, killing four emirs, one of whom was Rukn al-Din al-Hijawi, the victor over Amaury at Gaza. The boldness of the attack sent the garrison fleeing. Damietta, which had defied the Fifth Crusade for eighteen months, fell to Louis in one day. Otherwise his Seventh Crusade repeated the Fifth. Louis refused an offer to swap Damietta for Jerusalem and marched up the Nile without much clue of the terrain. They were stopped outside Mansourah on 6 February 1250 in a ferocious battle that killed among others Geoffrey of Chateaudun. Guy III de Montfort may also have been among the casualties, for his death is given in this year by Port Royal Abbey. He left no children.[9]

Louis held on, hoping in vain that the death of Ayyub from tuberculosis might revive his fortunes. He sent Philip de Montfort to negotiate a truce with one of the emirs, but the terms were unacceptable. By the time Louis gave the order to retreat, the army was plagued by illness again. The only food they had eaten were eels that had grown fat off the corpses of their comrades in the river. They were being hemmed in by the Egyptians when the king, by then suffering from dysentery, asked Philip to renew the negotiations. Philip arranged the truce with the emir, who as a token of faith removed his turban and ring.

All of a sudden hordes of crusaders started giving up. A treacherous sergeant named Marcel had gone among them demanding they surrender in order to save the life of the king. The emir saw no need to grant a truce when the enemy were already his prisoners and so put his turban back on. Normally Philip, as an envoy, would have been allowed to go free, but it was the Egyptian custom that if one of the leaders of the warring sides died during negotiation, as was the case of Ayyub, then the envoy became a prisoner too.

Philip was held in a pavilion with a group that included his Cypriot cousins Baldwin and Guy and Peter of Dreux. They were among those dispatched to hear the terms of deliverance offered by Ayyub's son Turanshah, the new sultan. Louis was to hand over Damietta, which was held by his wife Margaret of Provence, and pay a ransom of £100,000. Turanshah, however, had alienated the Mameluks, former slaves that had risen to become the warrior caste of Egypt, who remembered how Ayyub had put to death a number of them whenever he grew jealous of their success. The captors of Amaury de Montfort had met such a fate. On 2 May, the Mameluks cut down Turanshah in the presence of Louis and for a time it looked as if they might massacre the crusaders en masse. Four days later Turanshah's agreement was ratified by the new rulers. Damietta was surrendered, half the ransom paid, and Louis led the remnants of his army to their ships.

As they sailed away, all was quiet. The king had already lost one brother, Robert of Artois, and now a second one, Alphonse of Poitiers, had to be left behind with other prisoners as surety for the rest of the ransom. Suddenly a ship pulled up alongside with Philip de Montfort on deck shouting excitedly to Louis. 'Sire, sire, it's your brother. He is in this ship over here.' Alphonse had been released as a mark of goodwill and for a moment joy erupted in what was otherwise a sombre fleet heading to the

Holy Land. They were leaving behind the other prisoners and the most complete defeat of any crusade.

Louis spent the next four years in the Holy Land, doubtless his idea of atonement for the disastrous consequences of his failure. Fortunately for him, the Mameluk seizure of power started another war between the Syrians and Egyptians. Although the Syrians offered him Jerusalem for his support, he allied with the Egyptians to get back the remaining prisoners and the remission of the second part of his ransom. The Syrians responded with attacks that included the sacking of Sidon. Philip, who was likely born there, was in the relief force that found more than 2,000 corpses rotting in the city. When Louis arrived, he had a hand in burying them and doubtless Philip and the other lords joined him.[10]

Simon and Eleanor return from crusade, Henry's Poitevin expedition, a lawsuit and the de Montforts vow to go on crusade again

The English troops who joined the Seventh Crusade had been equally decimated. Their leader William Longespee was shamed by Robert of Artois into storming ahead with the French into Mansourah far ahead of the army. They were wiped out in the trap set by the Mameluks. Simon de Montfort should have been among them. He had taken the cross again in late 1247 with the intention of joining Louis's crusade. Matthew Paris says that he wished to be 'absolved from his sins and gain admission to heaven; from reflecting within himself he was in great alarm concerning the marriage he had contracted with his wife'. Eleanor also felt troubled by their private circumstances and 'flew with all speed' to assume the cross with him.[11]

The de Montforts never recovered from the humiliation of the churching and Henry's charges of premarital indiscretion. When they returned from Italy with their sons Henry and Simon and a newborn they called Amaury, they were in no hurry to go back to England. In the spring of 1242, they can be found as guests of the duke of Burgundy. It was then that Simon received a summons from Henry to report for duty. The king had landed with a small force in Gascony. He would again attempt to wrest Poitou back from the French. His chances were better this time because he was supported by the Poitevin lords and by Raymond VII of Toulouse and James I of Aragon. Six English earls sailed with the king, who ordered a seventh, Simon, to join his operations.[12]

Simon came, but he wanted compensation for the money Henry had wrung out of his lands to pay off his debts. The king agreed, if because he had bigger worries in front of him. His mother Isabella of Angoulême and stepfather Hugh Lusignan had bungled their revolt against the French Crown. By the time Henry reached Taillebourg, he found himself deserted by his allies and confronted by Louis's much larger army. He and his earls escaped capture and ransom thanks to Richard of Cornwall, whose efforts on behalf of French prisoners in the Holy Land earned them a one-day truce from Louis. In the limited engagement that there was, Simon and William Longespee were said to have distinguished themselves. Simon nevertheless found their flight to Gascony not to his liking and snapped that Henry should be locked up behind bars, as what had happened to the tenth-century king Charles the Simple after he lost the battle of Soissons.[13]

Louis was forced to call off his offensive after an epidemic swept through his army. Safe in Bordeaux with his queen, Henry decided to stay on for a year to bring Gascony under firmer control. Most of his nobles went back to England, but Simon remained with him. It could not have been his choice, however. He had been absent from his earldom for thirty months and it was expensive maintaining his family abroad. But he had insulted Henry with his outburst in the heat of battle. He was physically safe because it was not an age of political imprisonment or execution, but the cold shoulder of the king was still an effective tool of submission. Simon knew he had some grovelling to do.

Henry's erstwhile allies Raymond of Toulouse and James of Aragon came to Bordeaux to discuss their next move. Both noticed with disquiet the presence of Simon at court. All three had been children when their fathers fought it out at Muret nearly thirty years earlier. Neither of these southern princes was prepared to forget the terrible fate visited on their homelands by the Albigensian Crusade. They tried to drive a wedge between Henry and Simon during their visit and succeeded insofar as Simon lacked full restoration to favour by the time the court returned to England in the autumn of 1243.[14]

Queen Eleanor's mother Beatrice of Savoy arrived to marry her third daughter Sanchia of Provence to Richard of Cornwall. It will be remembered that Beatrice's brothers were William and Thomas of Savoy, but she had more. There was Peter, who rose to become one of Henry's leading councillors, and Boniface, who was elected archbishop of Canterbury in 1241 at Henry's prodding. Simon and Eleanor approached Beatrice to complain that it was unfair how the king lavished so much generosity on her family and yet he was ignoring his own sister. Henry might have felt he had been generous enough by allowing Simon to take possession of Leicester and the two of them to marry, not to mention all the money, deer and wine he had given them in the years before they fell out. Not wanting to look bad in front of his mother-in-law, he agreed to give the de Montforts £333 annually as a dowry for Eleanor, forgive nearly £2,000 of their debts, and give them both custody of Kenilworth Castle.[15]

Although the friendship between Henry and Simon was a thing of the past, they still needed each other. Henry came home to problems with Wales and Scotland and huge debts from his Continental expedition. Parliament met his request for a tax in 1244 by demanding he undertake reforms. They wanted to end his personal rule by appointing a chancellor and justiciar to manage the affairs of government outside the king's direct control. These and other conditions formed what became known as the 'paper constitution'. Henry was not prepared to go that far for the money and told his magnates to exert pressure on their men to come through with the tax. Simon was the only earl to lobby the clergy on behalf of the king. When parliament granted the king a feudal aid only, for the future marriage of his eldest daughter, Henry exempted Simon from paying it.[16]

Simon was also rewarded with the wardship of Gilbert de Umfraville, which is to say Henry sold it to him for £6,667. Since the yearly payments were fixed at £333, the wardship cancelled the fee Henry had recently granted him and Eleanor as her dowry. But Gilbert was just a baby, so the de Montforts could look forward to the earnings from his family estates for the next twenty years. That raised their total annual income to nearly £2,000, making them among the most affluent of baronial families. The problem was half that money came from Eleanor's Marshal dower. Like the Umfraville wardship, none of it could be passed on to their children, who now included a fourth son, named Guy. The only land they could inherit was Simon's Leicester domains and Odiham Castle from their mother.[17]

It was in these years that the remaining Marshal sons died without heirs, Gilbert in 1241 and both Walter and Anselm in 1245. The payment of Eleanor's £400 for her dower lands in Wales and Ireland fell to the eighteen heirs of the Marshal sisters, including Simon's fellow earls of Norfolk, Gloucester and Surrey. They not only consistently defaulted on their share of the payment, but the Marshal widows who followed Eleanor received dower settlements for Wales and Ireland as high as £770, almost double what she had been getting. In the spring of 1247, the de Montforts sued the heirs in the hope of receiving land from the Marshal estate as compensation. Six months later, when the case seemed to have stalled, they took the cross. Their opponents might have seen it as a publicity stunt, the earl and countess of Leicester presenting themselves as two wronged crusaders whose only wish was to put their house in order before leaving to win back Jerusalem.[18]

What the de Montforts could not deny is that they made their vow in the middle of their court case, long after Longespee and other notables had sworn to join Louis on crusade. These included Walter Cantilupe, the bishop of Worcester. Like Robert Grosseteste, who was now the bishop of Lincoln, and Adam Marsh, a Franciscan friar, Cantilupe became both a good friend and spiritual counsellor of the de Montforts. Surviving letters of Adam Marsh suggest Simon and Eleanor were going through a rough patch at this very time. Their decision to go on crusade may have had a mercenary motive to it, but it could also have been about saving their marriage as much as their souls.[19]

In the end, both their case and crusade were dropped. Henry was wary of the political implications from visiting his sister's dower again. Too many noble clans would be upset by a favourable ruling for the de Montforts. Eleanor had been swindled, but there was no helping it now. Instead he would try to make it up to her and Simon. He made himself surety for her dower payments and resumed the gifts of wine, deer and timber that had gone dormant over the past few years. Most importantly, he had a job for Simon. Gascony had again become restless and could well be lost without intervention, which was unthinkable to

Henry. The duchy was not only England's last Continental possession, a matter of pride to the Crown, but a source of revenue, patronage and the future proving ground for young Edward, the heir to the throne. Henry wanted Simon to go down there and restore order.[20]

He turned to him for several reasons. First, there was his status as a crusader. That gave Simon extra clout, as did being the brother-in-law of the king. His personal history also recommended him. He had grown up in the region, knew the people and their language, knew what it took to make them understand who was in charge. There was the risk that the name 'Simon de Montfort' might stir up old resentments, as the visit of Raymond of Toulouse and James of Aragon had shown, but also instill fear and respect in the governed. Matthew Paris says Simon VI had already carved out fame for himself as a warrior, but when and where remains a mystery. His presence in combat can be traced to no engagement other than the rearguard skirmish of the Taillebourg campaign.[21]

Lastly, Simon had withdrawn to the periphery of the court since returning from Gascony five years earlier. It could have been because of his own resentments, against the king or Marshal heirs, or because the spiritual world of his clerical friends now occupied his interests. But his diplomatic skills and connections to the court in Paris made him too valuable a magnate not to take a greater part in the affairs of the realm. He would not, moreover, be going to Gascony like the seneschals before him, as an official of the Crown. He would be the viceroy, with the power to issue commands as if they came from the king himself. He was offered fifty knights and all local revenue, plus more if he needed, and a term of office to last seven years. In another reminder of the elder Simon, who had made the legate and nobles beg him to take command of the Albigensian Crusade, the younger Simon refused the post until the queen and council pleaded with him to accept it.[22]

It was 1 May 1248 and Simon VI was 40 years old. His father at that age had been the top general of his day, his brother the constable of France, and his cousin commanded Christian forces for the crusader states. Philip's advancement had not only been impressive, but he had shown Simon how a baronial faction with effective leadership could take on the emperor and win. Simon had yet to make a similar mark. He had had his spectacular rise under Henry III, but it ended in disgrace. It took him nearly five years to climb back and now the king was offering him something big, the chance to be an independent ruler, to become something like the southern prince his father and brother had aspired to be. The key, however, was Henry, and whether these two men, each brilliant yet flawed in his own way, could cooperate and make it work.

Simon becomes the viceroy of Gascony, he rules with an iron hand, the king puts him on trial

Simon and Eleanor left England on 21 August 1248. His first assignment was to extend the truce with France. Since Louis was just then on the Mediterranean coast, preparing to set sail for Cyprus, Simon made the arrangement with Blanche of Castile, again serving as regent for her son. Once they reached Gascony, Simon went to the Pyrenees to meet Theobald IV of Champagne, who as the king of Navarre had clashed with Henry and his officials over their shared border. Theobald agreed to settle their differences through arbitration.

The two families that dominated the political and economic life of Bordeaux, the Delsolers and Columbines, had concluded a truce during the summer. With the capital quiet, Simon went around the four feudal courts of Gascony to announce his arrival and lock up the troublemakers, mostly on charges of highway robbery. Many were petty lords of the type that his father had constantly battled against and tried to legislate out of existence with his Statute of Pamiers. Now the son imprisoned them without trial and forced them to pay ransoms for their release. The viscount of Gramont did not walk free for six years.[23]

On a more personal level, there was Gaston VII, the viscount of Béarn. His great-uncle Gaston VI had been among the coalition of southern counts who fought against the Albigensian crusaders. It will be recalled how, following his death in 1214, his widow Perronelle, the countess of Bigorre, was married to Simon's brother Guy and had two daughters with him. She married twice after he was killed outside Castelnaudary in 1220. The daughter from her last marriage became the wife of the current Gaston. Perronelle intended to leave Bigorre to her grandson Esquivat, the son of Alice, her eldest daughter with Guy II. Displeased that his wife had been cut out, Gaston began raiding the frontier between their counties. Perronelle turned to Simon for help against her son-in-law. She and Simon had not seen each other for thirty years, since the siege of Toulouse in 1218, when he was 10 and she 34. They agreed that he would lease Bigorre from her and use it as a base of operations against Gaston.[24]

Returning to England for Christmas, Simon was feted at court for bringing the Gascons to submission. According to Paris, he had 'behaved with such bravery and fidelity that he deservedly obtained the praise and favour of all the king's friends, and was said to take after his father in all respects'. He and Eleanor made plans to have their 10-year-old son Henry and his 7-year-old brother Amaury educated in the household of Robert Grosseteste, the bishop of Lincoln. In June 1249, they went back, crossing at the same time as Longespee and his men, who were on their way to meet their dreadful end on the Nile. Within weeks of their arrival in Bordeaux, a riot broke out on the eve of the mayoral election between supporters of the Delsolers and Columbines. Simon intervened in force and lost three of his men in the fighting. He detained culprits on both sides, but was inclined to believe the Columbine side of the story. The Delsolers complained to Henry, who stood by his viceroy but nevertheless cautioned him to conduct himself in a manner befitting a 'consistent and just judge'.[25]

On 27 September 1249, Raymond VII of Toulouse died. In the twenty years since the end of the Albigensian Crusade, he had devoted himself to rehabilitating his father's memory and having a son to keep his family's dynastic lands from falling into the hands of the French. He had failed at both and Toulouse now went to his daughter and her husband Alphonse of Poitiers, who was then on his way to meet his brother Louis in Egypt. Alphonse's chaplain met Simon and Eleanor at La Réole to discuss matters of litigation involving the border between Gascony and Toulouse. He wrote to Alphonse that the de Montforts were planning to join the rest of them on the crusade next June. The duchy had been subdued and the chaplain seemed to agree. 'Know that he holds Gascony in good estate, and all obey him, and dare undertake nought against him.'[26]

The chaplain was writing after Simon had captured Gaston de Béarn and other Gascon lords and shipped them off to the king for judgement. Henry received them at Clarendon in mid-December and pardoned the lot of them. For Gaston, he could not do otherwise, for he was a first cousin of Queen Eleanor and she felt compelled to intercede for him. Henry ordered Simon 'not to move war against him or his adherents or molest him, knowing that the king's will is that his bailiffs and subjects be intimate (*familiares*) and friends with them as before'. The war, however, reignited after Gaston returned, and at the end of March, Simon informed Henry in a letter, the only one of his known to exist, that the situation was rapidly spiralling out of control.[27]

> Sir, I have heard for certain that some knights of Gascony have provided themselves with everything to demand their lands by war. And they are certainly leagued together, they and their friends; and I fully understand that they will begin soon to overrun the land; but what force they will have I cannot as yet be at all sure. And because the great men of the land bear me such ill will, because I uphold your rights and those of the poor against them, there would be danger and shame to me, and great damage to you, if I were to return to the land without instructions from you and without speaking to you.[28]

At the time Simon was in Paris managing Henry's business, which included renewing the truce with France for another five-year term. They could not know it, but Louis's army was just then on the verge of surrender to the Egyptians. On 3 May, Simon was back in England. He had asked for the personal meeting with Henry because he understood many 'sinister things' were being said of him. He wanted to reassure the king he was doing everything by the book. He also needed more money. This was a problem for Henry, because he had recently vowed to go on crusade and was already cutting costs to fund it. The king scraped together £2,000 and sent Simon on his way, but the viceroy returned to a land in full rebellion against his rule. Like his father before him, he had to go around reducing individual strongholds, some on inaccessible outcrops of rock. But also like his father, he never had enough resources for it and by the end of the year he was in full flight to England to seek aid.

He arrived on 6 January 1251 to announce that Gascony was as good as lost without more money. He reminded the king that these were the same people who had turned their backs on him after Taillebourg in 1242 and showed no mercy to the queen either when she was ill before and after she gave birth to a daughter in Bordeaux. Henry concurred that that had been the case, but he still could not ignore all these complaints he was hearing about Simon's conduct. The worst was his viceroy imprisoning people who had come to him in peace and good faith, even putting some of them to death. Simon dismissed the charges contemptuously. 'My lord, their treachery, which you have experienced, renders them unworthy of belief.' The king was willing to believe him for now and gave him another £2,000.

Simon raised more money from his estates and those of his ward Gilbert de Umfraville. With troops that included 300 irregulars, he returned to Gascony and put down the uprising. He faced a new threat, however, from a new crusade. Word of Louis's demise in Egypt had led thousands of shepherds and common folk to mass together under the preaching of a mad monk from Hungary. He would lead them to the Holy Land to accomplish what the clergy and nobility had failed to do. It was a tragic reminder of the Children's Crusade that swept through France in 1212 (the same year Simon's father was bringing his own crusade to what he had believed was a successful conclusion). Having rioted in most of the towns in their path, the shepherds who reached Bordeaux chose to heed Simon's warning to disperse lest he 'cut them to pieces'. Their movement had begun to melt away in any event after a butcher with an axe sent the Hungarian monk 'brainless to hell'.[29]

Otherwise the momentarily quiet situation in Gascony allowed Eleanor to rejoin her husband. In Bordeaux she gave birth for the first time in six years, to their first daughter no less, but the infant died and was buried at the Dominican priory there. The Dominicans, of course, had been founded by St Dominic, the spiritual guide and friend of the family who baptised Simon's sister Petronilla. His other sister Amicia had founded, in her widowhood, a Dominican nunnery at Montargis and was soon to die there, as a nun, in 1252. The only religious house Simon is thought to have founded was the Dominican friary in Leicester. Interestingly, though, all of his and Eleanor's close friends – Robert Grosseteste, Walter Cantilupe and Adam Marsh – were Franciscans.[30]

It was in Marsh's letters to the couple that we gain much insight into the difficulties of their years in Gascony. He informed them that the tide of complaints from the Gascons, led by Gaston, was starting to shift opinion at court. The king was becoming fed up with what he saw as a quagmire and money pit. In November 1251, the de Montforts returned to England, but Matthew Paris says that Henry cold-shouldered the couple. They nevertheless travelled with the court to York for the marriage of 11-year-old Princess Margaret to 10-year-old King Alexander III of Scotland. Sometime during the festivities, the king and viceroy had a row. Henry had learned that the Gascons were again in revolt and all on account of the man they called a 'most infamous traitor'. There was also the money Simon sought for the castles he had built. When Henry refused to reimburse him, the queen intervened and convinced him to relent, but he refused to take his brother-in-law any longer at his word. Much to Simon's disbelief and resentment, the king detained him in England while a commission was dispatched to find out what was really going on.[31]

The commissioners found a state of war between the Gascons and Simon's lieutenants, with all the fighting and anarchy endangering the truce with France. The commissioners told the Gascons to put down their arms and proceed to England, where they could present their case in person to the king. Henry had already allowed Simon to go back to Gascony when he received the commission's report. Furious it had come to this, he ordered him to return immediately. Simon himself was already in a high temper. According to Paris, 'the earl with all haste crossed the sea, but in no calm state of mind; for he proposed to have his vengeance for the injury done him by such serious accusations'. A large delegation of Gascons, led by the archbishop of Bordeaux, had answered the summons. On 9 May 1252, the adversaries gathered in the dining hall of the monks at Westminster Abbey to square off before the king.[32]

Simon made sure to have plenty of friends and supporters on hand, and one of them, Adam Marsh, sent a full description of the proceedings to Grosseteste. The Gascons accused Simon of 'harassment, pillaging, fraud and oppression', but Henry, rather than jumping to his defence, heaped vociferous abuse on Simon, who nevertheless took it with 'meekness and a mature magnanimity'. Only grudgingly was the accused and his advocates, who included a few Gascons, allowed to respond, and they countered that all his actions had been taken for 'the honour of the lord king and his heirs'. Where the accusers had provided no proof, the defence was ready to engage them in judicial combat to see who was telling the truth. They also insisted that both sides should accept whatever judgement was imposed by the king or his judges. When the Gascons replied that they would accept no judgement that did not include banishing the 'exterminating earl', the king had no choice but to vindicate Simon. That seemed the end of it.

The next day, however, Henry changed his mind. No one in the room knew Simon better than he did and he was not so convinced of his innocence. That led to a public shouting match between the two. According to Paris, Simon sneered at the king and questioned his piety, which in Henry's case was tantamount to slander. It was only thanks to the presence of peers like Richard of Cornwall, Peter of Savoy and Richard de Clare, who were all then well-disposed to Simon, that the earl was not seized and tossed in the Tower. In the end, Simon offered to rule the duchy with compassion or else resign his office with full indemnity and free of any guilt or reprisals. Henry rejected both out of hand. He ordered him and the Gascons to go back and observe a truce. He would make plans to come over himself and sort everything out. In the meantime, he was not yet finished with Simon and dismissed him with a parting shot: 'Go back to Gascony, you who are so fond of war and strife, and reap its rewards like your father did before you.'[33]

He left on 16 June 1252, taking his eldest son, 13-year-old Henry, with him. He raised a mercenary force along the way, says Paris, 'to take vengeance for the defamation of his character'. At one point Simon staged an ambush, but his enemies got the better of the fight and captured one of his knights. As his father before him, Simon rode into the fray to rescue him, but just barely escaped himself. A new royal commission reported back to Henry that the country was at war again. On 27 August, the king ordered the Gascons to observe the truce, and if Simon failed to do so, they were no longer to obey him. Even a stalwart friend like Adam Marsh was beginning to have doubts about Simon's conduct. In October 1252, Adam wrote to inform him that Eleanor was close to her term (birth of their fifth son Richard) but then savaged him for all but kidnapping a parish priest to serve with him in Gascony:

I am not a little disturbed to think of this. I do not know what obscured the clarity and prudence of your pious mind to cause such an error. It makes me more sorry that you have, as I hear, some absurd arguments by which you think it is possible to defend an act which deserves to be condemned. I pray the Lord may forgive those who took pains to persuade your kind heart of these arguments.[34]

Parliament was just then meeting and urged the king to let Simon finish what he had set out to do, saying the Gascons were only getting what they deserved. There were suspicions that it had become a vendetta for Henry and that he was motivated by no other desire than to have the earl of Leicester declared a traitor so he could strip him of his earldom and give it to one of his foreign relatives. Paris says Simon himself thought that was the case and that was the reason he was determined to hang on to their agreement. The Gascons, however, were equally determined to drive him out and managed to trap him at the castle of Montauban. He was forced to surrender prisoners in return for getting them to lift the siege. It was a humiliating setback and a sign to cut a deal. In November, Simon agreed to take £4,667 plus the payment of his debts to clear out.[35]

His first attempt at rule was over. It had met few expectations, least of all Henry's, but the French were impressed by what they saw as Simon's fidelity and courage. In the spring of 1253, they asked him to join their regency council, which had seemed rudderless following the death of Blanche of Castile the previous November. Says Paris: 'For they asserted that he, like his father Simon, who had fought for the Church against the Albigensians, loved the kingdom of France in his heart, nor was he an alien to France by blood.' Twice they made him the offer, twice he rejected it. 'No man can properly serve two masters', he told them, meaning his loyalty was to the king of England.

That loyalty, however, came at a price. When Henry sailed in August 1253, the duchy was again at war. The cause was the ambitions of the new king of Castile, Alfonso X, who had his own ancestral claims to Gascony, and Gaston de Béarn, who saw himself filling the role of viceroy for Alfonso. After reaching Bordeaux, Henry summoned all the men who owed him service, but got no response from Simon. On 4 October, as his campaign against the rebels was beginning to stall, the king summoned the earl of Leicester again, almost reaching out to him. Prompted by encouragement from his mentor Robert Grosseteste, who died around this time, Simon came and brought a body of troops with him, but it was just like his answer to Henry's summons after his crusade eleven years earlier. The king was going to have to pay to make things right between them.[36]

In the agreement worked out, Simon and Eleanor were given lifetime possession of Kenilworth and Odiham, a new annual fee that raised their combined income to £2,350, and £500 for his losses and expenses in Gascony. Simon stayed with Henry's forces until February 1254, longer than expected, but there still had to be some tension between the two men. Here they were hunting down Gaston, the same man the king had pardoned against Simon's wishes, and destroying vineyards and carrying out other harsh measures Henry had censured him for back in England. The irony of their situation now, with the reminders of the ill treatment he felt he had suffered on account of it, must have made Simon seethe on more than one occasion.[37]

It was not until August 1254 that the duchy was secure again. Simon was back in England by then and during that month undertook a secret mission to Scotland for Henry, probably connected to certain intrigues going on within the minority regency of the king's son-in-law Alexander III. It looked as if they had the nightmare of Gascony behind them and that the quarrels of the past were forgotten. And yet Paris offers a vague but instructive anecdote.

At one point during Henry's campaign, Alfonso began mobilising for war. The king wrote to his wife and regent, Eleanor of Provence, to summon parliament to ask for men and money to guard against it. The results were inconclusive, so in February 1254, Eleanor summoned another parliament, this time ordering the sheriffs to have two knights elected from their respective counties to come to London to discuss the aid she was seeking. These were the first elections to parliament, a constitutional innovation that did not go unnoticed at the time. The assembly turned out to be a raucous affair, with many in attendance believing there was no threat of war, that the king was simply trying to squeeze more money out of them.

In fact, Henry was at that very moment concluding a peace treaty with Castile, underpinned by the marriage of his son Edward to Alfonso's sister. If the assembly had learned about the treaty, it probably came from Simon, who had just arrived from the Continent. All Paris says is that Simon had informed his fellow parliamentarians of 'the truth of the matter' and that upon learning it the assembly 'departed in the greatest indignation'.[38] The question becomes whether Simon had not only sabotaged the king's request for assistance but knowingly made him look deceitful and untrustworthy in front of his peers.

Chapter 10

Realpolitik and Revolution
1254–1263

During the turmoil of the preceding years, Frederick II's misfortunes continued after the expulsion of his men from the crusader states. In 1245, the new pope, Innocent IV, succeeded in deposing the emperor at a special council he summoned to Lyon. Frederick was a pathetic, lonely figure when he died of a fever on 13 December 1250, aged 56. Innocent refused to recognise his son Conrad as his successor and looked for another European prince to become the king of Sicily. When his offer was declined by Richard of Cornwall and Louis's youngest brother Charles of Anjou, his choice fell to Edmund, the 9-year-old son of Henry III and Eleanor of Provence. Henry accepted for his son for reasons that were quite understandable at the time. He was vowed to go on crusade, but the war in Gascony had robbed him of all the treasure he had been saving for it. The pope would redirect his vow, and the Church subsidies being collected for his crusade, to Sicily instead.

Then in May 1254, Conrad too died of a fever, aged 26, and the pope felt he had been too rash in offering Sicily to England for the price of an invasion. It was, after all, one of the richest kingdoms in Europe. But Frederick had an illegitimate son named Manfred, who now vied for control of Sicily and Italy. In the battle that followed in December, papal forces were routed by Manfred's army, and Innocent IV died just days later, a broken pope. His successor Alexander IV felt compelled to continue the struggle, and in March 1255, he renewed the offer of Sicily to Henry, but at a price of £90,400 in addition to the invasion. Henry still accepted. He had to crusade somewhere and it was a bargain compared to the half a million pounds Louis had squandered on his failed crusade.[1]

The Sicilian business never became popular in England. The massacre of Longespee and his men in Egypt and Simon's woes in Gascony left the barons with little desire for foreign ventures. The clergy positively hated it. They objected to funding any crusade on principle, but this one, like the Albigensian Crusade before it, was against Christians. It was for political purposes only. But as the popes kept telling them, it was a new era. Crusades were no longer just about heretics or infidels, but excommunicates as well. The Raymonds of Toulouse and Frederick got their just desserts and now so too would Manfred.

The diversion of Henry's crusade probably caused the greatest concern in the kingdom of Jerusalem. In September 1254, Philip de Montfort joined other magnates in sending a letter to the king deploring their desolate condition following Louis's departure several months earlier. They urged Henry to fulfil the vow he made 'some time ago' and come to help them defend 'this tiny remnant of Christendom'.[2] They did not expect him to be any more competent at military leadership than Louis was or even they were. They were in fact enjoying a breathing spell. Pressure from the Mongols to the east kept the sultanates from devoting their energies to conquests along the seaboard. What the magnates needed was somebody with stature. Louis's greatest contribution was his royal majesty. With a king in their presence, the magnates were less inclined to bicker among themselves.

Even the united front of the Ibelins had begun to falter. After Balian of Beirut died in 1247, his brother John of Arsuf was named *bailie* of the kingdom by King Henry I of Cyprus, the regent for Conrad. He was soon ousted by the king, apparently at the suggestion of Philip, only to be reinstated the following year. In 1250, John wanted to have all the proceedings of the high court of Jerusalem written down, but the majority of barons, led by Philip, were against it. Then in early 1256, the Venetian and Genoese colonies in Acre came to blows over possession of the hilltop monastery of St Sabas. As the two maritime republics took their fight to the seas, all the Ibelins were drawn to the initial success of the Genoese. Philip had his own quarrels with the Venetians and in September expelled them from the third of Tyre that was theirs by treaty.

That upset his cousins John of Arsuf and John of Jaffa, who suspected that Philip was seeking to carve out his own independent enclave around Tyre. The military orders stepped in to try and restore peace between the Italians, and to show his good faith Philip offered his mansion in Acre for the talks. The meeting, however, broke up violently when the Venetian and Genoese envoys ended up in a near fatal swordfight. Afterwards the advantage swung to the Venetians, and the two Johns, the Pisans, Templars and Teutonic Knights threw their support to them. The Genoese had the Hospitallers and Philip, who ran supplies to their men besieged in Acre.[3]

In June 1258, a fleet of fifty-two ships from Genoa arrived in Tyre to coordinate an assault on Acre. Philip led eighty horsemen and thirty archers to a position outside the port city called 'New Vineyard'. There the master of the Hospitallers and several of his men joined them and together they waited for the Genoese to win their expected victory in the harbour. When that happened, they would move in and seize the Pisan and Venetian quarters. Superior seamanship, however, allowed the Venetians to capture twenty-four of the attacking vessels and drive off the rest. The raiding party watched the debacle in dismay, then returned to Tyre, where the master shortly died. The Genoese were forced to abandon Acre and trail after Philip to Tyre. They continued to get the worst of the conflict until 1261, when they helped the Greeks re-conquer Constantinople from Baldwin and the Venetians. The Latin Empire, established around the time of Philip's birth, was at an end.[4]

The 56-year-old Philip remained hostile to the Venetians and Acre, and Arab sources say that he and the Genoese entered into an alliance with Baybars, who had become the sultan of Cairo in 1260. If true, it may have had something to do with a sudden attack by Baybars on Acre in 1263. Philip's determination to stick by the losing side in the War of St Sabas, as the conflict was called, suggests his primary motive was commercial. Tyre was a thriving seaport and stood to gain whatever Acre lost. Twenty years earlier, when Amaury de Montfort was in the Holy Land, Acre was said to produce £50,000 in annual revenue through trade and taxes. If Tyre could be made to earn that much wealth, and Toron alone was worth 60,000 bezants (£10,000), Philip would be the beneficiary of a lordship worth a hundred times more than Simon's earldom of Leicester.[5]

There was contact between these de Montfort cousins at this time. In November 1259, Philip's son Philip II gave £120 to the abbey of Port Royal as the share of inheritance from the Albigensian conquests that belonged to his aunts Agnes and Alice, nuns of the house. The bequest, which was made at the request of his father, was seconded by Simon, who was in Paris at the time.[6] The younger Philip would have been in his thirties by now and events about to unfold suggest he was already a seasoned warrior. Described as a 'bold knight, adept at arms', he may have gained experience on Louis's crusade, but there is no evidence he participated in it.

Philip II had been the acting lord of Castres since his father went to the Holy Land and referred to himself as 'the successor in the Albigeois to the counts of Toulouse and Montfort'. The proximity of his lordships to Gascony makes it likely that there was some cooperation between him and Simon during the latter's stormy administration. On 9 April 1259, almost seven years after his recall as viceroy, Simon appointed Philip II to be his guardian for Bigorre. This action goes back to the death of Countess Perronelle in 1251. Her grandson and heir Esquivat had been unable to protect Bigorre from plundering by Gaston de Béarn. Exasperated, he gave his great-uncle Simon the county in August 1256, but then went on ruling it as before. Apparently the transfer of ownership had been a ruse. It was Esquivat's way of using the threat of Simon de Montfort to keep Gaston in line. As far as Simon was concerned, the county was still his, perhaps to be given to one of his younger sons someday.[7] Apart from keeping an eye on Gaston or Esquivat, the appointment of Philip II was meant to reinforce his claim to the lordship in an even more complicated scheme then being negotiated.

At this juncture the Sicilian business had ground to a halt. Henry III needed more money than what Church subsidies could provide for the venture, but his barons were not interested. His brother Richard of Cornwall had the capital, but having turned down the crown of Sicily for himself, he decided to buy Frederick's other vacant crown, the kingdom of Germany. Henry's only real assistance came from Louis. They had met for the first time in 1254 when the king of England went through Paris on his way home from Gascony. It was a grand occasion. Their queens, Margaret and Eleanor, were joined by their sisters Sanchia, Richard's wife, and Beatrice, the wife of Charles of Anjou. The two former boy kings hit it off well, which was essential because, if Sicily was going to work, the century-long state of war between England and France had to come to an end. Still haunted by his crusade, Louis came home not only ready to make peace with England but to offer concessions he might have otherwise not made had his mother been alive or his conscience not bothered him so much.[8]

It was natural for Henry to turn to Simon to work on the draft treaty. He was intimately familiar with Louis, his brothers and members of the council, and he was good friends with the chief negotiator for the French, Eudes Rigaud, the archbishop of Rouen. Henry authorised Simon to pursue any of his own claims in France, whether they involved Albigensian conquests or the ancestral lands of his forebears on the Norman frontier. The terms of the treaty called for Henry to renounce his claims to Normandy, Poitou and other English lands seized from him and his father King John, and in return Louis would cede several lordships around Gascony to Henry and pay him enough money to support 500 knights in the field for two years. The last concession was the work of Pope Alexander IV, who saw the knights as forming the core of the army Henry was supposed to send to Sicily.

In May 1258, Simon was part of a delegation that went to Paris to finalise the treaty. It was agreed that in November, Henry and Louis would meet in Cambrai, northern France, for the formal ratification. They would be joined by Richard of Cornwall, now the king of Germany. It would be a meeting of three kings, a reference to the *Magi* of the Bible, who brought charity, peace and devotion to the world. Henry put great store in state occasions imbued with such symbolism, but he never showed up. In the six months between the finalisation of the peace treaty in Paris and the meeting of three kings, a revolution had taken place in England. Henry had finally given in to parliament's demands for reforms and the barons used their ascendancy to take control of the realm. The now all-powerful council decided to send a delegation of magnates instead of the king to meet the other two kings. Louis saw no sense in treating with underlings on so important a matter and stayed away. The ratification of the treaty would have to wait.[9]

The Provisions of Oxford, ouster of the Lusignans, Simon's revenge and assumption of the baronial leadership

Everything had seemed to be going Henry's way. He restored order in Gascony, secured an alliance with Castile, established friendship with

Louis, had recently regained control of the Scottish regency council, and Wales had been peaceful for eight years. But huge problems abounded at home. The king's indebtedness was unsustainable, and this was outside his commitment to Sicily and rebuilding Westminster Abbey at the same time. The counties were becoming restless under pressure from fines imposed by eyres (itinerant justice), from the sheriffs, who were under pressure themselves from the exchequer to step up their collections, and from magnates, who were driving their peasants hard to increase their own margins. Denied taxation by parliament, Henry siphoned off the wealth of the Jews, but that created a credit crunch and unsavoury debt market, the kind that got Simon into trouble two decades previously. Not only was the prosperity that marked most of Henry's reign over, but it left behind a population boom that fell victim to famine when bad weather ruined harvests in the latter part of the 1250s.[10]

It was intrigue at court, however, that brought on the revolution. The origins went back to Richard Marshal's uprising a quarter of a century earlier. To head off any more baronial rebellions, Henry set out to tie the ancestral clans closer to the Crown by marrying their heirs and heiresses to his Lusignan half-siblings or the queen's Savoyard relatives. This generated criticism that he was putting the wealth of England into the hands of foreigners, a jibe Simon was likely to have heard when he married Eleanor, but everything worked as long as everyone received their share. Then in the following decade, Henry's stockpile of land became exhausted and his treasury struggled to support all the courtiers on the payroll. Those who obtained their land and fees were eyed warily by those still waiting in the queue.

Simon had his eye in particular on one fellow magnate. In 1247, Henry married his half-brother William de Valence to Joan, the heiress of Pembroke. This gave Valence a portion of the Marshal estate that was not only bigger than Leicester, but included lands that Simon and Eleanor felt belonged to her. Valence was soon the rising star of the court, the favourite Simon had been twenty years before. That would have been enough to arouse jealousy in him, but Valence and his Lusignan brothers were brash and impulsive, unapologetic for their good fortune and not cowed at all by the older aristocracy. During parliament in 1257, Simon accused Valence of raiding his property and carrying off booty. Valence responded by calling Simon a liar and traitor, even hinting that Simon's father had been a traitor. According to Paris, Henry had to restrain his brother-in-law from killing the impetuous younger man.[11]

On the other hand, Simon had good relations with the other foreign faction, the Savoyards. They too wanted to see the backs of the Lusignans because Edward, the 18-year-old heir to the throne, had recently become attached to their circle. It started when Wales revolted in late 1256. Only the Lusignans showed interest in helping Edward recover his lordship there. Like the rest of the court, the queen saw her Lusignan in-laws as rivals for her husband's patronage. She now looked on with dismay as her son came under their influence. An opportunity to put a stop to it occurred in April 1258 when the Lusignans were implicated in a deadly church brawl. A secret confederation of seven magnates, one of them Simon de Montfort, came together to oust them.[12]

Parliament was in session at the time, and when Henry made his appeal for the Sicilian business, the barons offered to lobby for the tax among their men if the king and Edward agreed to undertake reforms of the realm in partnership with them. Henry had always been loath to share power following the experience of his minority, when his regents looked after themselves first and foremost. He also felt it was unnatural for barons to tell a king what to do, but he had run out of options for Sicily and the famine had shaken his piety. Feeding the poor had always been one of the hallmarks of his kingship. Needing to put his house in order, he agreed to reconvene parliament in Oxford in June 1258 and swore to abide by whatever decisions were taken at it.[13]

Their work went far beyond what he or even most of the barons could have envisioned. Where Magna Carta was a charter of liberties concerned at most with the free people of the land, the 'Provisions of Oxford' was a constitution of government that covered everybody, including unfree peasants. It set up judicial commissions in the counties to investigate abuse by lords and officials, inviting anybody with a complaint (*querela*) to state their case for free and receive judgement on the spot. Parliament would no longer be an instrument of royal prerogative, rather an institution of state meeting at regular intervals. The appointment of ministers was also taken out of Henry's hands and entrusted to a permanent council of fifteen that would oversee all the affairs of the realm. It would technically be under the lordship of the king and so it was assumed that Henry would get his way on most matters, but he had no sooner given his blessing to these undertakings than the confederation struck. Working with the queen behind the scenes, they made sure the Lusignans were excluded from the council and pushed through an anti-alien measure requiring them to forfeit much of their patronage from the king. When they resisted, the newly formed council ordered their expulsion from the realm.[14]

Henry must have started second-guessing the whole business. Clearly certain barons had an agenda other than reforms and the profit of the realm. Simon in particular seemed to be everywhere and in charge of everything as the work of putting the reforms into effect began. From the outset it looked like he was in it for himself. As part of the committee tasked with drafting the reforms, he made his claims for land one of the first issues the committee took under advisement. He was far and away the most militant of the reformers. When Valence refused to hand over his castles as ordered by the council, Simon warned him to comply or risk losing his head. After the Lusignans went abroad, his son Henry de Montfort gathered up friends and family to pursue and harass them. Since their stated purpose was to avenge the insults Valence had heaped on Simon, it seems likely that the senior de Montfort had had a hand in their action.

Simon's hand can also be seen in the official proclamation of Henry's support for the council and the clause at the end that branded anyone who opposed the Provisions of Oxford a 'mortal enemy'. It fit nicely with his uncompromising nature. Finally, there was a chance encounter between Henry and Simon after a thunderstorm in July 1258, just after the Lusignans and their retainers had been expelled. Henry, whose fear of thunder and lightning was well known, told Simon that he feared him more than all the thunder and lightning in the world. Paris, who reports the incident, says that Henry was not joking. The implication here was his fear that Simon, if given the opportunity, would take their experiment in government too far for their own good (Paris died the next summer and so never saw just how far it ended up going).[15]

More ominous was Simon's sense of personal grievance. Besides all the scrounging and begging he and Eleanor had had to do over her dower, his experience of the royal wrath had left him bitter and resentful.

Twenty years on after the queen's churching and he was still unable to repeat Henry's 'extremely coarse and shameful language' to him. His trial over Gascony was such a humiliation that, if Paris can be believed, Simon actually threatened Henry's life during the proceedings. Now was his chance to get back at the king, and two opportunities immediately presented themselves.[16]

First, he got his fellow councillors to give him custody of Winchester Castle. Henry loved Winchester. It was the city of his birth and his home for nearly every Christmas. In 1250, he pressured the monks there to elect his Lusignan half-brother Aymer de Valence as their new bishop. By taking possession of the castle and securing Aymer's banishment, Simon was all but announcing to Henry that Winchester was his town now. Then there was Cambrai and the meeting of three kings. The council decided to prevent Henry from going there for fear that he might return with the Lusignans. It was an unfounded argument. The Lusignans had put the blame for their exile on the queen and were saying some unpleasant things about her, which earned them her ire and that of her sister, Queen Margaret of France. Henry would have problems with more than just the council if he tried to reinstate his brothers any time soon. As for who might have raised these concerns about the king's integrity, Simon is the most likely candidate. The council was packed with his allies and they chose him and his friends Walter Cantilupe and Richard Gravesend, who had lately become the bishop of Lincoln, for the delegation to ratify the treaty. In usurping Henry's position for this crowning moment of his reign, Simon was having his vengeance for those past humiliations.[17]

Louis had been friends with the de Montforts for a long time, but he refused to get caught up in this unseemly business. Simon was not deterred. While the other treaty delegates went home, he stayed on in France for the next couple of months. His sons Henry and Simon VII were with him and he wanted to arrange some personal affairs. There was the £333 he owed to the estate of Peter of Dreux, who had died on the return voyage from Louis's crusade. Perhaps as an incentive to make Simon pay the debt, Peter's executors assigned it to the convent of Saint-Antoine in Paris, where Simon's sister Petronilla had risen to become the abbess. Simon went there to see her and begin payments to the convent of £22 a year until the debt was clear.[18]

Since Simon had done nothing about his debt in the eight years since Peter's death, nor in the twenty years before it, he had to feel that the reform era imposed obligations on everyone, not just the king. The barons could not reasonably expect Henry to sacrifice much of his authority for the betterment of the realm while they continued to be oppressive lords in their own right. This emerging attitude can be seen in the will he dictated to his son Henry de Montfort on 1 January 1259. In it he names Eleanor his executor and asks her to address 'the wrongs I have committed in whatever way, wherever and in whatever country'. He wanted to do right by the 'poor people' of his land. His newfound awakening also included rigorous spiritual purification. He began wearing a hair shirt, he prayed by candlelight at midnight, and stopped sleeping with Eleanor. (Their last child, a daughter named after Eleanor, had been born a year earlier.)[19]

The man who reappeared for the first parliament of the year in February 1259 had become an idealist, not a welcome development to the barons who were worried about their own power and privileges coming under scrutiny. When Richard de Clare, the earl of Gloucester, proved recalcitrant about new laws to this effect, Simon denounced him in front of their peers, saying he did not care to 'live and deal with people so fickle and deceitful'. But instead of sticking around to ensure the passage of the laws, Simon left again for France. The issue again was the peace treaty. One point that had gone unaddressed in all the activity of the previous year was the renunciation of claims to Normandy and other lordships of King John by members of the royal family. Henry and Richard of Cornwall, who had landed in England after the conference in Cambrai failed to take place, renounced theirs in February, but Eleanor refused. She wanted satisfaction for her dower claims and also the land that had been promised to her and Simon. Clare led a group of magnates to France to negotiate with Simon, but it ended with the two earls nearly getting into a fistfight. The de Montforts refused to budge. It seemed to Clare and others that the new idealist was really the same self-serving Simon from the beginning of the reform movement.[20]

Henry and the council tried placating them. First, they paid off all money owed to the de Montforts going back to their time in Gascony, £237 in all. Then they were given nine manors to replace their £400 fee. Here Simon had to tread lightly. In 1257, the year before the reform movement began, he and other councillors had taken an oath not to receive any grants from the royal demesne, as some of these manors clearly were. When later called to account, Simon wriggled out of this ethical lapse by saying the arrangement had only been temporary. But the transfer of the manors saw the eviction of one Savoyard retainer. Together with what was now plain obstruction of the peace treaty, Simon was risking his long-standing alliance with the Savoyards, and Eleanor her friendship with the queen. Nothing, however, could have prepared them for Simon and Eleanor's next demand, which was presented to the arbitration panel appointed to adjudicate their case. They wanted her dower for Wales and Ireland adjusted to a value they believed was right. It was worth £1,333 a year, not £400, and they wanted the difference going back every year to the beginning of her agreement with Richard Marshal. That meant £933 annually for 26 years, or £24,258.[21]

It was a fantastic sum of money, equal to all of royal revenue for one year, and under normal circumstances nobody would have been so foolish to demand such an amount. But Simon had been one of the negotiators of the peace treaty and knew that Louis was obliged to pay Henry a sum of money equivalent to maintaining a force of 500 knights for two years, which in the end was set at £33,500. Instead of wasting that money on an army for Sicily, he perhaps figured it might as well be used to satisfy his and Eleanor's claims. Henry was beside himself when informed of this latest twist and came to believe that Simon had deliberately included Eleanor's renunciation in the treaty so that the two of them might blackmail him in this fashion. He believed that, as an official envoy, Simon's actions were nothing short of treachery. Henry countered by offering Louis indemnification for any claims Eleanor might make against him later on. That put ratification back on track and Henry made plans to travel to France in August. Suddenly he received word that the deal was off. What happened is not clear, but we know that Simon was then in Normandy socialising with Archbishop Rigaud, the lead French negotiator on the treaty.[22]

Simon did not return from France until the parliament of October 1259. So diminished had his role in the reform movement become that when a group of knights and freeholders protested against the slow pace of legislation they did not look to him for leadership, rather to Clare and Edward. The laws they wanted enacted clamped down on abuses by magnates and extended the availability of free justice. Because these 'Provisions of Westminster' affected local society, they became more popular than the Provisions of Oxford, which regulated rule at the top. Having been absent for most of the year, Simon could not have contributed much to the final form of these new provisions, although their aims were in keeping with his own beliefs about good government. His main interest in this parliament was Edward and recognising the force he had become in politics.

It had been a harsh year for the heir to the throne. When the move was made against his Lusignan uncles, he stood by them and refused to take the oath to the Provisions. This resulted in their banishment and in Edward finding himself a ward of the state. He was the only member of the royal family besides his aunt Eleanor who opposed the renunciation of claims to Normandy. His reasons were equally mercenary, but more in the hope of someday re-conquering the territories when he became king. Now 20 years old, he longed for his freedom and saw his uncle Simon as a man who got things done. Sometime before parliament wound up its business, he and Edward entered into a private agreement to support each other in the battles ahead.[23]

Simon then left for France again and Eleanor went with him. It was decided that the best way to get her to make her treaty renunciation was to bring all the parties together and find a compromise. Henry and the English court arrived in Paris and more talks ensued. Louis broke the impasse by giving the de Montforts a fief-rent worth £120 a year, presumably for Simon renouncing his own rights in France, and offering to withhold £10,000 of the treaty money he owed to Henry until her dower issue had been settled. Henry agreed and Eleanor renounced her claims on 4 December 1259. Archbishop Rigaud then read the treaty aloud before both kings and their courts in the garden of Louis's palace and Henry did homage to Louis for Gascony and other lands. The king of England was again a peer of France and for the first time in nearly a century there was peace between the two countries.[24]

That kicked off a round of celebrations, but Eleanor left for Normandy and Simon stuck around only to cause trouble. The king and queen of

England used their stay in Paris to see through the marriage arrangements of their daughter Beatrice to John of Brittany, the grandson of Peter of Dreux. Beatrice's dowry was a sensitive issue because it was supposed to comprise the earldom of Richmond, which was then in the custody of Peter of Savoy. Seeing a chance to undermine Henry's authority and Peter's position on the council, Simon told John's father, the duke of Brittany, that the marriage might have to be negotiated anew because the full council was never consulted on the matter. Since the marriage went through anyway, the only thing Simon accomplished by this subversive act was to upset both the king and queen further.[25]

Eleanor of Provence would be even angrier if she learned what else Simon was up to while in Paris. Apparently at his own initiative, he sought out William de Valence and his brothers and became reconciled with them. Simon later claimed that the king had asked him to do it, but it seems more likely it was something he had arranged with Edward, who never stopped championing his Lusignan uncles. For Simon to swallow his pride and ally himself with his former enemies is a measure of how embittered he had become against the king and queen. When he left Paris in late December, he took his leave of Louis but completely ignored Henry.[26]

Parliament becomes the battleground of reform, Simon faces another trial, Henry goes on the offensive, Simon goes into exile

Henry suspected that Simon might be up to no good and ordered Hugh Bigod, his justiciar and regent, to arrest anyone who tried to enter the kingdom with men and arms. The king's own return was delayed by the wedding of his daughter and sudden death of Louis's 15-year-old heir. He sent Clare home to explain these matters, with instructions to Bigod that parliament was not to meet until he returned. This was Simon's chance. It was not up to Henry to decide when parliament should meet, he declared, rather the Provisions of Oxford. They were the constitution of the land and they stipulated Candlemas (2 February) as one of the three regular meetings. At first, Simon and his supporters allowed for a delay of a couple of weeks, but then appeared in London at the end of February with mounted troops. He and Edward were going to force parliament to meet with or without the king. By this point Clare was a determined enemy of both men and arrived with his own troops. It took the efforts of Richard of Cornwall and the magistrates of London to keep war from breaking out between the two sides. Meanwhile, Henry had learned that his Lusignan half-brothers were planning to land with men and arms to come to Simon's assistance. With part of the treaty money Louis had given him, he hired a contingent of 300 foreign knights and made ready to sail in April.[27]

Simon told Bigod that if Henry landed with troops, he would greet them in such a way that 'none would have any great desire to follow them'. But he was not in the welcoming party that met the king in Dover. Henry and his troops rode unopposed to London where, after a tense standoff for two weeks, he readmitted Edward to favour and the threat of civil war was over. Henry was furious at Simon, however, and ordered him to stand trial for sedition. A panel of six bishops was convened to hear his answers to the charges prepared by royal proctors. Simon's cool demeanour throughout was a mark of his natural self-confidence but also the presence in England at that time of his friend Archbishop Rigaud, who had been sent by Louis to make sure he received a fair trial. The proceedings came to a halt when the Welsh struck again in July. As a 'mighty and prudent warrior of England', says the *Flores* chronicler, Simon was appointed commander of the army mustering for a counterattack, but a truce was arranged before any operations took place.[28]

Parliament of October 1260 was supposed to be a grand affair for Henry. He was going to knight his son-in-law John of Brittany and other young men of noble stock, and his other son-in-law Alexander III was visiting from Scotland. With Richard of Cornwall in attendance, he at last secured his meeting of three kings. As for the man who in all likelihood was responsible for the aborted meeting two years before that, Henry would put him on trial in front of parliament. Only Simon was way ahead of him. Knowing Clare was unhappy with reforms aimed at the barons themselves, Simon agreed to water down the programme so that it was less invasive for earls like them, and in return Clare helped him get his trial scrapped. Edward, whose reconciliation with his parents had been superficial, lent his support in return for a lucrative wardship. Together the three of them convinced parliament to appoint ministers from among Simon's friends. Finally, as a deliberate snub to Henry, Simon handed over his duties as the steward to his nephew Henry of Almain (Richard of Cornwall's son) so he would not be seen attending to the king during the feast.[29]

Simon did not see his concession to Clare as a betrayal of the reform movement. Important was to keep tight control of the king and his ministers. Hugh Bigod had struck Simon as not tough enough for the job of justiciar, so he arranged to have him replaced by Hugh Despenser, one of his strongest adherents. Despenser validated their reform credentials by undertaking an eyre that cited Richard of Cornwall and Peter of Savoy among others as oppressive landlords, although disinterested observers would have pointed out that he was targeting the magnates closest to the king. But having regained the initiative, Simon suddenly took off for the Continent. Edward had gone there to tourney with the new knights, including his cousins Henry and Simon VII de Montfort, both of whom he had knighted. Simon needed his help with Bigorre. Esquivat had allied with Gaston and together the two of them moved to take back full control of the county. Edward appealed to his Lusignan uncles, who went to Bigorre from Poitou to prevent the whole county from slipping out of Simon's hands.[30]

It was an interesting development, because Eleanor accompanied Simon to Paris for the purpose of suing her Lusignan siblings. Their mother Isabella of Angoulême had died in 1246 without leaving any of her estate to her children with King John. One of the brothers, Aymer de Valence, was not included in her suit because, as the bishop-elect of Winchester, he was a churchman. He was also the most objectionable of the Lusignans, so when he died suddenly in Paris in December 1260, the path towards reconciliation between them and the queen was possible. It was a step Eleanor of Provence had to take in order to win Edward away from Simon, who, as she now saw it, was the greater evil.[31]

This move was part of a broader plan by Henry to take back all power into his hands. He had had enough of the Provisions of Oxford. The barons had not kept their promise to help him find funding for Sicily or reduce his indebtedness. In March 1261, he harangued them at a parliament specially convened to hear these and other grievances. He complained that the council made decisions of state in his absence or else ignored his input. As the lord king, his opinions should carry the most weight in their discussions, he argued. The barons agreed that they should defer to him, but only when, and here we can hear Simon's voice speaking, 'he talks sense'. Henry also lambasted them for allowing Edward to run rampant and associate with the Lusignans, the very concerns that gave the reform movement its initial impetus.

Even now Edward was on his way home with William de Valence. It was part of the new alliance between the Lusignans and the queen. Edward himself was ready to give up his rebellion. He had squandered so much money abroad that he needed his parents to bail him out, but their price was his absolute obedience and an end to his infatuation with Simon. At the beginning of May, Henry broke off talks with the barons and headed to Dover. There he secured the castle for the arrival of both mercenaries and an envoy he had dispatched to Rome back in January. The envoy was bringing back a bull from Pope Alexander absolving Henry and everyone else in the kingdom of their oaths to the Provisions of Oxford. The experiment in constitutional government was over.[32]

Henry made the announcement at Winchester on 12 June 1261. The barons began mobilising for action, but were unable to confront him because he had since moved to the Tower of London. As in the original summer of reform three years earlier, Simon again took the lead in everything. He directed the struggle to the countryside, where the king's new appointments for sheriffs were opposed by 'anti-sheriffs' installed by the barons. Learning that the pope had died even before his absolution of Henry was published, Simon arranged to have baronial agents in Rome get the papal chancery to confirm Henry's oath to the Provisions. It would take several months for the new pope, Urban IV, to figure out what was going on and confirm Henry's absolution instead. (Urban was no friend of Philip de Montfort. He was the former Patriarch of Jerusalem who, upon arriving in the crusader states in 1260 to take up his duties, supported Acre and the Venetians against Tyre and the Genoese. He happened to be in Rome on business when Alexander died and, when the cardinals were unable to agree on a successor, they chose him as a compromise.)[33]

More dangerous to Henry were Simon's connections on the Continent, where he went to raise money and troops. In early September, the king wrote to Louis not to receive or succour him. Simon was back soon enough, for he conceived his boldest act of defiance yet. He sent orders to the anti-sheriffs to send knights representing their counties to an anti-parliament he was going to convene on 21 September in St Albans with Clare and Cantilupe. Henry, however, found out what was afoot and ordered his sheriffs to send the same knights to a special, legitimate parliament he was convening on that same day in Windsor. He also summoned 150 barons he felt he could trust to come to the regular October parliament in London. They were told to bring their military service with them.

War was averted when Clare and other barons were won over, probably as the result of an intensive lobbying campaign. During this time, fourteen kilograms of sealing wax were being consumed every week by the chancery for all the writs going out, compared to a quarter of that figure two and a half years earlier during the height of reform legislation. The agreement reached on 21 November 1261 in Kingston-on-Thames provided for a committee of three royalists and three barons to discuss the major points of dispute, particularly the appointment of sheriffs, and if compromise failed, then Richard of Cornwall would decide, which all but guaranteed victory to Henry. Simon saw it as a sell-out and refused to go along. According to the Dunstable annals, he declared he would rather die landless than abjure from the truth and perjure himself. He packed up his family and went to live in Normandy, where Louis made one of his castles available to them.[34]

For Henry, it was galling to see Louis so supportive of a seditious subject, but he had to admit he would do anything to get Simon on his side. He was, quite simply, a host in himself, a leader very much like his father the crusader. Although Henry had re-established his personal rule, his grip on the realm was tenuous. That was thanks to Simon and the masterful propaganda campaign he ran in the counties against the king. Henry could argue that he had had the Provisions of Oxford annulled because disaffected barons like Simon had used them to rob him of dignity. On the other hand, the Provisions of Westminster, which provided the greatest relief to the people as a whole, were still very much in effect. Simon, however, had removed the distinction between the two. The king, he said, had annulled the Provisions period. He was trying to roll back reforms in their entirety. It was the barons who got rid of the oppressive sheriffs in the first place. Now the king was free to bring them back because the barons had buckled under pressure from him. All but one, the earl of Leicester.

Simon was able to make this point so effectively across the kingdom because he had the support of the English Church. Everywhere friars and pastors were preaching in the villages and fields, educating the peasants about a new grassroots concept. They were told that, by pulling together as a community, they had a real voice in their everyday lives. They could finally enjoy some of the power that had always been skewed against them by their lords and officials. This 'community of the realm' as it was called was in fact the first 'commons' in the modern sense. It gave rise to the first political party in England, with Simon as the unstated head of it. John Mansel, the king and queen's top adviser, noticed all this activity going on in Sussex and lamented that their own side lacked similar outreach. In the spring of 1262, Henry moved to quash it by ordering the sheriffs to arrest anyone undertaking preaching against him.[35]

The situation might have been different had Robert Grosseteste been alive. He came from the old school of bishops who believed in strict separation between worldly and temporal affairs. Walter Cantilupe, on the other hand, had no such qualms. He came from a family of royal servants and was one himself until he turned religious. His elitist background was behind his election as bishop of Worcester in 1236. He carried on Grosseteste's opposition to papal preferment for foreign clergy in England, but not necessarily for the same reason Grosseteste had argued, namely that the inability of foreign priests to speak English disqualified them from administering to the needs of the parish. Cantilupe's main concern was financial. He was a firm believer in holding multiple benefices, which is to say clerics like him appearing on more than one payroll. He had spent his whole career resisting attempts by the Church to crack down on pluralism and so spread the wealth among all members of the spiritual community.

Apart from the friendship between their families, Cantilupe saw in Simon the baronial leader able to get him and other senior English churchmen what they wanted most, independence from the king and pope. The new bishops who came along as the reform movement got underway, in Lincoln, London and Winchester, either joined the cause or were recruited for it. Some of it was due to Simon's personality and that certain aura that drew people into his orbit. There were of course his strong beliefs and determination, but doubtless other factors invisible to us today, like his appearance, charisma and silver-tongue oratory. It had been the same with his father. The hold of Simon V over the bishops of southern France had been remarkable and was ultimately key to the success of his crusade. Now here it was a half century later and another group of bishops was lining up behind his son, also with a mixed bag of motives.[36]

Failed arbitration, war breaks out, the Montfortians take over, their regime collapses

While abroad in France, Simon had appealed to the French royal pair to put an end to his quarrel with Henry through mediation. Queen Margaret offered to arbitrate, and in July 1262 Henry and Queen Eleanor arrived in Paris. The problem as Henry saw it was that Simon was an ingrate with a chip on his shoulder. The king had been generous in giving him the earldom of Leicester and his sister in marriage, but he received only rancour and insults from him in return. Simon's replies seemingly confirmed this was the case. Leicester was his by right, he insisted. If anything, Henry should be apologetic for the poor state he found it in. As for his sister, Simon implied that he was doing Henry a favour. It pleased the king, he said, to give him Eleanor in marriage. (Writing at the time of the secret wedding, Matthew Paris says that Simon was 'most grateful' to receive such a distinguished bride.) Simon next parried Henry's charges that he nearly lost Gascony through his repressive government by saying he did down there what he had to do. It was the same with his opposition to Henry's own repressive government.[37]

Margaret must have been stunned by the acrimony between the two men, both of whom were friends. Before she had to render what could only have been a difficult decision, an epidemic swept through the English court. By the time Henry recovered, he learned that Simon was on his way to England, angry and intent on stirring up trouble. The king warned the justiciar, Philip Basset, to be on the lookout for him. Simon suddenly appeared at the opening of parliament on 13 October to confer with his supporters and he disappeared just as quickly. The fact that parliament was sitting in the absence of the king, a sign that Henry had adopted some aspects of the Provisions of Oxford, did not seem to impress him.

Prior to leaving France in December, Henry implored Louis to talk to Simon, find some way to pacify him. Louis tried, but reported that Simon found reconciliation impossible. He believed that Henry meant him well, but there were others at court who were out to get him and his wife. In February 1263, envoys were dispatched to Paris with a last-ditch deal for Eleanor's dower. Simon demanded more than what they put on the table and the envoys returned home exasperated. Henry then reached out to Simon by reissuing the Provisions of Westminster and inviting him and other baronial cohorts to discuss further reforms, but there was no response from him.[38] The consensus among the king and his advisers must have been unanimous. There was simply no doing business with the man.

In all likelihood, Simon was already set on returning to England to raise rebellion against Henry. The circumstances were certainly encouraging. Wales was again in revolt, but many of the lords of the borderlands, called Marchers, had done nothing to reverse their advance. These men had once been friends and retainers of Edward, drawn together by the proximity of their lordships around Wales and their love for the tournament. But when Edward submitted to his parents in 1261, he made a clean break with his past. The Marchers saw this as the queen's work. She had singled them out as a bad influence on her son's behaviour, much like the Lusignans had been. Edward only confirmed he was through with them when he arrived in the spring of 1263 to take control of the situation in Wales. Instead of asking his former retainers for help, he had a troop of foreign knights with him. They were his friends now. Incensed, the Marchers turned to Simon to come home and together they would teach the royal family a lesson.[39]

Henry himself did not go to Wales because he had been ill since returning to England. It was a brutally cold winter that year and making matters worse, part of Westminster Palace burned down while he was convalescing there. In March 1263, the annalist of Tewkesbury Abbey wrote up his obituary. The monk assumed he had died because the sheriffs were ordered to take oaths of fealty to Edward from local officials. But just as the annals of Tewkesbury was the only historical record to describe the beginnings of the reform movement as a palace revolution, so it was the only one to report Henry's premature demise. The patrons of the abbey were the Clare family. In July 1262, Richard de Clare, one of the confederates against the Lusignans, did in fact die, after a protracted illness, and his 19-year-old son Gilbert was outraged when Henry told him to be patient about being named the next earl of Gloucester. Gilbert responded by refusing to do homage to Edward. Although not part of the Marcher gang, he joined them at a special meeting convened with other malcontents. The venue was Oxford, chosen for its symbolic value to the reform movement.[40]

In addition to Simon, who had landed on 25 April 1263, Richard of Cornwall was also at the meeting. The presence of Henry's brother in what was a plot to overthrow him has never been adequately explained. He may have aspired to the throne if the deposition of Henry and his sons was taken under consideration. His own pretensions to be the king of Germany had been wholly underwhelming. He had spent vast sums of money and yet six years later his election was still being contested by the only other candidate, Henry's ally Alfonso of Castile. But if Richard did become king of England, his son Henry of Almain would be next in line, and he too was at this meeting.[41]

Simon was nevertheless the undisputed leader of this disgruntled lot at Oxford. Apart from his personal qualities, he had the name, prestige and connections to pull off what was a risky endeavour for them all. In planning and waging war against the king, they were violating their oaths of fealty to him. Under feudal law and custom, they were traitors and so faced disinheritance. They certainly did not see their actions in terms of disloyalty. They had taken an oath to the king, but also one to protect and preserve the Provisions of Oxford. It had a higher purpose because it was an oath to God, not just to the Vicar of God, as Henry liked to call himself. Simon informed the men who gathered around him that what they were about to do was nothing less than a crusade. They were an 'army of God' ordained to bring justice and good government to everybody. It was going to be violent, but then the Provisions had always been underpinned by a clause that held anyone who opposed them as a mortal enemy.[42]

In late May 1263, everything was ready. A letter was sent to the king demanding that he abide by the Provisions of Oxford. His refusal, when it came, was the signal to launch their offensive. They attacked the properties of royalists and Savoyards, anyone suspected of having helped the king overthrow the Provisions. The uprising drew widespread support from the peasants, middling classes and clergy thanks not only to the recent cultivation of political power in local communities, but national identity as well. Where the original reform movement had targeted only one set of foreigners, the Lusignans, this movement went after all of them. The Savoyards, Flemish merchants, French moneylenders and Italian priests were attacked, usually after they failed a litmus test of Anglo–Saxon comprehension. The Jews spoke English, but were also assaulted and robbed, doubtless in many cases by the people who owed them money.

The speed of the offensive took the royal family by surprise. Lacking the time and money to put together an effective response, they retreated to the Tower of London, while key advisors and adherents, like the archbishop of Canterbury, fled abroad. Edward left the Tower with his foreign knights, first to plunder the vaults of the New Temple for the money he needed to pay his men, then to try and cut Simon off as he approached London. Simon, however, had turned his forces southeast in order to secure the Channel ports to prevent any help getting to Henry from the Continent. Edward's heist put London in an uproar, leaving royalists and foreigners vulnerable to attack. On 13 July, his mother Eleanor of Provence attempted to flee the violence by taking a boat upriver to Windsor, where Edward had stationed himself, but a crowd on London Bridge unleashed a volley of debris and filth at her with such vehemence that Mayor Thomas Fitz-Thomas and his militia, who supported Simon, had to intervene before the boat sank and took the queen to the bottom of the river.[43]

On 15 July, the Montfortians marched into London and the next day Henry accepted an agreement that reinstalled conciliar rule, only this time with Simon, and not the king, at the head of it. To enhance his authority, he called himself the steward of England. This attempt to exalt his status with the ceremonial title he held as the earl of Leicester struck some observers as presumptuous and boastful. Simon further stumbled with the grants that were immediately made to family and friends. All the lands of John Mansel, who had fled abroad, were committed to his second son Simon VII. His third son Amaury VIII, who was raised to become a churchman, was given a prebend at St Paul's that should have gone to an Italian chaplain. Another purloined prebend went to Walter Cantilupe's nephew Thomas. Richard of Cornwall received a prized wardship, but also a stern letter of rebuke from the pope when he learned of his collaboration with the rebels.[44]

On 9 September, Simon convened parliament to discuss this new state of affairs. The major issue was whether to let the king go abroad. Louis was gathering his nobles in Boulogne on the north Channel coast to discuss a new crusade, and Henry, as the duke of Aquitaine, received a summons (the Dunstable annalist says the king and queen had secretly arranged it with him). Not wanting to alienate Louis, the council agreed that the royal family could cross over, but Simon and a baronial delegation would go over as well to justify the turn of events in England. They prepared themselves for a hostile reception from the exiles, and Queen Margaret in particular, who was aghast at the ill treatment of her sister. There were calls for Louis to put the delegation on trial for treason, but Simon scoffed at the notion of any authority outside England having jurisdiction over the matter. Louis refused to condemn their usurpation of power in any event. As he understood it, the Provisions were all about ensuring that England was ruled by native Englishmen, not foreigners, and he saw nothing wrong with that in principle.[45]

The Montfortians came home from France cheering, but as Henry had probably hoped, the sideshow in Boulogne broke up their momentum. When parliament of October 1263 opened, they found themselves on the defensive from aggrieved victims of the violence and spoliations, and from Henry insisting that only he had the right to name his ministers. In a coordinated plan, Edward stole away from the assembly and seized Windsor. Henry arrived the next day and there issued a proclamation to the barons who had held aloof until now. They were either for or against him. Within a month his ranks were swelling with supporters while Simon's were plagued by defections. The Marchers and Richard of Cornwall had been lured away by promises of patronage and other favours. Richard's son Henry of Almain struggled with his decision to desert and felt obliged to inform Simon of it in person. Rather than appreciate the gesture and send the young man, who was his nephew, on his way with a chivalric handshake, Simon called him a liability and jeered at his promise to never take up arms against him. He was angry at what he saw was an innate lack of trust all around him. 'Nowhere have I found such infidelity and deceit as I have met in England', he thundered indignantly.[46]

By November, the Montfortians were in full retreat. Simon stayed away from a special parliament the king summoned to Reading for fear of being arrested. When Henry next moved to retake Dover, Simon gathered up his forces in London to prevent him from bringing in troops that the queen, who had stayed behind at Boulogne, was recruiting on the Continent. Henry was at Croyden, fifteen kilometres to the south, when he was informed by supporters that the gates of London Bridge had been secretly barred against Simon and his men, who were encamped south of the river. He sent word to Edward and his forces at Merton and together they closed in. When called upon to surrender, Simon declared they would rather die first. At the last moment, the people of London came to their rescue by breaking open the gates and allowing them to escape inside the city.

To prevent an all-out civil war from erupting, Richard of Cornwall arranged for both sides to submit to arbitration by Louis at Amiens after Christmas. Where the proceedings at Boulogne had been unofficial, here the king of France was given full authority to adjudicate their dispute.[47] The Montfortians recognised the risk involved in it. Louis was under sustained pressure from the sister queens to defend the concept of absolute monarchy and he would be loath to formally approve the Provisions of Oxford when two popes had already quashed them. But just as Boulogne had broken up their party's momentum, so Amiens would stop the king's juggernaut long enough for them to regroup. The problem was they had to swear on the Bible that they would accept whatever verdict Louis rendered. If he ruled against them and they ignored it, they would be perjurers, a word Simon liked to use to describe those who had fallen away from their oaths to uphold the Provisions.

To get around this dilemma, Simon and his team devised an elaborate line of defence. They would inextricably link the Provisions of Oxford to Magna Carta. The king had repeatedly violated the charter of liberties, they would assert, because it lacked executive enforcement. The Provisions remedied that abuse. Any judgement that nullified the Provisions meant leaving Magna Carta again exposed to the machinations of the Crown. By arguing in this manner, they would tie Louis's hands before their case had even rested. Simon, moreover, would make the presentation. His renown and integrity and that of his family carried such weight in France that nobody could accuse him of trying to subvert the arbitration, at least not any more than what Louis himself might have in mind.

In the end, however, it seemed a higher judge got involved first. On his way to catch the boat over, Simon's horse tumbled and fell on top of him, breaking his leg. It was the only injury he is known to have sustained in his lifetime and was serious enough to keep him immobilised for the next three months. He was forced to go back to Kenilworth and await Louis's decision there.[48]

Chapter 11

Tried and Tested in the World
1264–1300

Henry and his party breathed a sigh of relief when they reached France just after New Year's. They had encountered a terrifying winter storm in the Channel that left Edward, for one, trembling and praying for deliverance. Making the royalist case at Amiens was Walter Merton, the chancellor and later founder of Merton College in Oxford. He kept it simple. The barons had usurped the king's power and authority through 'constitutions' that used violence to enforce their own rule. The Montfortians argued that these constitutions had to be enacted, with the king's blessing no less, because his kingdom had become overrun with aliens and corrupt officials. Their very able advocate was Thomas Cantilupe, Bishop Walter's nephew and a former chancellor of Oxford. Thomas contended that everything was the fault of an untrustworthy king who had failed to observe Magna Carta as he had sworn to do on many occasions. The Provisions were the safeguards against that ever happening again.[1]

Louis's mandate gave him until summer to decide, but he wasted no time about it. Reform fatigue was setting in across Europe and he and the pope wanted done with it. They were eager for another crusade and all this infighting among Christians was only hindering it. On 23 January 1264, Louis issued his ruling. 'We quash and invalidate all these provisions, ordinances, and obligations, or whatever else they may be called, and whatever has arisen from them or has been occasioned by them.' He saw through the trap the Montfortians tried to spring and so noted that his decision had nothing to do with Magna Carta or other statutes and customs in place before the Provisions. He called on both parties to drop their rancour towards each other and for Henry to make the first move by offering a full pardon to his opponents, which he did the next day. It made no difference. The country was at war when he returned three weeks later.[2]

The monastic chroniclers, almost all wholly committed to the Montfortian cause, were outraged by Louis's judgement. At the priory in Dunstable, the king of France was said to have no regard for his own honour. The annalist at Tewkesbury says that he had weakly given in to the feminine wiles of the queen of England, who was still based in Paris.[3] There was no call to arms because none was needed. As soon as Simon was informed of the 'Mise of Amiens', as Louis's ruling is known today, he made no statement as he was wont to do on other occasions. He sent his two oldest sons, 25-year-old Henry and 23-year-old Simon VII at the head of a body of troops to the Welsh March to attack Roger Mortimer, a senior Marcher who had raided three of Simon's manors in the area back in December. Simon had acquired these manors from the royal demesne in 1259 as part of the attempt to satisfy him and his wife for the Treaty of Paris. Henry had always considered it extortion and before leaving for France he told Mortimer, who had sat on the fence for much of the reform period, that they were his if he could take them.[4]

As in the previous summer, the outbreak of war occurred in the Severn Valley. Mortimer fled at the approach of the Montfortians, who laid waste to his lands before moving on to Gloucester. There they were joined by the youthful Robert de Ferrers, the earl of Derby, whose men had just sacked Worcester and the Jewish community there. Ferrers's grievances against the Crown went back to his wardship under Edward. He now had the chance to imprison him, for Edward and Henry of Almain were just then holed up in the castle at Gloucester. They appealed to their cousin Henry de Montfort for a truce. Young Henry was advised to reject it by Ferrers, but Walter Cantilupe convinced him otherwise. Edward broke the terms of the truce and escaped to his father at Oxford, where King Henry had summoned the feudal host to deal with this new rebellion. Ferrers left in disgust and Simon raged at his son for being so naive. Young Henry set out to make up for it by capturing the earl of Warwick and his wife at their castle, while young Simon went to Northampton to bolster its defences.[5]

Louis hoped peace might yet be achieved and sent a trusted hand John de Valenciennes to England. John had spent many years as the lord of Haifa in the crusader states and was well known to Philip de Montfort. Valenciennes had come west with the archbishop of Tyre to seek funds for the Holy Land, and in 1263 Louis employed him as his mediator between Simon and Henry. His mission now was to tell the two antagonists that their war was with the Saracens, not each other. Still laid up at Kenilworth, Simon sent his troop of bishops to meet the king and Valenciennes at Brackley near Oxford. On his behalf, they offered to accept Louis's award at Amiens in its entirety if the king agreed to appoint only Englishmen as his ministers. To Henry, it was Simon at his cynical worst. He was not making a serious offer, just playing to his base while at the same time pretending to Louis, through his envoy, that he wanted peace. Henry ordered the bishops out of his sight and not to return unless he summoned them.[6]

By the end of March, Simon's leg had healed enough for him to move around in a special carriage. He arrived in London, where his top lieutenants Hugh Despenser and Mayor Fitz-Thomas had already organised demonstrations against crown officials. They also turned their backs as the properties of high-profile royalists were ransacked. The first hit was Richard of Cornwall's mansion at Isleworth. Having helped bring the Montfortians to power a year ago, the king of Germany was now considered a traitor, although Simon might have seen it coming all along. Richard was famous for deserting rebellious causes, going back as far as the Marshal uprising three decades earlier and, a few years after that, to the uproar over Simon's secret wedding to his sister.[7]

On 3 April 1264, Henry unfurled his dragon standard and marched his army north to assault the Montfortian stronghold at Northampton. As one of the commanders of the garrison, Simon VII repelled two attempts by royalists to get through a breached wall, then fought in their midst until his horse was brought down. It was said that only the appearance of Edward on the scene saved him from being killed by his captors. His father Simon VI had set out from London with a relief force, but got only as far as St Albans when he was informed of Northampton's fall. According to William Rishanger, he took the setback stoically. In an echo of his great-great-grandfather Amaury III nearly a century and a half earlier, he declared that 'superiority sometimes goes to these, sometimes to those' (see p. 4).[8] But his return to London marked a complete reversal of last summer's offensive. Now he was the one stuck in the capital while the king marched about triumphantly, perhaps taking special pleasure in pillaging Leicester.

The Montfortians also had no money, but where Edward had robbed the Templars the previous summer, they went after the Jews. How to go about it seems to have divided the leadership. Rumours that the Jews were planning to betray the city led the hardliners to plan an all-out assault on their community, which was situated near Guildhall. Despenser and Mayor Fitz-Thomas sent word to them of the horror about to be unleashed and some managed to reach the Tower for safety. They did not include Kok, the son of Abraham and the most preeminent Jew in the city. In the savagery that followed, he was killed by Despenser's own brother-in-law John Fitz-John. Other Jews caught up in the tumult were able to ransom their lives or forced to endure baptism, but by morning more than 500 people of all ages had been stripped, despoiled and slaughtered. Chronicler and London resident Thomas Wykes says Fitz-John walked away with the most plunder, but afterwards 'he gave, though unwillingly, no small amount to the earl of Leicester, so that neither of them should be free from the guilt of robbery and murder'.[9]

At this point the Montfortians obtained an unexpected ally in Gilbert de Clare. He was still angry at the king for making him wait for his earldom, but he held off joining the rebellion in the hope of dislodging Simon as the leader of the party. A circular connected to his family was put out earlier in the year questioning Simon's fitness for command because he was old, already 56, and he had shown he was ready to enrich his family once in power. Gilbert moved up from his castle at Tonbridge to assault the royalist garrison at Rochester in coordination with Simon leading troops there from London. They breached the riverside defences and sacked the town, but were unable to take the massive keep. The approach of Henry's army from the north led them to give up the siege on 25 April and fall back to London.[10]

There was little Simon could do as the king went about securing the southeast coast. Henry's plan was to blockade Dover and use the fleets of the Channel ports against London. Simon realised he had no choice but to leave the city and risk everything on one decisive battle. He led his men south on 6 May and took up position around his own manor of Fletching. Henry learned of their advance three days later and moved his forces to Lewes, about thirteen kilometres away. On 12 May, Henry received two delegations. The first one, led by Stephen Berksted, the bishop of Chichester, said that Simon was willing to submit the Provisions of Oxford to arbitration by a panel of bishops and other churchmen. Given that most of the clergy stood completely behind the Montfortians, Henry had to wonder if it was just more of Simon taunting him. The second delegation, led by Walter Cantilupe, was also rejected. They offered £30,000 in compensation, clearly meant for consumption by Richard of Cornwall, whose greed was well known. The king of Germany, however, reminded his brother that the Provisions in any form meant a depression of royal authority and power.[11]

The next day Simon and Gilbert sent a letter to 'his excellent majesty lord Henry, by the grace of God, illustrious king of England, lord of Ireland, and duke of Aquitaine'. Henry was impressed with neither their overwrought salutation nor their assurance that their fight was with his 'evil advisers', not with him. By return letter he informed 'Simon de Montfort and Gilbert de Clare and their accomplices' that all the late disturbances of the realm were their fault and their protestations of loyalty were fooling no one. 'We do not care for your safety or your affection, but defy you as our enemies.' That was the answer the Montfortians had been expecting. Since facing the king in battle was now inevitable, they went through the formality of renouncing their homage and fealty to him.

As night fell, they ascended the hills running west of the town. Simon knighted Gilbert and several other young nobles and addressed the troops. They were fighting for England, God, the Virgin Mary and their oath to the Provisions, he told them. The men then threw themselves on the ground and prayed while the bishops of Worcester and Chichester absolved them. They arose, fashioned white crosses on their outer garments, and waited for the dawn of 14 May 1264. It was the forty-fifth anniversary of the death of William Marshal, who had knighted Henry and served as his first regent. He had famously mourned on his deathbed that no people were more divided against themselves than the English.[12]

The approaching Montfortian army was spotted by foragers. Henry and Richard of Cornwall emerged from the priory where they were staying, Edward from the castle at Lewes. They moved their men into three divisions with Henry on the left, Richard in the middle, and Edward on the right. They had about 500 knights, 1,500 cavalry and 7,000 foot soldiers. That was twice the number of men on the high ground in front of them. Simon would have felt that it made no difference at all. Fifty years before on 12 September 1213, his father went up against similar odds at Muret. The disparity in numbers was greater during that earlier battle, but Simon the crusader put all his faith in the Lord above and won a smashing victory. His son too believed that divine will would ultimately decide this contest, but he kept a fourth division in reserve to exploit any weakness he noticed in Henry's lines.

The battle began with Edward leading the cream of the royalist fighting force against the Montfortian left. They were so successful in scattering the light cavalry and foot soldiers that had Edward wheeled to the left and hit Simon squarely in the flank, it might have been over soon after that. Instead he rode off the field in pursuit of the London irregulars, who he blamed for the assault on his mother at the bridge, and he took with him William de Valence and the Marchers. Seeing Edward's flight, Simon threw his fourth division against Henry and Richard's divisions, which were struggling to fight uphill. It was enough to cause their ranks to collapse. Henry was in the thick of the hand-to-hand combat and lost two horses under him. For Simon's father, the death of King Peter in battle had been instrumental in his victory at Muret. At Lewes, Henry's death would be disastrous. Simon's authority to rule rested solely on the king's observance of the Provisions of Oxford. If Henry died, so did the Provisions. As it was, the king and his household guard were able to fight their way back to the priory. By the time Edward returned to the battlefield, it was over. His attempt at counterattacking with the men he still had available failed and he ended up trapped in the priory with his father.[13]

Richard of Cornwall was made a prisoner after he was found hiding in a windmill. Simon tried to get Henry to surrender by threatening to execute his brother, but that came to nothing. At last he was forced to offer him a surprising concession. He agreed that the Provisions could be modified through arbitration, something he swore he would never do because it went against his oath. He probably had no intention of going through with it in any case, just meant it as a face-saving gesture to get Henry to come out. The scheme of arbitration he drew up was not only complex, but it required Louis's participation, which would be like the king of France admitting his judgement at Amiens had been in error. Henry must have realised the arbitration was never going to happen and so made sure to get another, more important concession, the release of prisoners on both sides. Although his son and other members of the royal family were not included, freeing the Marchers would pose a serious risk to Simon's regime.[14]

The terms for the treaty, known as the Mise of Lewes, were formalised the next day. Henry and Edward walked out of the priory and into captivity. The two kings were taken to London, Henry to St Paul's, Richard to the Tower, while their sons Edward and Henry of Almain were confined at Richard's castle of Wallingford. Richard was soon to join them there, but Henry remained safely ensconced behind the walls of London.[15] The lesson Simon had learned from his first regime was to never let the king out of his sight. As long as he had Henry, he had his Great Seal, and that was all he needed to rule legally.

Unlike 1258 and 1263, the king was now truly a figurehead and England a constitutional monarchy. A nine-man council consisting only of Montfortians did the day-to-day governing while policy and major decisions were made by a triumvirate of Simon, Gilbert, and Stephen Berksted. These arrangements were codified in a special ordinance passed by parliament at St Paul's in June 1264. Henry was told not to make trouble about it or else face deposition and the election of a new king. It was no idle threat. Both he and Simon were probably aware that a renegade group of barons had elected Simon's father king back in 1212.[16] Had that somehow panned out, the Plantagenet dynasty would have been extinguished, replaced by the de Montforts. King John and his sons would have been killed off, Amaury VII would have been in line to succeed as king of England, while Simon VI, as a younger son, would have been forced into a career in the Church.

Now, in the real world fifty-two years later, Simon was supreme in England, with more power and control over it than his father or brother ever had over Toulouse. He enjoyed far more popular support than they had had and his bishops were more beholden to him. None of them ever turned against him the way Arnaud-Amalric did against Simon the crusader. What he lacked compared to his father or brother was recognition from above. Both had been legitimate princes in the eyes of the pope and king of France, who willingly backed them with men and money even as fortune turned against them. Simon VI, on the other hand, was a usurper who offended their sense of dignity. They found his pretension to govern in the king's name, while holding his son hostage for his compliance, simply outrageous. The republicanism of the Montfortians, if it could be called that, was anathema to everything they believed in. Echoing the ghost of Achilles, Louis declared that he would rather toil in the fields than rule the kind of kingdom that England had become under this new order.[17]

Of course, none was more offended than Queen Eleanor. She learned about the disaster at Lewes from William de Valence and other barons who had fled the field. With Louis's help, she began putting an invasion force together in Flanders. Simon warned her, through a letter sent to Louis in Henry's name, that she was putting her son's life at risk. She already had a plan for that. The queen had received information that Edward was being held at Wallingford, where her sister-in-law Eleanor de Montfort was in charge. She encouraged the royalist garrison at Bristol to try and spring him. Their surprise dawn assault ultimately failed and saw the captives moved to the more secure compound of Kenilworth, but she was not deterred and continued amassing men and equipment on the coast.[18] Simon responded on 6 July with a nationwide summons to defend England from alien invaders:

> Let no one plead that the harvest is at hand or that some private duty calls him. It is better to suffer a little loss and be safe than to be delivered to a cruel death, with the loss of all your lands and goods, at the impious hands of men thirsting for your blood, who will spare neither sex nor age.

In addition to the feudal host, he wanted every village to provide from four to eight men depending on the size of the community. The peasants that gathered on the coast between Canterbury and Dover arrived in such a multitude that *Flores* says 'you would not have believed so many men ready for war existed in England'.[19] Consciously or not, the political awareness and turbulence of these years had been transformed into a new awakening in national identity. The irony of course is that neither Simon de Montfort nor Eleanor of Provence, the two antagonists about to go to war for the English soul, was actually from England.

Impressive as the call to arms was, those who saw the invasion force believed it would prevail. The queen, however, stayed the launch of her fleet while negotiations went back and forth between Simon's regime and Cardinal Guy Foulquois, a papal legate dispatched by Pope Urban to restore Henry to full authority. Simon had barred Foulquois from entering the realm, which would have been enough for a legate like Arnaud-Amalric to order the invasion, but Foulquois lacked the same zeal and militancy. From his base in Boulogne, he insisted on finding a peaceful solution despite all the signs that Simon and the bishops had no intention of relinquishing power. By the time his patience ran out, the queen's funds were exhausted and her army disappeared. Foulquois disappeared too, called back to Rome after Urban died on 2 October. Before leaving, he excommunicated the Montfortians, but was unable to get the sentence published in England. It was not the last they heard of him, however. In February 1265, he was elected the new pope, Clement IV, and his determination to punish Simon and his cohort of bishops for their defiance had not abated in the least.[20]

Simon summons his Great Parliament, Edward escapes, the battle of Evesham, Simon is killed and mutilated, his legend lives on

Although England had been saved from invasion and interdict, internal problems continued to mount. The economy was a wreck. The wool trade, which accounted for much of the prosperity of Henry's reign, was disrupted by the disorders of the past year. Piracy flourished in the Channel. The regime was said to support it because it received a third of the booty. To stop all the 'plunderings, burnings and other enormities' besetting the counties, keepers of the peace were appointed to serve alongside the sheriffs, but some of these keepers engaged in lawless activity themselves and the sheriffs were forced to go after them instead. Since the Jewish communities were vulnerable in these circumstances, a stream of orders went out to protect them in London, Lincoln and other cities. Simon warned despoilers of Church property that if any of them were caught, he would cut their heads off. According to Rishanger, who was a teenager at the time, it had no impact.[21]

The Marchers also held up the recovery. They staged two uprisings, each one requiring Simon to seek help from his ally Llywelyn of Wales. After suppressing them for a second time, he banished the Marchers to Ireland in a deal worked out at Worcester, but he agreed to their demand that he put a plan in effect for releasing Edward. On 14 December 1264, Simon sent out a summons for parliament to meet the following month for this expressed purpose, but went to work on it himself beforehand by arranging to have Edward grant him his lordship of Chester in return for some of Simon's manors elsewhere. It was ostensibly a security measure. Removing Edward from proximity to the Marchers prevented them from making war on the regime in the future.[22]

The swap was announced on Christmas Eve at Woodstock, where the court had stopped on the way from Worcester. Christmas court had always been a hallmark of Henry's reign, often culminating in the knighting of young nobles on the day itself. There would be none of that this year. The king was in fact alone, save for his household. As Simon had appropriated his kingdom, so it seems his Christmas court as well. He took it to Kenilworth along with the feast of five boars, thirty oxen and 100 sheep. He needed it for the 140 knights he kept in his train, twice the number Henry ever had, and a similar number of servants and other officials. This was in addition to his wife, six children and the royal captives, who were doubtless encouraged to enjoy themselves.[23]

There is no record of the entertainment, but a special reading may have been held for a select body of guests, for those at least who understood Latin. A new composition came out at this time, *The Song of Lewes*, a rhyming poem of nearly a thousand lines celebrating their victory that year. Latin seems like an odd choice for a work where one of the themes is England for the English, but the *Song* was not meant to provide jingoes for the party faithful, rather to justify the radical state of things to a wider audience. They wanted the clergy and aristocracy across Europe to understand that Montfortianism stood for good government for all people and that kings were neither infallible nor above the law. Loyal were the men who stepped in to correct their monarch when he erred, not those who obeyed him blindly. It was thanks to one man that 'the sword waxed strong, many fell, truth prevailed, and the false fled'. It was thanks to Simon de Montfort that 'England breathes again'.

The author of *The Song of Lewes* remains unknown to this day, but his knowledge of the negotiations conducted by Stephen Berksted, the bishop of Chichester, prior to Lewes suggests he was a friar attached to his household.[24] It may have been Berksted himself, although the idea for the undertaking could have been Simon's. There were a lot of propaganda songs in circulation at the time, many of them extolling him and his cause, but he wanted something epic, something to immortalise him much the way his father had been by Peter of Vaux-de-Cernay. Of course, the bishop could not put his name to it like Peter did to his *The History of the Albigensian Crusade*. Innocent III would have been delighted to receive a laudatory tribute to the deeds of Simon V the crusader, Clement IV decidedly not to the deeds of Simon VI the revolutionary.

Berksted's authorship can also be deduced from the fact that he was one of the triumvirs and yet completely disappeared from view. Unlike the other Montfortian bishops, he played no role in the standoff with the legate. Simon may have intended it that way. He had the bishop named to the triumvirate knowing his work on the poem would keep him absent from government. This encumbered Simon with one less associate to consult. But he had a harder time trying to ignore the other triumvir, Gilbert de Clare. The earl of Gloucester was young, younger than Simon's older sons, and lacked experience, but he craved recognition and respect. It was under the first Montfortian regime that Gilbert received his earldom and Simon made sure he was well rewarded for his services at Lewes.

What Gilbert noticed was how much more Simon, and, disturbingly, his sons received. Henry de Montfort was made warden of the Channel ports and would inherit Chester, which was worth three times the value of Leicester. Simon VII was given the extensive properties of John Mansel, who died abroad in January 1265. He was also granted the marriage of Isabella de Forz, the countess of Devon. She was one of the wealthiest widows in the land and Henry had intended her marriage for his own son Edmund. The churchman Amaury VIII was awarded the rectory of St Wendron and treasurership of York, two of the richest benefices in England, and Guy IV retained the custody of the lands of his uncle Richard of Cornwall.[25]

In looking after his family, Simon was doing nothing more than anyone else in his position would do, but his overweening ambition was worrisome to some. It was visible the moment parliament opened on 20 January 1265 at Westminster Palace. Summonses had been sent out to 120 churchmen, more than five times the number of barons. Other participants included the knights of the counties and, for the first time on record, delegates of the towns, which were also solidly behind him. It was this increase in parliamentary representation that earned Simon his immortality, more than *The Song of Lewes* ever did. It was seen in modern times as the beginning of the House of Commons, even though Simon had no overt intentions in this direction. He needed people he could count on to support his programme. An equally far-reaching innovation had already occurred a decade earlier in any case when Queen Eleanor ordered the counties to hold local elections. That made it the first parliament to meet with a democratic mandate.[26]

But the queen's parliament had been exclusively concerned with obtaining an emergency subsidy. Simon's dealt with the future of the kingdom. Where most parliaments lasted two weeks at most, this one stretched out to nearly two months. Clearly not everyone was there to rubberstamp his proposals. It took more than three weeks just to get the king to give his assent to rule by constitutional monarchy and promise not to seek retribution against the Montfortians.[27] To punish him and his supporters for not being more cooperative, Simon had the announcement made in the chapter house of Westminster Abbey. He chose this venue because Henry had had the chapter house built for the purpose of gathering the great men of the realm together to bask in the glory of his kingship. He certainly never imagined they would be witnessing its debasement instead.

Looking around at the hundreds of prelates, knights and bourgeoisie, as opposed to just five earls (including himself), Gilbert could see that it was not just the king finished under Montfortianism, but the ancestral nobility as well. Power in the land had shifted to the priestly class and community of the realm. The baronial ranks were diminished further by the unexpected arrest of Robert de Ferrers, the earl of Derby, sometime before 23 February. The official reason for sending him to the Tower was the private warfare he had been conducting since Lewes, but that had been fuelled in large part by his feud with Edward over the ownership of lands adjacent to Cheshire. Now that Simon was claiming these lands as part of his swap with Edward, he decided to get rid of Ferrers before he inherited their feud.[28]

Gilbert and his brother Thomas had their own feud with the de Montfort sons at the same time. They were jealous of their arrogance and wealth, which rivalled their own, and challenged them to a tournament in Dunstable, northwest of London. Simon had it cancelled at the last minute and rounded on his sons for being so foolhardy as to endanger the security of the realm at so important a time. Gilbert was furious over the money he had spent organising it and lashed out at his fellow triumvir. Suddenly remembering how the Provisions of Oxford, as he understood them, were about getting rid of all foreigners, he professed his outrage that one like Simon should 'presume to put the whole realm under his yoke'. The tipping point was the arrest of Ferrers a few days later. Fearing he might be next, Gilbert left parliament without license and went back to Gloucester.[29]

Simon pressed ahead, and on 11 March 1265 he staged a grand finale in Westminster Hall. With Henry seated in gloomy silence, it was announced that Edward and Henry of Almain were no longer hostages for his compliance. They were henceforth released to his household, which meant under direct supervision of the Montfortian council. The oath of the king and heir to observe the peace and tranquillity of the realm was read out loud, followed by nine bishops pronouncing penalties against anyone, king or otherwise, who transgressed Magna Carta or the constitutions of previous years. Lastly, it was instructed that homage to Henry should be renewed, and it was Mayor Fitz-Thomas who spoke for this new dawn when he told the king, 'So long as you will be a good lord, we will be faithful and duteous to you'.[30]

Edward and Henry of Almain were then led away by their cousin Henry de Montfort and taken under armed escort to Odiham, which Eleanor de Montfort used as her base for cultivating political support for her husband's regime. They arrived with 128 horses in their train. Leaving the king at Westminster, Simon followed a couple days later with another 162 horses carrying knights, officials and attendants. The household had to scramble to feed so many people. Eleanor's accounts show that on the day of her husband's arrival, 19 March, more than 1,000 loaves of bread were consumed, 280 litres of wine drunk and 900 of beer. All the de Montfort children were there except the young Simon, who was fruitlessly engaged in besieging the royalist garrison at Pevensey. The guests stayed for nearly two weeks, Henry of Almain a little longer because Simon was sending him to France to reopen negotiations with Louis. The main discussion was the course of action Simon ought to take with Gilbert. He had scheduled a tournament in Northampton for 20 April to make up for the one cancelled at Dunstable. It was hoped they could work out their differences there. On 1 April, the party left Odiham to pick up the king and head north. It was the last time Simon and Eleanor saw each other.[31]

They waited five days for Gilbert to show up, then set off for Gloucester for the fateful confrontation. They found him gathering forces with the Marchers, who had ignored Simon's repeated orders to abjure the realm as per their agreement in Worcester back in December. A new threat emerged when, in coordination with the queen's efforts on the Continent, a troop of 120 mounted men disembarked at Pembroke under William de Valence. Loath to retreat in the face of surmounting odds, Simon moved the court to Hereford to keep Valence from linking up with the Marchers. He was still confidant of reaching a deal with Gilbert, and as a sign of his good faith he retained his brother Thomas de Clare at court, even allowing him personal access to Edward. On 28 May, Thomas and Edward were outside Hereford for some galloping gamesmanship when the two of them and several other defectors in Henry de Montfort's escort guard dashed away. As prearranged by Thomas, they met up with Roger Mortimer lurking nearby in the woods and together they rode to meet Gilbert at Ludlow. Although the earl of Gloucester had played as big a role as anyone in Edward's humiliations over the past year, all was forgiven now that he was ready to stamp out the Montfortians and Provisions of Oxford forever. His only condition was the banishment of all foreigners from government, which was not practical for a man of Edward's international pedigree, but the future king agreed and they swiftly went down the line of the Severn from Worcester to Gloucester to cut off Simon from the rest of England.[32]

Simon sent word to his namesake son to raise all the troops he could and head west to his aid. He too went west, about thirty kilometres, to conclude a quick treaty with Llywelyn in order to get immediate help from him. The Welsh prince was in a good position to extract concessions he might otherwise never get, but he provided Simon with much needed reinforcements as the court moved south on 24 June to catch a flotilla of boats across the river to Bristol. They were too late. They found the boats either sunk or on the other side, but worse, Edward was on their side with a much larger army. With Llywelyn covering his retreat, Simon led his dwindling forces back to Hereford. Edward was prevented from following them after word reached him that his cousin had arrived in the theatre with an army. He went to Gloucester to watch his movements.[33]

Simon VII had left London in a southwest direction, as if a rendezvous with his father had been planned at Bristol. Their destination turned out to be Winchester, which they reached on 16 July. Most of the men were Londoners who viewed Winchester as rich and royal, and having a free go at it and its Jewish community was apparently the price for their support. They spent three days sacking the town before heading north to Kenilworth, where other Montfortian troops were gathering. Edward also moved north, to Worcester, to stay between both Simons. He now had to decide which one to deal with before they joined forces and turned the tables on him.

His spies made it an easy call for him. They reported that many of the men at Kenilworth were billeted in the town, not behind the castle walls, because the bathing facilities were better. Late in the afternoon of 1 August, Edward and his cavalry left Worcester. They traversed the fifty-four kilometres to Kenilworth and surprised the Montfortians at dawn. Some they killed in their sleep, others they captured, but many more escaped to the castle, including Simon VII, who ran for it completely naked. Having given Simon VI a free pass to cross the river, Edward now hurried back to Worcester, where he found them just six kilometres to the south. They had marched thirty-five kilometres from Hereford to get there and were exhausted, but so too were Edward's men after their night raid. In the morning, Simon's troops were gone, but they were spotted by spies crossing the River Avon into the town of Evesham. They were heading north to unite forces with Simon VII, who still had a sizeable body of troops with him.[34]

Had they kept moving, they might have made it, but hunger and exhaustion forced them to pause at Evesham. Pushing his men with all speed, Edward arrived on the heights north of the town around eight-thirty on the morning of 4 August 1265. They were flying the Montfortian banners they had captured at Kenilworth, either to lure the smaller army into their grasps or perhaps to taunt Simon. At first, he believed it was his son, but a closer look by his barber revealed that the men on the hill were Edward's forces. After pausing to admire their displacements, which he took credit for, he prepared his men for an uphill lurch, hoping his son was just behind Edward ready to strike. He lacked his usual confidence, however, and urged his men to flee, something he himself would never do:

> Fair lords, there are many among you who are not as yet tried and tested in the world, and who are young; you have wives and children, and for this reason look to how you might save yourselves and them; cross the bridge and you will escape from the great peril that is to come.[35]

Walter Cantilupe was there, having made his own journey in the night. He preached to the men so that 'they had less fear of death', then gave Simon a farewell embrace and left. There is no record of him offering to take the king into his custody in order to spare him the battle ahead, but Simon was not about to give him up in any case. Henry was all that was left of his authority. He decided he was to go into battle with them wearing only ordinary armour, like Peter of Aragon at Muret, to keep the royalists from snatching him away.

As they moved forward, the sky grew dark and ominous. It was Henry de Montfort who led the charge. He managed to open up a wedge, but Edward's men were quickly on top of him. He was pulled off his horse and hacked to death. His brother Guy IV fell, but survived. Close associates like Despenser were killed in the mayhem and the king nearly too. Henry was wounded in the shoulder before he made his attackers understand who he was. One tradition, too mawkish for credulity, has Edward hearing his father's cries over the din of battle and coming to his rescue. Simon was the only Montfortian deliberately targeted for assassination, by a twelve-man death squad personally chosen by Edward and Gilbert. Despite their orders to do nothing else except find the earl of Leicester and mow him down, it was Roger Mortimer, coming up from behind, who drove the lance through his neck that killed him.[36]

He had fought and died for his cause as he imagined he would someday. When he was 10 years old, he was at Narbonnais Palace next to Toulouse when his father, who had also laboured long and hard for his own cause, was borne before him and the rest of the family. His head had been crushed by a stone, but his body was otherwise intact. He was given a grand funeral in Carcassonne, then later reinterred at the family mausoleum in Hautes-Bruyères. His brother Guy II had died in enemy hands, but was honourably turned over for burial next to his father.

There would be none of this for Simon VI. First, Mortimer and his men stripped his corpse of armour. They found he was wearing a hair shirt underneath, which probably made them laugh. Simon de Montfort, conscious of his public image to the last! They then set about chopping up his body, with Mortimer taking Simon's head and private parts to present to his wife. The others took their trophies, although not for sinister purposes in every case. One of his feet ended up at a priory near Scotland, where it was encased in silver and became an object of local veneration.[37]

His torso was buried next to his son Henry at Evesham Abbey, but was later disinterred and buried in secret elsewhere because, like Raymond VI of Toulouse, Simon had been an excommunicate at the time of his death. It did not stop a miracle cult from flourishing around a spring that bubbled up on the spot where he was cut down. Gilbert's own mother attested to the healing powers of the water there. Miracles had also been reported at his father's tomb in Carcassonne, but nothing exact of them is known. Of the cures worked by Simon in Evesham, at least 198 had been recorded by the time his shrine was suppressed in 1279. His legend lived on, however, well into the next century. In 1323, King Edward II was entertained in Yorkshire by two peasant women singing songs about Simon de Montfort. One was called Alice de Whorlton, the other Agnes the Redhead, and they received four shillings for their work.[38]

The surviving de Montforts leave England, the family helps in the conquest of Sicily, the murder of Henry of Almain, the crusader states fall

How quickly the kingdom returned to peace depended to a certain degree on Simon VII. He had set out towards Evesham on the morning of the battle, but did not arrive until after the carnage was over and his father's head was being paraded around on a pike. Upon their return to Kenilworth, his men were angry enough by what they had seen to want to dismember Richard of Cornwall in retaliation. Simon saved his uncle's life and let him go free, then proceeded under safe-conduct to Winchester, the town he had recently plundered, for a parliament summoned there by Henry for 8 September 1265.

At issue was whether to fine the Montfortians for their rebellion or disinherit them entirely. The inability to reach an agreement for the surrender of Kenilworth settled the matter in favour of disinheritance despite resistance from Richard of Cornwall and other senior barons who were not at Evesham. The earldom of Leicester was forfeited by Simon VII, who was in line to succeed his father, and given to the king's son Edmund. Simon went back north to carry on the struggle with other disinherited families, but tired of the life of an insurgent. In December, he went to Henry at Northampton to cut a deal. He agreed to abjure the realm in return for a pension from the revenues of Leicester. He was taken to London by Edward, but suspected that imprisonment awaited him and escaped to France early the next year.[39]

He found his mother and siblings Amaury, Richard and Eleanor already there. They had spent the crisis period before Evesham at Dover, ready to flee if disaster should strike. Amaury and Richard were the first to go over, taking with them almost £7,000 in cash. Eleanor arranged leniency for her friends and household with Edward and then left with her daughter on 28 October, one day before the queen returned after more than two years of exile. Eleanor of Provence was accompanied by a new legate, whose first task was to deal with the Montfortian bishops. Walter Cantilupe died in February 1266, but not before, reports one chronicler, admitting his error in espousing Simon's cause and asking for absolution. The only bishop to remain a firm Montfortian to the end was Stephen Berksted, who died blind and infirm in 1287.[40]

Guy IV de Montfort had been imprisoned at Windsor following Evesham, but was moved to Dover after his mother vacated the castle. He escaped from there in the spring of 1266 and can be found with his mother, brother Simon and sister Eleanor later in December at Montargis, the nunnery founded by his aunt Amicia, where his mother had gone to retire. Amaury was then in Italy, where he had gone to study medicine and to plead with the pope to obtain a Christian burial for his father. Clement was still sufficiently angry at Simon by the time of Evesham to refer to him as 'that pestilent man', but he agreed to look into Amaury's request. Fourteen-year-old Richard was in Navarre serving in the royal court. Eleanor had angled that position for him by ceding the family claim to Bigorre to King Theobald II. Richard disappeared from the records at this point, probably perishing in Theobald's ill-fated attempt to take Bigorre.[41]

By this time the war carried on by Simon's disinherited followers was coming to an end. Under the Dictum of Kenilworth issued by Henry on 31 October 1266, they were allowed to redeem their properties at a value based on their involvement in the rebellion. The case of the de Montforts themselves was given to Louis to decide. In May 1267, he sent John of Brienne to England to discuss the matter. John was no longer the count of Montfort, having relinquished the title to his stepdaughter Beatrice, but he had since become the butler of France and that gave him plenty of clout with Louis. Henry agreed to give Leicester back to the de Montforts, but provided that they sold it to him or his sons when asked to do so. Louis himself was to set the value, but Henry asked him to consider the damages caused by them to the realm. Simon VII could come back to England to sue for a better deal if he wished, but he would have to stand trial first. Henry also offered his sister £500 for her dower and the right to sue as well if she felt this was unfair. The case dragged on for more than a year and in the end Louis made no award. By the autumn of 1268, Simon had left to join his brother Guy, who had taken the warlike skills he inherited from his father to a new campaign.[42]

The way to this new venture went all the way back to the beginning of the reform period a decade earlier. The barons had promised Henry to work for his Sicilian tax but did nothing except write the pope an impertinent letter. In the summer of 1263, as the Montfortians were marching on London, Pope Urban cancelled Edmund's claim to the throne of Sicily and transferred it to Louis's brother Charles of Anjou. In October 1265, as Guy IV was lying wounded in a dungeon at Windsor Castle, Charles mustered his troops at Lyon with Philip II de Montfort leading them through Lombardy. They defeated and killed Manfred at Benevento on 26 February 1266. Philip was at the head of the Angevin troops that crossed into Sicily that spring. The following year he negotiated the surrender of Florence and was named Charles's imperial vicar of Tuscany. It was around this time that Guy arrived in Italy. He may have been invited by Philip, who was a second cousin 15–20 years older than him, or by Charles, who had sworn a mysterious pact of brotherhood with Simon VI, probably during the latter's last visit to France in September 1263.[43]

Charles needed all the support he could get, for Conrad's 17-year-old son Conradin made a bid for the imperial throne. In April 1267, Guy was given command of 800 knights in Florence to secure it against the passage of Conradin's German forces. The inevitable battle took place on 23 August 1268 at Tagliacozzo (Alba). At first, things went badly for Charles, but a late counterattack eventually won it for him. Guy was said to have distinguished himself in the fierce hand-to-hand fighting. He was like a 'wild boar among dogs' and at one point his helmet became twisted around. Unable to breathe or see, he flailed his arms around like a madman until a comrade set his helmet aright again. Conradin was later caught and executed, finishing off the Hohenstaufens for good. In August of the following year, Philip and Guy de Montfort together led reinforcements to Sicily to put down a revolt there.

On 24 March 1270, Charles named Guy as his vicar-general for Tuscany. In this capacity he negotiated the submission of Pisa and Sienna and was so highly respected in Florence that Charles made him the acting *podestà*, or chief magistrate, of the city. On 10 August, he married 17-year-old Margherita Aldobrandesca, the heiress of one of the richest and most powerful clans in Tuscany. He was about 26 and the first of Simon and Eleanor's six children to get married. His father would have been envious of not only the power and authority he had achieved, and so rapidly, but the legitimacy behind it and the future that lay ahead of it. Dante was a 5-year-old boy in Florence at the time and may have caught a glimpse of Guy riding by on a splendid warhorse with a procession of knights behind him. His brother Simon VII followed him into service for Charles at the end of 1268 and two years later he received the county of Avellino.[44]

Throughout this time, Charles and Philip made plans to join Louis on his new crusade. It would not take them far from home because Louis decided to strike at the emir of Tunis. He seems to have been urged in this direction by Charles, who wanted to reduce Tunis to a tribute state of his new Sicilian empire, but Louis was also looking for an easy victory to atone for his Egyptian crusade. The Holy Land needed help more than ever, but the Mameluks who crushed him last time were at the peak of their strength and had even defeated the invincible Mongols. Louis, however, did not count on the African heat or the usual poor supplies and sanitation when he landed in the summer of 1270. Within two months, dysentery killed most of the army, including the king himself on 25 August. Philip II also succumbed to the disease. He was taken back to Castres and buried at the church of Saint-Vincent.[45]

Edward and Henry of Almain arrived later from England with a contingent of crusaders, but Charles told them it was over. After all the money spent organising his crusade, Edward despaired going back with nothing to show for it. He decided to continue eastward, but not with Almain. He detached him so he could look after affairs in Gascony before returning to England. Henry would accompany Charles and the new king of France, Philip III, on the overland route and stop with them in Viterbo, where the cardinals had been deadlocked for more than two years trying to find a successor for Clement IV. Since Charles summoned Guy to meet him in Viterbo for talks, perhaps Guy could also meet his Plantagenet cousin Henry of Almain to discuss reconciliation between their families.[46]

That was the problem Edward and the Plantagenets had to face with the mutilation of Simon de Montfort's body. It saddled them with a blood feud with their de Montfort cousins. Guy IV and Simon VII had not been a part of Louis's crusade because letting them near Edward or other veterans of Evesham was out of the question. Experience with the now martyred Simon had shown that the de Montforts were not an easy clan to conciliate and there was no better living example than Philip I.

His grudge against Acre had gone on for more than a decade despite the danger it posed to the crusader states as a whole. The dissension aided Baybars in his relentless conquests, and in 1266 he took Toron from Philip. Tyre next came under threat, but it was from the west and King Hugh III of Cyprus. Conradin's death in 1268 had allowed Hugh, a near relative, to pursue the title of king of Jerusalem, and Tyre was technically part of the kingdom. Since Philip was not about to give it up without a fight, they agreed on a marriage alliance. Philip's son with Maria of Antioch, John II de Montfort, would marry Hugh's sister Margaret. Philip would then cede his lordship to the couple and their expected children. John and Margaret were married in Cyprus and returned to the mainland with Hugh, who was crowned king of Jerusalem in Tyre in September 1269.[47]

When Baybars learned that Louis was not coming east with his army, he decided to renew his attacks against the crusader states, beginning with a covert operation. He dispatched two men from the Order of Assassins to gain access to Tyre by posing as Saracen men-at-arms looking to convert to Christianity. They were taken to Philip and his nephew Julian, who was the lord of Sidon. The men were baptised, with each taking the name of one of the lords. Philip was warned about a plot to kill him, but he trusted the converts and took them into his household. One of his Syrian servants discovered the men were carrying poisoned daggers, but agreed to keep quiet if they paid him 100 bezants by the end of the week. Since they did not have the money, and it was already Thursday, they decided to carry out their act on Sunday. Julian had left for Sidon and Julian the assassin followed him there. Philip the assassin found his benefactor standing at the door to his chapel, fiddling with one of the rings on his fingers, and stabbed him in the chest. He then drew his sword and ran into the chapel to kill his son John, but was restrained by a knight who was with the younger de Montfort. Philip collapsed onto a stone bench outside the entrance. The guards brought in by all the commotion pounced on the assassin and killed him straightaway. John rushed out to his father, who opened his eyes, saw that his son was safe, and died. It was 17 August 1270, right around the time Philip's son from his first marriage lay dying in Tunisia.

Philip I was buried in the church of the Holy Cross in Tyre. Julian's assassin had still not acted when the plot was uncovered and fled to safety. The Syrian servant admitted under torture what had happened and was executed.[48] In May 1271, Edward arrived at Acre with a few hundred knights, hardly a threat to Baybars, but the sultan was disturbed by his attempt to establish a joint operation with the Mongols. In June of the following year, he sent another agent to deal with him. It was the same ruse, a Saracen man-at-arms asking for baptism. Although Edward was based at Acre, it seems he would have heard the details of Philip's assassination in Tyre and yet he took the man into his confidence. He even used him as a spy, with orders that he should report to him at any time. One night the agent gained admittance to his bed chamber even though Edward and his wife were asleep. He stabbed Edward in the hip, but was instantly floored by one punch. Edward grabbed his own knife and stabbed the would-be assassin to death. Fearing the spy's dagger was poisoned, doctors were brought in and had slaves suck on Edward's wound before they sutured it.[49]

Edward recovered and sailed for home. Stopping in Sicily, he met Charles of Anjou, who informed him that, Henry III having died, he was now King Edward I of England. Doubtless they discussed a scandalous murder that had occurred just before he left for Acre. On 12 March 1271, Guy and Simon de Montfort arrived in Viterbo with Guy's father-in-law Count Rosso and a retinue of fifty knights. It is unclear if they knew of Henry of Almain's presence in the city and sought him out or they chanced upon him at worship the next day in the church of St Silvestro. Either way, Guy shouted from the doorway, 'Henry of Almain, you traitor! You shall not escape me'. Dagger drawn, he dashed towards his cousin, who ran for the altar but was cut down there. It was reported that Almain was then dragged out of the church, perhaps still alive, and finished off with a hail of blows on the plaza outside. The assailants jumped on their horses and rode north, where the de Montforts were given shelter by Guy's Tuscan in-laws. Simon VII died later that year, in a castle near Siena, just over 30 years old.[50]

King Philip of France wrote to Richard of Cornwall to express his grief and anguish over the slaying of his son, adding that the de Montforts had acted 'at the instigation of the devil'. In his own letter announcing the tragedy, Richard calls his dead brother-in-law Simon and his sons 'satellites of Satan'. The general condemnation did not arouse any judicial action against Guy, however, until Edward took up the case with the new pope, Gregory X, who had served with him in the Holy Land before his election to the holy see. Gregory ordered Guy to appear before him, but Amaury arrived instead to say that his brother preferred to wait until Edward had left the country. Amaury, who was the family lawyer, doctor and chaplain all in one, offered various excuses for the murder, none of them pleasing to the pope's ear. He excommunicated Guy with orders for his arrest by anyone who encountered him.[51]

In July 1274, it was the pope himself who met Guy, along with his wife and several friends, at the gates of Florence, barefoot and wearing only a smock with a rope around his neck. For three kilometres he begged his holiness for forgiveness. The sentence was duly lifted, but he was ordered to remain under close confinement at Lecco on Lake Como. It seems that Guy was still able to move about and had at least one secret meeting with Charles of Anjou. In 1280, Edward was informed that Guy was a fugitive and had been apprehended in Norway. He asked King Eric II to deliver him, but when the officials went to get the prisoner, he was gone. By the following year, Guy had been fully rehabilitated by the latest pope, Martin IV, the fifth since Gregory X died in 1276. He was reunited with Margherita and their two daughters. On 11 May 1283, he was put in command of papal forces at Romagna, but when his father-in-law died the next year, he obtained leave to go north and defend his wife's inheritance in Tuscany.[52]

Were it not for Edward, Guy might never have faced justice. So horrific was the mutilation of Simon's body that there was some sympathy for the equally horrific response. It did not matter that Henry of Almain had not been at the battle of Evesham. The people who heard about his murder naturally assumed he must have had something to do with Simon's demise. A case in point was an account of Evesham written up by the anonymous chronicler known as the Templar of Tyre, who was not a Templar but had spent his whole life in the crusader states and in Cyprus:

The battle was very bitter and many men were killed on each side. In the end Earl Simon de Montfort was defeated and taken alive. Once he had come from the battle, the Lord Edward sought counsel from his cousin who was named Henry of Almain and who was also cousin to Earl Simon's children, the children of two sisters, as to what he should do to Earl Simon. The Lord Henry advised him that if he wanted peace and an end to the war, he should cut off Earl Simon's head and have it said that he was killed in battle since it would have been regarded as shameful to have him killed after he had been captured. So that night the Lord Edward, on the advice of the Lord Henry of Almain, had Earl Simon de Montfort's head cut off and had him thrown on the field among the other dead bodies.

How the Templar came to this distorted conclusion can be gleaned from his close acquaintance with the de Montfort household in Tyre. As he informs the reader, the Templar was in Margaret's service in Cyprus prior to her marriage to John II, then went to Tyre and worked for them there for a year. Visitors from the west who passed through the de Montfort household doubtless carried news of the murder in one form or another. Whatever the de Montforts heard, they could not believe that Guy would have sacrificed his brilliant career unless he was sure his vengeance was in the right place. By the time the Templar committed the story to writing, many decades later, the plotline was clear: Henry of Almain had it coming to him.[53]

John and Margaret de Montfort turned out to be effective lords amidst an increasingly deteriorating situation. Baybars resumed his offensive, taking all the great inland castles of the Templar, Hospitaller and Teutonic orders, and reached the hinterland of Tyre. In 1271, the de Montforts surrendered the revenues of several outlying villages in order to get the sultan to agree to a truce. They acted alone because King Hugh had been unable to unify the kingdom of Jerusalem. Matters were made worse for him by Charles of Anjou, who aimed to recover both Jerusalem and Constantinople for his much desired empire. In March 1277, Charles purchased the rights of another relative of Conradin whose claim to the kingdom of Jerusalem was stronger than Hugh's. Charles sent his Angevin deputies to seize control of Acre, which they pulled off with the help of the Templars. They then began to eye Tyre. To avoid a struggle, John agreed to end his family's 20-year-long feud with Acre and give the Venetians back their share of Tyre that had been seized by his father Philip.

After suffering from gout for many years, John II died on 27 November 1283 and was buried within the tomb of his father. The Templar of Tyre says he was 'most sagacious in all matters, both to God and man, and for this he was loved by all manner of people'. He and Margaret had no children, but because Hugh lacked the money to indemnify the de Montfort family for their expenses on fortifications, Tyre went to John's next of kin, his younger brother Humphrey. He was the lord of Beirut by right of his marriage to Eschiva, another Ibelin. According to the Templar, Humphrey de Montfort had 'great presence' and was the handsomest knight of his age. King Louis IX was moved to make the same judgement when he met him. Humphrey died within a few months of John and was buried with his father and brother. He left two sons, Amaury IX and Rupin, but Margaret ruled alone as the lady of Tyre. The Templar says she was a 'truly good woman, most wise and generous' but later on she became fat 'quite beyond reason'. She and her nephews had all fled to Cyprus by the time Tyre and the kingdom of Jerusalem fell in 1291. The crusade era was over.[54]

The Final Act

Edward had vowed to return to the Holy Land with real help, but it took him over a year and a half just to get around to his own coronation in August 1274. His fear and mistrust of the de Montfort brood continued and was confirmed at Christmas 1275 when a boat off Bristol was stopped and searched. Discovered among the passengers were Amaury VIII and his sister Eleanor, who was then about 17 years old. They were on their way to Llywelyn, whom Eleanor had married by proxy earlier that year. The match had been negotiated by Simon VI, when his alliance with Llywelyn was one of the mainstays of his regime. The prince of Wales, already in his fifties but with no heir to succeed him, was anxious for the marriage to go forward, but the ceremony was not performed until shortly before the death of Eleanor's namesake mother at Montargis in April 1275. Given Edward's recent troubles with Llywelyn, any intention to create a Welsh-Montfort bloodline naturally filled him with unease. He ordered Eleanor's captors to bring her to Windsor, where her brother Guy had been imprisoned after Evesham a decade before.

Her confinement was certainly comfortable. Despite the nearly twenty-year age gap between them, Edward and Eleanor had long enjoyed a close relationship. When the tables were turned and he was the captive, the cousins exchanged letters and gifts and they remained on friendly terms even after the murder of Henry of Almain. It was a whole different story with her brother, however. Although Amaury had proved he was in Padua on the day of the murder, Edward remembered his impertinence back in Italy when he sought to bring Guy to justice. Amaury wound up at the fortress of Corfe in Dorset, locked away without trial but not denied the writing materials he requested. This most scholarly of the de Montforts, who had studied under Robert Grosseteste, passed the time in his cell writing a theological treatise and jotting down musings that reflected the anguish of the fate that had befallen their family.

Edward was not opposed to Eleanor's marriage, but he wanted an end to both Llywelyn's incursions and his refusal to pay homage to the king of England. Llywelyn responded to the capture of his young wife by digging in; war was on between Wales and England. The hard-fought campaign ended not quite two years later with Llywelyn's total submission. He accompanied Edward to Westminster, where on Christmas Day in 1277 he finally knelt before the king. One of his men was allowed to visit Eleanor at Windsor, but her release was delayed pending the prince's probation. When it did happen, Edward decided they were to marry in an official ceremony to make it clear that it was by his hand and grace that Eleanor de Montfort became the princess of Wales. The wedding was held in Worcester on 13 October 1278. The bride was given away by her cousin Edmund of Lancaster while her other cousin the king paid for the feast. As a wedding present, she received a kerchief from Edward and his queen Eleanor of Castile.[55]

Troubles nevertheless persisted and in July 1279 Eleanor felt compelled to write Edward a letter assuring him of their fidelity. She asked him not to believe certain calumnies being said of her and Llywelyn, or at least to give them a chance to explain themselves. Her worrisome tone echoes the letter written by her father Simon VI in 1250, when he asked Henry

III for an interview so he could refute 'many sinister things' being said of him. In another letter Eleanor took up her brother's plight and implored Edward to release him by appealing to their bond of kinship:

> With bended knees and tearful groanings, we supplicate your highness that, reverencing from your inmost soul the divine mercy (which holds out the hand of pity to all, especially to those who seek him with their whole heart), you would deign mercifully to take again to your grace and favour our aforesaid brother and your kinsman, who humbly craves, as we understand, your kindness. For if your Excellency, as we have often known, mercifully condescends to strangers, with much more reason, as we think, ought you to hold out the hand of pity to one so near to you by the ties of nature.[56]

Three successive popes also got involved in the case, but the king would not budge. He and some of his barons were convinced that Amaury and other de Montforts were still plotting against them. It took the personal intervention of the archbishop of Canterbury and bishop of Winchester to disabuse them of these suspicions, and in April 1282, after more than six years of incarceration, Amaury was handed over to a papal agent and taken to France. He never saw his sister again. Eleanor died on 19 June 1282 giving birth to a daughter and was buried at Llanfaes, a Franciscan house in Anglesey that had been founded in memory of Eleanor's aunt Joan, a natural daughter of King John. In revolt again, Llywelyn was killed later that year in an ambush and all Wales conquered afterwards. Edward had the seal matrix used by Eleanor to imprint her heartfelt letters to him melted down and fashioned, along with her husband's, into a silver chalice. Their infant daughter Gwenllian was taken to Lincolnshire and placed in the priory of St Mary in Sempringham, where like so many of her female de Montfort cousins she grew up to be a nun. What she may have known or thought about her Welsh and Montfortian heritage went unrecorded at her death on 7 June 1337. She was just shy of 55 years old.[57]

After his release, Amaury went to Paris, where he kept busy as the executor of his mother's will. He drove Edward to distraction by suing for reinstatement of his family lands and titles in England. Impertinent as ever, he did not drop the suit until 1285, and only then because he was grieved to think of the worry that it caused Edward. In 1289, he was back at Montargis making his will, where he calls himself, among other titles, the earl of Leicester and Chester and steward of England. He bequeathed his books to the Dominican house of Saint-Jacques, which had represented his parents in the negotiations over his mother's dower thirty years earlier. A copy of his will in the Vatican archives is dated 1300, suggesting he lived at least until the end of the century.[58]

He was most likely in Italy for the remainder of his life. Just as his brother Guy had found a new career there thanks to a kinsman, so it was with Amaury two decades after him. The relative this time was John III de Montfort, the son of Philip II and so Amaury's second cousin once removed. John had inherited not just his father's estates in France and Italy but also the trust and patronage of Charles of Anjou. By 1273, he was Charles's chamberlain, an office that was predominantly military in function. His younger brother Simon VIII was also in Italy, serving as the castellan of Misiano. In 1275, he became embroiled in a duel and died, along with his Italian opponent, from the wounds he received. Charles had to forbid John, now the count of Squillace in Calabria, from exacting revenge on the local population. The uprising of the Sicilian Vespers in 1282 deprived the Angevins of the island kingdom. After Charles's death in 1285, John was the captain-general in charge of trying to retake Sicily from the Aragonese. Two years after that he called Guy back into service for an assault on Augusta near Syracuse, but their fleet was captured in the bay of Naples.[59]

John and other prisoners were able to buy their freedom, but negotiations for Guy floundered. John informed Amaury that Guy's ransom was set at 8,000 ounces of gold, a small treasure. When it was then raised to 10,000 ounces, it was clear that his captors were not acting in good faith. Edward was in Gascony at the time and likely using his influence with neighbouring Aragon to keep Guy locked up forever. Guy's wife Margherita started living with another man and arranged to have her and Guy's eldest daughter Tomasina, who was barely 10 years old, married to a large landowner in Viterbo. Guy protested that his consent was never sought but Tomasina died soon afterwards. By 21 March 1292, Guy was also dead, having never emerged from prison. He was in his late forties. Margherita went on to marry four more times. Her other daughter with Guy, Anastasia, was taken from her by the pope and married to Romanello Orsini. In October 1293, Anastasia was restored the fiefs that had been granted to her father.[60]

The defeat did not cost John his high standing in the royal Angevin household and it was here that he arranged for Amaury to be given a house and to serve as tutor to Guy's children. John III, who was married three times but with no offspring, died around 1300.[61] Together with Amaury VIII, he closed out the century for the de Montforts, but the family name itself was revived in the early part of the fourteenth century through Yolande of Dreux, the daughter of Beatrice, granddaugther of John I, and great-granddaughter of Amaury VII. After a short time as the queen of Scotland, she became the second wife of Arthur II of Brittany, himself a grandson of Henry III. Their son inherited Montfort l'Amaury and later fought the children of Arthur's first marriage for control of Brittany. The war of succession was eventually won by his son John of Montfort in 1365, a hundred years after Evesham.

Had John sought inspiration for his victory, a visit to the family mausoleum at Hautes-Bruyères would have easily sufficed. His ancestors buried there, and the services held for those absent, were a reminder of not just the scale of their ambitions, but how far afield their fortunes had risen and fallen. There were of course the two Simons, father and son, the crusader and the revolutionary, both architects and implementers of the most far-reaching constitutions of their ages, one in Languedoc, the other in England. Between them was Amaury VII, whose rather subdued record as a crusader nevertheless earned him the respect of kings and popes and honour as the constable of France. His son John I died before he could prove his own crusade credentials, but in the last outposts of Christendom in the east, it was his shrine on Cyprus that pilgrims thought of whenever the name 'de Montfort' was mentioned.

Those not in the direct line of the new duke of Brittany had their own remarkable stories to tell. Philip I, following in the footsteps of his father Guy I, was the dominant lord of the crusader states during their twilight years. His son Philip II was one of the ablest generals of the lot, leading Angevin forces in the conquest of Italy and Sicily. Unlike the two Simons, he did not live to see his victories undone. He was helped immensely by Guy IV, the fiercest of all the de Montforts in battle. That was no mean feat given all the warriors that preceded him, as far back as Isabella, the granddaughter of Amaury I, the founder of the house of Montfort. She rode around in armour and showed as much daring and courage as the knights under her command. Her sister Bertrade, on the other hand, preferred the power of intrigue. The mother of a king and a queen herself, though by different connections, her scandals reigned supreme until Guy IV avenged the family on their English cousins.

How much John of Montfort knew of the colourful and turbulent history that followed the establishment of Montfort l'Amaury in the eleventh century can only be conjectured. At their peak, the de Montforts had set themselves up as rulers in England, Wales, France, Italy, Sicily and the Holy Land. By the fourteenth century, they had all been swept away, their influence of no longer any account. After the death of Simon the crusader, the language and culture of Languedoc went on as before. It was the steady crawl of the Inquisition that finally did away with heresy. His son's legacy was more lasting, but his imposition of a constitutional monarchy, brief as it was, made England a profoundly dangerous place for political dissent. The monarchs who followed Henry III started using the axe and gallows to get rid of troublesome malcontents like Simon the revolutionary.

Knowing all this would not have deterred John of Montfort in any case. He was as much caught up in the forces of his day as his ancestors were in theirs. Whether he too came out of it a hero or villain in the end would be largely beyond his control. It was up to the historians, poets and popular imagination to decide that outcome.

Appendix

Seals of the de Montforts

These sketches were made of the seals found in the family archives now part of Clairambault collection 1188 at the Bibliothèque nationale de France. Bémont's *Simon de Montfort*, pages 285–7 for compete details.

Simon V, 1209 (fol. 2v)

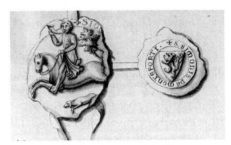

Simon VI, 1261 (fol. 20)

Eleanor I, Simon VII, Guy IV, Eleanor II, 1266 (fol. 25)

Henry de Montfort, 1264 (fol. 24r.)

Amaury VIII, 1274 (fol. 17)

Notes

Chapter 1: The Forebears

1. *Orderic II*, p. 399; *Peerage VII*, p. 708; Prothero, *Montfort*, pp. 31–2.
2. Robinson, *Gilbert Crispin*, pp. 7, 15–16.
3. *Orderic I*, pp. 441, 462; *II*, 188–90; *Peerage XII-2*, pp. 168, 759–60; Power, *Norman Frontier*, p. 225.
4. *Orderic II*, pp. 485, 494–5.
5. *Orderic III*, pp. 212, 426; *Cartulaire général de Paris I*, pp. 153–4; *Peerage VII*, p. 711.
6. *Orderic II*, pp. 475–7; *III*, p. 3; *Suger*, p. 41.
7. *Orderic III*, pp. 4–5, 63, 352–5; *Suger*, pp. 41, 81.
8. *Orderic I*, p. 484; *II*, p. 50; *III*, pp. 420, 448, 449, 465, 471, 477–8.
9. *Orderic III*, pp. 480, 483–4, 486.
10. *Orderic IV*, pp. 18–19, 59, 60. The main aim of the conspiracy was to promote the claims of William Clito, the son of Robert Curthose, still imprisoned in England, as the rightful duke of Normandy. Clito's death in 1127, followed by Robert's six years later, extinguished their claim.
11. *Orderic IV*, pp. 61–2, 70, 72–5, 78; Hollister, *Henry I*, pp. 292–302.
12. *Orderic IV*, pp. 79; *Suger*, pp. 132, 136, 144; Power, *Norman Frontier*, p. 229.
13. *Orderic III*, pp. 348, 428. As the heir presumptive to Count William of Evreux, Amaury was betrothed in 1103 to the infant daughter of Count Robert I of Meulan. It was hoped that the match would secure peace between the 'belligerent' lords of this region, but it was called off the next year after the twins Waleran and Robert were born to Count Robert. The infant was thought to be their sister Adeline, who was married to an unrelated Montfort, Hugh, the lord of Montfort-sur-Risle, but more likely she died in infancy and her name became lost (White, 'Career of Waleran', p. 20). Hugh was captured along with his brother-in-law Waleran and not released until after Henry's death twelve years later.
14. *Peerage VII*, pp. 715–16; *Torigni*, pp. 714, 764; Power, *Norman Frontier*, p. 229. Waleran seems to have had his eye on the Garlande lands of his mother-in-law and appropriated them after her death. He was said to have become a monk just prior to his own death in 1166.
15. *Torigni*, p. 753. Simon III married a woman named Matilda, whose origins are unknown. In 1158, she lay ill at the family priory of Hautes-Bruyères and Simon made two grants there for her recovery.

16. *Torigni*, p. 775; Power, *Norman Frontier*, p. 290. The common ancestor of King Henry II of England and Simon III was Simon I, the father of Amaury III and Bertrade, who was Henry II's great-grandmother. For Henry II and Hugh, the common ancestor was King Henry I of England, whose natural son Robert, the earl of Gloucester, was the father of Hugh's mother Maud.

17. *Torigni*, p. 753; *Howden I*, p. 369; *Peerage III*, p. 167; Church, *King John*, p. 17. Bertrade and Hugh had five children, the most famous of them the next earl of Chester, Ranulf de Blondeville. Their four daughters made illustrious matches: Maud to David of Scotland, the 8th earl of Huntingdon–their son John the Scot for a time was the heir to the Scottish throne; Mabel was wed to William d'Aubigny, the 3rd earl of Arundel; Agnes to William de Ferrers, the 4th earl of Derby; and Hawise to Robert de Quincy, the son of Saher, the 1st earl of Winchester. Robert's mother was Margaret de Beaumont, the younger sister of the Amicia who married Simon IV.

18. *Torigni*, p. 780; *Peerage VII*, pp. 715–16; Power, *Norman Frontier*, pp. 331–2.

19. *Howden II*, p. 418.

20. *Orderic IV*, p. 44; *Howden II*, p. 165. The witness to Richard's treaty may have been a Breton noble also named Amaury de Montfort. The substance of the treaty was the marriage of Tancred's daughter to Richard's nephew Arthur of Brittany, whom he had named as his successor. My thanks to Daniel Power for this information about Amaury V and the crusade.

21. Power, *Norman Frontier*, pp. 239, 291; Lippiatt, *Simon V of Montfort*, pp. 1, 83.

22. *Howden II*, pp. 191–2; *Vinsauf*, pp. 217–18, 242.

23. Lippiatt, *Simon V of Montfort*, pp. 1, 56, 104–05.

24. *Howden II*, pp. 326, 387, 431–2; Lippiatt, *Simon V of Montfort*, pp. 20–1; *Peerage VII*, pp. 534, 538. Robert IV de Beaumont had been part of the tournament of cane poles in Sicily when things turned nasty between King Richard and William III des Barres. He had to be restrained from jumping into the fray to pound his brother-in-law Barres himself. He then distinguished himself on more than one occasion after the host moved on to Syria. In one engagement, he charged the Turkish line to rescue several of his men (to be something of a refrain for the earls of Leicester). Courage and honour were big things for him, and Philip was counting on this through his choice of sureties. Robert would not subject his nephew Simon V and other kinfolk to disinheritance just to get his castle back (*Vinsauf*, pp. 239, 251, 254–5; Power, *Norman Frontier*, pp. 259–61).

25. *Howden II*, pp. 327, 429–32; Baldwin, *Government of Philip Augustus*, pp. 89–90, 280–1. There was a codicil in the agreement between Philip and Robert that made Robert's promise conditioned on war not breaking out between the two kings, which evidently had (Powicke, *Loss of Normandy*, p. 430).

26. Baldwin, *Government of Philip Augustus*, pp. 110–1, 483.

27. *Actes de Simon et d'Amauri de Montfort*, p. 447; Lippiatt, *Simon V of Montfort*, p. 110.
28. *Howden II*, pp. 430, 447–8; Queller and Madden, *Fourth Crusade*, pp. 2–3.
29. *Peerage V*, pp. 692–3; Power, *Norman Frontier*, pp. 294–5.
30. *Villehardouin*, pp. 1–2; Lippiatt, *Simon V of Montfort*, pp. 79–80.
31. Queller and Madden, *Fourth Crusade*, pp. 2–4.
32. Lippiatt, *Simon V of Montfort*, pp. 105–07.

Chapter 2: The Fourth Crusade
1. *Innocent III, Reg. 1:398*, Sources, pp. 19–21. For a complete overview and analysis of these events, see Queller, Compton and Campbell, 'The Fourth Crusade: The Neglected Majority, *Speculum*, Vol. 49, no. 3 (1974).
2. *Villehardouin*, pp. 4–10. Villehardouin and Geoffrey of Joinville also made up the embassy to the duke of Burgundy.
3. *Villehardouin*, pp. 11–12; Lippiatt, *Simon V of Montfort*, p. 57.
4. Lippiatt, *Simon V of Montfort*, pp. 110–2, 120; *Peerage VII*, p. 538.
5. Lippiatt, *Simon V of Montfort*, p. 75.
6. *Villehardouin*, pp. 14; *Robert of Clari*, pp. 7, 10; *Devastatio*, Sources, p. 214. The figures according to Villehardouin: 9,000 squires, 4,500 knights, and 20,000 foot soldiers. Robert of Clari: 4,000 knights and 100,000 foot soldiers.
7. *Villehardouin*, p. 6.
8. *Villehardouin*, p. 8; Queller and Madden, *Fourth Crusade*, pp. 14–15.
9. *Villehardouin*, p. 14.
10. *Devastatio*, Sources, p. 213, n. 32; *Villehardouin*, p. 18; Queller and Madden, *Fourth Crusade*, p. 50.
11. *Villehardouin*, pp. 15–16; *Halberstadt*, Sources, p. 249, n. 35; Queller and Madden, *Fourth Crusade*, pp. 17, 51.
12. *Halberstadt*, Sources, p. 250; Queller and Madden, *Fourth Crusade*, pp. 56–8.
13. *Villehardouin*, p. 16; *Robert of Clari*, p. 11; *Halberstadt*, Sources, p. 250. For a full analysis of this discussion, see Lippiatt, 'Duty and desertion: Simon of Montfort and the Fourth Crusade', pp. 75–88.
14. *Devastatio*, Sources, p. 214; *Villehardouin*, pp. 16–17, 19; Queller and Madden, *Fourth Crusade*, pp. 9, 60–1, 64–5. Dandolo lost his sight from a blow to the head, probably when he was already in his seventies.
15. *Innocent III, Reg. 5:160 (161)*, Sources, pp. 39–45. Robert of Clari (p. 14) says the Zarans had secured such a letter themselves and sent it to Dandolo and the crusaders. For an explanation how the letter came into Abbot Guy's hands, see Queller and Madden, *Fourth Crusade*, p. 244, n. 105.
16. Lippiatt, *Simon V of Montfort*, pp. 82–3; *History*, p. 147. Peter of Vaux-de-Cernay writes of Abbot Guy that Simon had 'listened to his advice and followed his wishes ever since childhood.'

17. *Devastatio*, Sources, pp. 214–15; *Robert of Clari*, pp. 12–13; *Villehardouin*, p. 19; Queller and Madden, *Fourth Crusade*, pp. 69–71.

18. *Villehardouin*, p. 20; Queller and Madden, *Fourth Crusade*, p. 73.

19. *Villehardouin*, p. 20.

20. *History*, p. 58.

21. *Villehardouin*, p. 21. Villehardouin makes the absurd claim that sabotaging the crusade was the ultimate goal of Simon and his party.

22. *History*, pp. 58–9; *Robert of Clari*, pp. 13–14.

23. *Halberstadt*, Sources, p. 251; *Innocent III, Reg. 5:160 (161)*, Sources, p. 41–5; *Villehardouin*, p. 21; Queller and Madden, *Fourth Crusade*, p. 77.

24. *Devastatio*, Sources, pp. 215–16; *Villehardouin*, pp. 22, 25.

25. *Robert of Clari*, p. 14; *Villehardouin*, p. 26.

26. *Villehardouin*, pp. 19, 22; *Devastatio*, Sources, pp. 216; Queller and Madden, *Fourth Crusade*, pp. 26–7.

27. *Innocent III, Reg. 5:121, Sources*, pp. 35–9; *Villehardouin*, pp. 17–18; Queller and Madden, *Fourth Crusade*, pp. 33–8.

28. *Villehardouin*, pp. 22–3; *Count Hugh of St Pol*, Sources, p. 189; *Anonymous of Soissons*, Sources, p. 233; *Robert of Clari*, p. 26–7.

29. *Halberstadt*, Sources, p. 253; *Count Hugh of St Pol*, Sources, p. 189; *Villehardouin*, p. 24. Strangely, Villehardouin says the chieftains accepted the offer because they would be ashamed if they refused.

30. *Count Hugh of St Pol*, Sources, p. 188.

31. *Villehardouin*, p. 26; *Innocent III, Reg. 5:161 (162)*, Sources, pp. 46–9; *Halberstadt*, Sources, p. 252.

32. *Villehardouin*, pp. 23–4; Queller and Madden, *Fourth Crusade*, pp. 89–92.

33. *Villehardouin*, p. 27; *Devastatio*, Sources, p. 216 *Count Hugh of St Pol*, Sources, pp. 198–9; Lippiatt, *Simon V of Montfort*, p. 120.

34. *History*, p. 59; *Guibert of Nogent*, VII, xxiv; *Albert of Aachen*, VIII, xxii; *Oderic III*, pp. 290–7.

35. *Halberstadt*, Sources, p. 253–4; *Villehardouin*, pp. 27–9; *Robert of Clari*, p. 27.

36. *Villehardouin*, p. 30; Lippiatt, *Simon V of Montfort*, p. 71. Simon, Guy of Vaux-de-Cernay and Robert Mauvoisin, one of the knights who defected with them, are recorded making a donation to the Templars in Acre.

37. *Ernoul*, pp. 337, 341–3; *Alberic of Trois Fontaines*, Sources, pp. 294, 296. *Villehardouin*, p. 9, 58.

38. *Ernoul*, pp. 352–3; Queller and Madden, *Fourth Crusade*, pp. 93–4; Edbury, *Kingdom of Cyprus*, p. 10. Thierry is last heard in 1207, in Constantinople fighting for Emperor Henry against the Bulgarians (*Villehardouin*, p. 131). His wife, who was Greek, probably ended her days thereabouts. She has an interesting history for a woman with no name. In 1191, after Richard the Lionheart deposed her father as the emperor of Cyprus, she was brought to Acre as part of the court of Richard's sister Joanna and his wife Berengaria.

After the crusade, she went west with Joanna and Berengaria and was betrothed to Leopold of Austria, the son of Richard the Lionheart's captor, as part of the deal to release the English king. She joined Richard's niece Eleanor of Brittany, who was betrothed to Leopold's older brother, for the journey to Vienna. The death of the duke of Austria upset those plans and both women returned to France. She married Raymond VI of Toulouse shortly after the death of his third wife, who was none other than Joanna, and they divorced in 1202, shortly before she met Thierry. See *Howden II*, pp. 205, 220, 307, 345; http://fmg.ac/Projects/MedLands/CYPRUS.htm.

39. *Ernoul*, p. 360.
41. *Devastatio*, Sources, pp. 216–21; *Villehardouin*, pp. 37–57, 58–65; *Robert of Clari*, pp. 33–43, 45–51, 55–72; Queller and Madden, *Fourth Crusade*, pp. 119–203.
42. *Innocent III, Reg. 7:152, 153, 201, 203, 204, 205, 206, 207, 208, 223, 8:56*, Sources, pp. 98–131.
43. *Villehardouin*, p. 50, 91–5, 102; *Innocent III, Reg. 7:202*, Sources, pp. 128–30; Lippiatt, *Simon V of Montfort*, p. 31.

Chapter 3: Inheritance and Heresy

1. *History of William the Marshal*, lines 12698–13278; Church, *King John*, pp. 72–116.
2. *Peerage V*, pp. 692–3; Carlin and Crouch, *Lost Letters of Medieval Life*, pp. 32–6, 48. Little is known about the life of Amaury VI in England other than he married Millicent de Gurnay sometime before 1203. Surviving correspondence with his wine merchant suggests he was an affable and reliable customer, always paying his bills on time. Other letters attributed to him show he was conscious about celebrating Easter in style, with new garments made from furs, skins and scarlet. In one letter to his skinner, he admits being hard up at that moment, but asks him to supply the material from his own stock and he will make sure he gets his money 'without any dispute'.
3. Powicke, *Loss of Normandy*, p. 145; Crouch, 'Countesses', pp. 179–80.
4. *Peerage VII*, pp. 536–7, note i), Crouch, 'Countesses', pp. 181–3.
5. *Peerage VII*, pp. 532–3, note h); Crouch, 'Countesses', pp. 184–5.
6. Crouch, 'Countesses', pp. 186–7; Lippiatt, *Simon V of Montfort*, pp. 25–6, 37, 38, 122–3.
7. *Peerage XII, Vol II*, p. 749; Lippiatt, *Simon V of Montfort*, pp. 26, 39–40, 118.
8. Lippiatt, *Simon V of Montfort*, p. 108. In his chronicle of the Fourth Crusade, Robert of Clari calls Simon the count of Montfort, evidently assuming that a man whose authority and prestige rivalled the other chieftains must have been of the same noble rank.

9. Ibid., pp. 87, 112–13, 115, 117–18, 123–4; *Actes de Simon et d'Amauri de Montfort*, p. 450.

10. Oldenbourg, *Massacre at Montségur*, pp. 30–7; Sumption, *Albigensian Crusade*, pp. 32–5.

11. *Innocent III, Reg. 5:160 (161)*, p. 43; *History*, p. 59. Peter only mentions that it was a 'deserted land where no roads led'. He adds no specific encounters with heretics or other details following the intervention at Zara.

12. Biller 'Heresy and Dissent', p. 256.

13. *Puylaurens*, p. 10; Sumption, *Albigensian Crusade*, pp. 38–40.

14. Sumption, *Albigensian Crusade*, pp. 41, 48–9; Oldenbourg, *Massacre at Montségur*, pp. 38–9.

15. Peters, *Heresy and Authority in Medieval Europe*, pp. 66–71.

16. *Puylaurens*, pp. 7–8; Sumption, *Albigensian Crusade*, pp. 15–31.

17. *History*, pp. 10–14; Oldenbourg, *Massacre at Montségur*, pp. 44–52. As for the number of perfects in the region, there is an estimate of 4,000 in the second quarter of the thirteenth century, meaning after the two-decade long crusade aimed at wiping them out was over (Evans, *History of the Crusades*, p. 281).

18. Peters, *Heresy and Authority in Medieval Europe*, p. 121.

19. Lippiatt, *Simon V of Montfort*, p. 112.

20. *Puylaurens*, pp. 9, 25–6; *History*, pp. 10, 29; Oldenbourg, *Massacre at Montségur*, p. 37.

21. *History*, pp. 16–19; *Song*, p. 14; *Puylaurens*, pp. 23–4, 29.

22. *Puylaurens*, p. 18–19; Sibly, *History of the Albigensian Crusade*, pp. 313–17. Raymond's wives were 1) Ermessende of Pelet, who died without issue in 1176; 2) Beatrice of Béziers, whom he repudiated and who later became a Cathar perfect; 3) Joanna, the sister of Richard the Lionheart and mother of Raymond VII of Toulouse, who died in 1199; 4) the daughter of Emperor Isaac of Cyprus, see. pp. 221–2 and 5) Eleanor, the sister of King Peter II of Aragon. Peter of Vaux-de-Cernay (pp. 23–4) gives Raymond as only having four wives and puts his marriage to 'the daughter of the duke of Cyprus' before Joanna, although this is refuted in other sources.

23. *History*, pp. 22–5; Sibly, *History of the Albigensian Crusade*, pp. 304–05; Sumption, *Albigensian Crusade*, p. 74.

24. *History*, pp. 31–3; *Song*, p. 13; Evans, 'Albigensian Crusade', pp. 284–5. William of Tudela says a sword, Peter of Vaux-de-Cernay a lance.

25. *Puylaurens*, pp. 21, 27.

26. *History*, pp. 31–8, 41–2, 45; Sibly, *History of the Albigensian Crusade*, pp. 305–06. Raymond's mother Constance was the younger sister of Philip's father Louis VII. Philip of Swabia was assassinated in June 1208. Otto was now supreme and Innocent crowned him Holy Roman Emperor in October 1209.

27. *History*, p. 56. The phrase is from Psalm 91.

28. *History*, pp. 28–9; Bird, 'Paris Masters and the Justification of the Albigensian Crusade', p. 124.
29. *Song*, p. 12; Sibly, *History of the Albigensian Crusade*, p. 16, n. 4.
30. *History*, pp. 42–5; *Song*, pp. 15–16.
31. *Song*, pp. 16–19.
32. *History*, p. 50; *Song*, pp. 19–20.
33. *Song*, pp. 20–2; *History*, pp. 50–1; *Puylaurens*, p. 33. Both Peter of Vaux-de-Cernay and William of Puylaurens report that the people of Béziers got their just desserts for having lynched their lord Raymond I Trencavel, Raymond-Roger's grandfather, in 1167 and kicked in the teeth of the bishop who tried to defend him. Peter's figure of 7,000 perishing in the fire of the cathedral church is unsustainable because the structure was not large enough to hold so many.
34. *Song*, p. 19; Sibly, *History of the Albigensian Crusade*, pp. 289–93. The phrase appeared forty years after these events in the work of a Cistercian monk, Caesar of Heisterbach. He writes that the crusaders, worried the heretics were mingling with Catholics in order to escape, were told by Arnaud-Amalric, '*Caedite eos. Novit enim Dominus qui sunt eius*', literally, 'Kill them. The Lord knows who are his own'. Lacking sufficient mellifluousness, over time it became, 'Kill them all, God will know his own'.
35. *History*, pp. 52–3. Marvin, *Occitan War*, pp. 43–5.
36. *Song*, pp. 23–6; *History*, p. 54; *Puylaurens*, pp. 33–4; Sibly, *History of the Albigensian Crusade*, p. 290.
37. *History*, p. 55; *Song*, p. 26; *Puylaurens*, p. 34.
38. Sibly, *Chronicle of William of Puylaurens*, pp. 128–9.
39. *Song*, pp. 26–7; *History*, pp. 56–7.
40. *History*, p. 59; Queller and Madden, *Fourth Crusade*, p. 246, n. 16.
41. *Actes de Simon et d'Amauri de Montfort*, pp. 452–3. The houses belonged to Bernard de Lérida of Carcassonne, Amels de Rieussec of Beziers, and the 'late lady Filesars' of Sallèles, which lies between Beziers and Carcassonne.
42. *History*, pp. 55, 59–60.
43. *Song*, pp. 27–8; *History*, pp. 64, 71; Lippiatt, *Simon V of Montfort*, pp. 124, 146, 159.

Chapter 4: Lest Your Foot Stumble on a Stone
1. *History*, pp. 62–3; *Song*, pp. 17–18.
2. *History*, p. 64; Lippiatt, *Simon V of Montfort*, pp. 65–6.
3. *History*, pp. 65–6; *Puylaurens*, p. 24. Pamiers hosted a debate between Catholic preachers and Waldensians in 1207. When the count of Foix's sister arrived for the debate, one of the preachers snapped that she should go tend her distaff.
4. *History*, pp. 65–6; *Song*, p. 29.
5. *Song*, pp. 28–9; *History*, pp. 67–9; *Actes de Simon et d'Amauri de Montfort*, p. 455.

6. Sibly, *History of the Albigensian Crusade*, pp. 313–20.
7. *History*, pp. 68–9, 71–3; *Song*, p. 30.
8. *History*, pp. 69–70; *Song*, p. 30.
9. *History*, p. 74
10. Ibid., pp. 87–8. The actual absolution of the city was negotiated in the spring of 1210 by the legates and Bishop Fulk. The council agreed to pay 1,000 livres (£250) and turned over ten hostages, who were released in August.
11. *Song*, pp. 28–9, 30–1; *History*, pp. 74–7; *Puylaurens*, p. 32. Raymond's visit to Philip Augustus was not a success. Philip was displeased that Raymond, on his return from Rome, had met his enemy Otto, the emperor, even though Otto was Raymond's overlord for the marquisate of Provence.
12. *History*, pp. 70–1; *Song*, p. 32.
13. *History*, p. 78; *Song*, p. 33.
14. *History*, pp. 73–4, 78–9.
15. Ibid., pp. 80–2.
16. Ibid., pp. 82–5; *Song*, p. 33.
17. *Song*, pp. 34–5; *History*, pp. 90–1; Duffy, 'Ung sage et valent home', pp. 70–3. King John invaded Ireland in the summer of 1210 in pursuit of his enemy William de Braose and his family, whom Lacy and his brother Walter were accused of harbouring. Walter surrendered, but Hugh fled to France.
18. *Song*, pp. 36–7; *History*, pp. 91–100.
19. *History*, pp. 101; Bird, 'Paris Masters and the Justification of the Albigensian Crusade', p. 120.
20. *Puylaurens*, pp. 22, 35–7.
21. *History*, pp. 87–9; *Song*, p. 37. Peter of Vaux-de-Cernay says that Raymond started weeping when he heard their judgement (medieval man was not afraid to cry), but Thedisius was moved to contempt and recited Psalm 32, v.6 to him: 'In the flood of great waters thou shalt not come nigh unto God.' William of Tudela says Raymond rode back to Toulouse with all speed and 'in anger and distress'.
22. *History*, p. 101.
23. Ibid., pp. 101–02; *Song*, pp. 37–8.
24. *History*, pp. 107–08; *Puylaurens*, p. 37.
25. *Song*, pp. 38–9.
26. Sibly, *History of the Albigensian Crusade*, pp. 108–09, n. 38.
27. *Song*, p. 39; *History*, p. 108.
28. *Song*, pp. 39–40; *History*, pp. 110–11.
29. *Puylaurens*, pp. 11–12, 38; *Song*, p. 41.
30. *History*, pp. 111–15; *Puylaurens*, p. 38–9; *Song*, p. 41. It was Bishop Fulk who organised the White Brotherhood into a militia to join the crusaders at the siege. At their muster, Raymond went among them, ordering them to disband and at one gate physically blocked their path out of the city. They

found another way out and marched the thirty-five kilometres northeast to Lavaur.

31. *Song*, p. 42; *History*, pp. 112–13.
32. *Song*, pp. 41–2; *History*, pp. 116–17; *Puylaurens*, p. 40; Bird, 'Paris Masters and the Justification of the Albigensian Crusade', p. 151. None of the primary sources provides a reason Giraude came to be executed in this style. Since Lavaur was her lordship, she faced the same fate as her brother and the garrison, but perhaps Simon wanted to spare her the public shame of hanging or beheading. He could also have been haunted by his order to bury a compatriot alive in a vain attempt to appease Giraud de Pépieux (*Song*, p. 30). Learning that Giraud was among the southerners who massacred the crusaders at Montgey, Simon may have avenged himself by burying Giraude alive. Finally, Peter of Vaux-de-Cernay calls Giraude a 'heretic of the worst sort', suggesting she had engaged in incest (*History*, p. 14) or in a 'crime' of a sexual nature that, since time immemorial, ended with the woman being stoned to death. See also Marvin, *Occitan War*, pp. 103–04.
33. *Song*, p. 43; Sumption, *Albigensian Crusade*, pp. 132–3; Marvin, *Occitan War*, pp. 104–05.
34. *Song*, p. 48; *History*, pp. 119–20; *Puylaurens*, pp. 40–1. Peter of Vaux-de-Cernay says Les Cassés was proof Raymond harboured heretics, but William of Tudela claims they had been taken in by the local lord against Raymond's wishes.
35. *Puylaurens*, pp. 31, 41; *Song*, pp. 43–4.
36. *History*, p. 120; *Song*, p. 48; Sibly, *History of the Albigensian Crusade*, p. 120, n. 11; Sumption, *Albigensian Crusade*, p. 135.
37. *Song*, pp. 11, 44–5; *History*, pp. 121–2.
38. *Song*, pp. 45–8; *History*, pp. 121–5; *Puylaurens*, p. 42.
39. *Song*, p. 48; *History*, pp. 125–6.
40. *History*, pp. 127–8.
41. *Song*, pp. 48–9; *History*, p. 131.

Chapter 5: North versus South

1. *Song*, pp. 28, 50; *History*, p. 132.
2. *History*, pp. 129–31.
3. Ibid., pp. 132–3; *Song*, p. 51.
4. *History*, pp. 133–5; *Puylaurens*, p. 42; Marvin, *Occitan War*, pp. 121–5; Sumption, *Albigensian Crusade*, pp. 139–40. The crusaders were now used to the 'Montfort' trick and told the desperate men to prove their loyalty to Simon by cutting down one of their own, which they did, but the crusaders slew them anyway.
5. *Song*, pp. 51, 124; Lippiatt, *Simon V of Montfort*, pp. 156–7.
6. *Song*, p. 52; *History*, p. 117.

7. *Song*, pp. 6–7, 55; *History*, p. 139. In her translation of *The Song of the Cathar Wars*, Janet Shirley explains *paratge* this way: 'In derivation it is the same word as our "peerage" and has a general meaning of "equality", of being level with one's peers, that everything is all right because rank and order are decently observed, just as in cases of "disparagement" (once meaning "to marry out of one's class") rank is put under threat and society destabilised … *Paratge*, then, is seriously threatened by the disinheriting of the counts of Toulouse.'

8. *Song*, pp. 28, 55–6; *History*, p. 141.

9. *History*, pp. 141–4.

10. *Song*, p. 56; *History*, p. 145; Marvin, *Occitan War*, p. 133.

11. *Song*, p. 56; *History*, pp. 145–6; Marvin, *Occitan War*, pp. 134–5.

12. *History*, pp. xxiii–xxvi, 147–8.

13. Ibid., pp. 147, 149–50; Marvin, *Occitan War*, pp. 137–8.

14. *Puylaurens*, p. 43; O'Callaghan, *History of Medieval Spain*, pp. 245–9; Smith, *Crusade, Heresy and Inquisition*, pp. 35–6.

15. *History*, pp. 142, 151–3; *Song*, p. 57.

16. *History*, pp. 153–7; *Song*, p. 58.

17. *History*, pp. 158–60; *Song*, p. 59.

18. *History*, p. 161; *Song*, p. 60.

19. *History*, pp. 162–3; *Song*, pp. 60–1.

20. *History*, pp. 163–4. Peter of Vaux-de-Cernay reports that during the siege of Mossaic he himself just missed being struck by an arrow that went through his habit and lodged in the saddle. It harmed neither him nor the horse, but left him highly indignant. He felt his monk's attire entitled him to the status of a non-combatant, but the crossbowman, seeing how he was encouraging the men working the siege engines, took a different view.

21. *History*, pp. 164–5; *Song*, p. 62; Marvin, *Occitan War*, pp. 137–8.

22. *History*, p. 154; *Song*, pp. 17–8; Sibly, *History of the Albigensian Crusade*, p. 154, n. 67; Lippiatt, *Simon V of Montfort*, pp. 40–1.

23. *Dunstable*, pp. 34, 192; *Peerage V*, p. 693; Carlin and Crouch, *Lost Letters of Medieval Life*, p. 33. Amaury's widow Millicent later married William Cantilupe II, a royal servant and brother of Walter, bishop of Worcester. After the death of her second husband in 1251, Millicent went north to watch over the newly married Queen of Scotland, 11-year-old Margaret, daughter of Henry III. Matthew Paris calls Millicent, who died in 1260, 'a lady endowed with every honourable feeling' (*Paris II*, p. 472). Simon VI de Montfort became good friends of the Cantilupe family and was a pall bearer at the funeral of her son William III in 1254.

24. *History*, p. 169; *Song*, pp. 11, 62.

25. *History*, pp. 166–7.

26. Ibid., pp. 161, 167–8; *Actes de Simon et d'Amauri de Montfort*, p. 464; see p. .

27. *History*, pp. 170–1; *Song*, p. 63.

28. Sibly, *History of the Albigensian Crusade*, Appendix H, pp. 321–9; Lippiatt, *Simon V of Montfort*, pp. 161–8.
29. Sibly, *History of the Albigensian Crusade*, p. 173 n. 5 and Appendix: Innocent the Third and the Crusade, p. 318.
30. *Song*, p. 61; *History*, p. 168.
31. Sibly, *History of the Albigensian Crusade*, Appendix: Papal Correspondence, pp. 308–11.
32. *History*, pp. 24, 173–4.
33. Ibid., pp. 174–9; Sibly, *History of the Albigensian Crusade*, n. 35. Raymond's own emissaries to the council, swearing he would do whatever it was they commanded, were rebuffed.
34. *History*, pp. 181–4.
35. Ibid., pp. 180–1; Sibly, *History of the Albigensian Crusade*, n. 40. Lambert was imprisoned at Peter of Aragon's orders but eventually released through the intervention of some acquaintances he had at court.
36. *History*, pp. 192–4; Sibly, *History of the Albigensian Crusade*, n. 39.
37. Sibly, *History of the Albigensian Crusade*, p. 192; Lippiatt, *Simon V of Montfort*, pp. 68–9.
38. *History*, pp. 191, 193–4; Sibly, *History of the Albigensian Crusade*, nos. 34, 49; *Wendover*, pp. 265–70; *Waverly*, p. 278; Lippiatt, *Simon V of Montfort*, p. 53.
39. *Wendover*, pp. 271–3.
40. *History*, pp. 186–9.
41. Ibid., pp. 194–6, 199–200.
42. Ibid., p. 197; Sumption, *Albigensian Crusade*, pp. 161–2.
43. *Puylaurens*, pp. 43–4; *Song*, pp. 66–7; *History*, pp. 197–8. *The Song of the Cathar Wars*, authored by the anonymous poet, says the entire garrison was hanged or put to the sword on the spot. William of Puylaurens and Peter of Vaux-de-Cernay make it clear the Toulousains had committed an atrocity equal to all the others of this war, but this episode strangely tends to elicit an underdog sympathy for the Toulousains among historians. See Marvin, *Occitan War*, p. 174.
44. *History*, pp. 201–02; Sibly, *History of the Albigensian Crusade*, n. 92.
45. *Song*, pp. 68–9; *History*, pp. 204–05.
46. *History*, pp. 201, 205; *Puylaurens*, p. 46.

Chapter 6: Supremacy
1. *History*, p. 206.
2. *Puylaurens*, p. 47; *History*, p. 206; *Waverly*, p. 279; *Actes de Simon et d'Amauri de Montfort*, p. 468; Lippiatt, *Simon V of Montfort*, p. 115.
3. *Puylaurens*, p. 46; *History*, pp. 205–06; Sibly, *History of the Albigensian Crusade*, n. 16.
4. *Puylaurens*, p. 47; *History*, pp. 208–09; *Philippide*, pp. 238–40.

5. Marvin, *Occitan War*, pp. 182–7; Sibly, *History of the Albigensian Crusade*, p. 213, n. 54.
6. *History*, pp. 210–11; Sibly, *History of the Albigensian Crusade*, n. 42, 46.
7. *Puylaurens*, p. 48; *Song*, p. 70; *History*, p. 211.
8. *History*, p. 211–12.
9. Ibid., p. 212.
10. *Puylaurens*, pp. 48–9; *Song*, p. 71.
11. *History*, pp. 212–13, 217; Marvin, *Occitan War*, pp. 183, n. 92.
12. *Song*, p. 71; *Coggeshall*, pp. 164, 168; *Dunstable*, p. 39; *Waverly*, p. 280.
13. *History*, pp. 218–21.
14. Ibid., pp. 226–7; Sibly, *History of the Albigensian Crusade*, n. 44.
15. *Puylaurens*, pp. 50–1; *History*, pp. 222–5.
16. *Song*, p. 66. Peter of Vaux-de-Cernay places William of Contres with Baldwin at Lolmie when the covert operation took place. William of Contres may have been good friends of William of Tudela, or at least a good source of information, because he figures prominently in the *Song* and most of the final section Tudela wrote is given over to his exploits.
17. *History*, pp. 225–6.
18. Ibid., pp. 227–9 (Sibly, *History of the Albigensian Crusade*, n. 45, 55).
19. *History*, pp. 222, 231; Lippiatt, *Simon V of Montfort*, p. 97.
20. *History*, pp. 229–31.
21. Ibid., pp. 233–7; Marvin, *Occitan War*, pp. 208–13.
22. *Actes de Simon et d'Amauri de Montfort*, pp. 464, 467, 469, 470; Lippiatt, *Simon V of Montfort*, pp. 96–7.
23. *History*, p. 234; Lippiatt, *Simon V of Montfort*, pp. 43–4.
24. *History*, pp. 237–8; *Song*, p. 158. Marvin calls the incident at Sarlat Abbey an 'odd and unsubstantiated tale' that should be discounted (p. 214).
25. *History*, pp. 235, 239; Sibly, *History of the Albigensian Crusade*, n. 91 on p. 235.
26. *History*, pp. 241–4, 248–50; Sibly, *History of the Albigensian Crusade*, notes 122, 133, 135 in the cited pages.
27. Ibid., pp. 242, 244.
28. *Puylaurens*, pp. 51–2; *History*, pp. 244–5, 252; *Song*, p. 72.
29. *History*, pp. 246–8, 251–2; *Song*, p. 71.
30. *History*, pp. 250–1.
31. Lippiatt, *Simon V of Montfort*, pp. 186–7; Sumption, *Albigensian Crusade*, p. 179.
32. *Song*, pp. 72–81; *Puylaurens*, pp. 53–4; *History*, pp. 253–5.
33. Sibly, *History of the Albigensian Crusade*, pp. 311–12; *Song*, p. 82; Marvin, *Occitan War*, pp. 228–36.
34. *Song*, p. 78; Lippiatt, *Simon V of Montfort*, p. 188.
35. *Puylaurens*, pp. 54–5; Lippiatt, *Simon V of Montfort*, p. 191.

36. *History*, pp. 255–6; *Actes de Simon et d'Amauri de Montfort*, p. 482; *Wendover*, pp. 357–64.
37. *Actes de Simon et d'Amauri de Montfort*, p. 482; Lippiatt, *Simon V of Montfort*, p. 115.
38. *Song*, pp. 83–7; *History*, pp. 257–8; *Puylaurens*, p. 55.
39. *Song*, pp. 88–94; *History*, pp. 259–61.
40. *Song*, pp. 97, 100.
41. Ibid., pp. 94, 100, 105; *History*, pp. 261–2.
42. *Song*, p. 105; *History*, p. 262; *Puylaurens*, p. 57; Sumption, *Albigensian Crusade*, p. 186. Jacques de Vitry was in Italy at the time of Innocent III's death and reported that he did not find the body lying in state as might be expected, rather stripped of vestments and decaying in the summer heat.
43. *Song*, pp. 106–17; *History*, pp. 262–3; *Puylaurens*, pp. 58–9. Throughout these fictitious speeches, the Anonymous shows Simon continuously shunning the counsel of his brother and leading men to go easy on the city, which stands at odds to his ordinary conduct. It is clearly an attempt by the poet to portray him as a singular, evil force descending on the hapless residents. Marvin (pp. 260–1) and Sumption (pp. 188–9) are nevertheless inclined to agree, perhaps needing to see Simon as a tragic case of power gone amok, a tyrant isolated in his folly.
44. *History*, p. 263; Sibly, *History of the Albigensian Crusade*, n. 42, 43 on the cited page; *Song*, p. 118.

Chapter 7: Twilight of the Albigensian Crusade
1. *History*, pp. 264–5; Sibly, *History of the Albigensian Crusade*, n. 46, 47 in the cited pages; *Song*, p. 118.
2. *History*, pp. 266–8.
3. Ibid., pp. 268–9; *Song*, p. 130; Lippiatt, *Simon V of Montfort*, pp. 201–02.
4. *Song*, pp. 119–23, 128–9; *Puylaurens*, pp. 59–60; Lippiatt, *Simon V of Montfort*, p. 97.
5. *Song*, pp. 124–6; *History*, p. 270. The Anonymous makes Alice out to be a silly woman during the revolt, bemoaning, 'And yesterday all was going so well for me!'
6. *Song*, pp. 130–3; *History*, p. 271. The Anonymous has Guy's father-in-law Bernard of Comminges shooting the arrow, then following it up with a rude quip. 'The county is all yours, my boy.'
7. *Song*, pp. 134–6.
8. Ibid., pp. 137–9; *History*, pp. 271–2. Given that the poet takes pleasure in mocking Simon from the mouths of his own men, this would have been a good place for it. They watch as their leader sinks out of sight, then one of them observes, 'That's it, boys. The crusade's over. We can all go home'.
9. *Song*, pp. 142, 146–7; *History*, p. 272; *Puylaurens*, p. 60.
10. *Song*, pp. 148–9; *History*, p. 273.
11. *Song*, pp. 151–5; *History*, pp. 273–4.

12. *Song*, pp. 155–7; *History*, p. 274.
13. *Song*, pp. 159–61; *History*, p. 274.
14. *Song*, pp. 158, 161–4; *History*, p. 274.
15. *Song*, pp. 166–70; *History*, p. 272; *Puylaurens*, p. 60.
16. *Puylaurens*, p. 61. Describing Toulouse in this manner was a favourite pun of Peter of Vaux-de-Cernay, see Sibly, *History of the Albigensian Crusade*, p. xxvi.
17. *Song*, pp. 170–2; *History*, pp. 275–7; *Puylaurens*, p. 61. Peter of Vaux-de-Cernay says Simon lived long enough to commend his soul to God.
18. *Song*, p. 172. The Anonymous says the stone was fired from a mangonel worked by 'noblewomen, little girls and men's wives'. True as it may have been, the poet is clearly implying that the feared and invincible crusader was brought down in an 'unmanly' fashion.
19. Ibid., pp. 172–3; *Actes de Simon et d'Amauri de Montfort*, p. 490.
20. *Song*, pp. 174–6; *History*, p. 277.
21. *Song*, p. 176; *History*, p. 278; *Puylaurens*, p. 62. In an anecdote related by King Louis IX, Simon V supposedly told a group of heretics that he would have a crown in heaven, above the angels, because he held fast to the teachings of the Church, particularly the sacraments. See *Joinville*, p. 147.
22. *History*, p. 277; *Puylaurens*, pp. 61–2.
23. Kay, *Council of Bourges*, p. 9.
24. *History*, p. 278; Sumption, *Albigensian Crusade*, p. 201; Lippiatt, *Simon V of Montfort*, pp. 170–2.
25. *History*, p. 278; *Song*, pp. 176–7; Kay, *Council of Bourges*, pp. 7–8.
26. *Wendover*, pp. 357–402.
27. *Song*, pp. 181–6; *History*, pp. 278–9; *Puylaurens*, pp. 63–4.
28. *Song*, pp. 187–94; *Puylaurens*, pp. 64–5.
29. *Puylaurens*, pp. 63, 65–6; *Dunstable*, p. 61.
30. *Puylaurens*, pp. 63, 66.
31. *Actes de Simon et d'Amauri de Montfort*, pp. 496–7; *HGL XXIII*, p. 318.
32. *Necrologe de Port-Roial des Champs*, p. 101; *Obituaires de la Province de Sens*, p. 224.
33. *History*, p. 59; *Song*, p. 33.
34. *Dunstable*, p. 75; *Puylaurens*, p. 66; Duffy, 'Ung sage et valent home', pp. 83–4.
35. Cleve, *History of the Crusades*, pp. 418–28; Bird, 'Paris Masters and the Justification of the Albigensian Crusade', p. 142.
36. *HGL VI*, pp. 546–8, VIII, col. 759; *Puylaurens*, p. 70; Kay, *Council of Bourges*, pp. 10–13.
37. *Puylaurens*, pp. 66–8.
38. Ibid., pp. 68–9.
39. *Puylaurens*, p. 68; *HGL VIII*, col. 794–6; Sibly, *The Chronicle of William of Puylaurens*, Appendix B, pp. 134–6.

40. *Puylaurens*, p. 69; *HGL VIII*, 782–6; *Peerage* VII, p. 546; Sumption, *Albigensian Crusade*, pp. 209–10.
41. *Actes de Simon et d'Amauri de Montfort*, pp. 498–9; *Obituaires de la Province de Sens*, p. 224.
42. *HGL VIII*, pp. 599–601, 789, 792–4; *Actes de Simon et d'Amauri de Montfort*, p. 499; Sibly, *The Chronicle of William of Puylaurens*, Appendix B, pp. 132–3; Lippiatt, *Simon V of Montfort*, pp. 141–2. The king wanted a lot to renew the crusade, including £22,000 a year from the Church for a ten-year period, money that might have tipped the balance in Simon V's favour throughout his decade in the south.
43. *HGL VIII*, pp. 804–07; *Actes de Simon et d'Amauri de Montfort*, p. 500; Kay, *Council of Bourges*, pp. 18–20.
44. *Wendover*, p. 450; *Dunstable*, p. 91.
45. Kay, *Council of Bourges*, pp. 22–30.
46. *Puylaurens*, pp. 70–1; *HGL VIII*, pp. 774–6; *Wendover*, p. 470; *Dunstable*, p. 101.
47. *Puylaurens*, pp. 71–5; *Actes de Simon et d'Amauri de Montfort*, p. 501; *Layettes ii*, pp. 80, 87–9, 96–7, 101.
48. *Puylaurens*, pp. 75–81; *HGL VIII*, pp. 778–83; Sibly, *The Chronicle of William of Puylaurens*, Appendix C, pp. 138–44.
49. *Puylaurens*, p. 76; *Necrologe de Port-Roial des Champs*, pp. 260–1; *Cartulaire de l'abbaye de Porrois*, pp. 94–5; *Obituaires de la Province de Sens*, p. 224; *Layettes ii*, p. 144; *HGL VIII*, p. 728. Lambert's other properties went to the three children he had with Briende.

Chapter 8: New Lords in the Family

1. *Rishanger Barons' War*, p. 6.
2. Sibly, *History of the Albigensian Crusade*, pp. xxv, 71–2, n. 30. Bishop Guy of Carcassonne died in 1223 and was replaced by the man he succeeded, Bernard-Raymond de Rochefort. In 1226, the new bishop of Carcassonne was Clarin, the former chancellor and chaplain of Simon V.
3. *Cartulaire de l'abbaye de Notre-Dame des Vaux de Cernay*, pp. 254–5.
4. *Paris I*, p. 378.
5. *CPR, 1225–32*, p. 124; *Layettes ii*, p. 287.
6. *CR 1227–31*, p. 316; *Lanercost*, p. 39.
7. *Wendover*, p. 534–8; *Clairambault*, 1188, f. 80; Baker, *Montfort*, pp. 225–6.
8. *CPR, 1232–47*, p. 185; *Layettes ii*, pp. 193, 194–5; *Puylaurens*, p. 71.
9. *Dunstable*, p. 128; *CR 1227–31*, p. 543; *Clairambault*, 1188, f. 80; Baker, *Montfort*, p. 226.
10. *CChR, 1227–57*, p. 139; *CR, 1227–31*, pp. 550, 570; *Royal Letters I*, p. 407; *Wendover*, p. 552–62; Maddicott, *Montfort*, pp. 11–13; Ellis, *Hubert de Burgh*, pp. 127–43.
11. *Letters of Robert Grosseteste*, pp. 65–9; Mundill, *King's Jews*, pp. 132–3.

12. *Wendover*, pp. 539, 541; *CR, 1231–34*, p. 152; *CR, 1234–37*, p. 425; Wilkinson, *Eleanor de Montfort*, pp. 41–2.
13. *Wendover*, pp. 566–93; *Dunstable*, pp. 135–6.
14. *Rishanger Barons' War*, p. 6; Duffy, 'Ung sage et valent home', pp. 84–6; Baker, *Henry III* (2nd edition), pp. 126–7, 363–5; Maddicott, *Montfort*, p. 18.
15. *CPR, 1232–47*, p. 74; *Foedera I*, pp. 216, 217–20.
16. *Nangis I*, p. 192; *Layettes ii*, pp. 336–7 (2492); Bémont, *Montfort*, pp. 53–4.
17. *English Coronation Records*, p. 63; *Dunstable*, pp. 145–6; Duffy, 'Ung sage et valent home', pp. 85–6.
18. *CChR, 1227–57*, p. 230; *Dunstable*, pp. 144, 146–7; *Paris I*, pp. 29, 34, 49, 54–5, 68, 73; *Chronica Majora III*, p. 418 (Simon's presence as one of Otto's bodyguard is missing in the Giles translation of *CM*); Stacey, *Politics*, pp. 112–13. Because Siward had sworn to go on crusade, he was soon released. Paris finds the behaviour of the councillors perplexing because they were Englishmen and not foreigners, whom he typically holds in contempt. This may seem curious in Simon's case, but his claim to Leicester was through his English grandmother Amicia.
19. *CPR, 1232–47*, pp. 119, 155, 185; *Cartulaire de l'abbaye de Notre-Dame des Vaux de Cernay*, pp. 252–3; Powicke, 'Loretta, Countess of Leicester', pp. 269–70.
20. *CPR, 1232–47*, p. 155; *Wendover*, pp. 604–06; *Paris I*, pp. 34, 160; Maddicott, *Montfort*, pp. 8–9.
21. *Les Registres de Gregoire IX, Vol. III*, pp. 798–9 (3923, 3926); *Alberic of Trois-Fontaines*, p. 946; Lippiatt, *Simon V of Montfort*, pp. 116–19; Lower, *Barons' Crusade*, pp. 43, 50, 153.
22. *Wendover*, pp. 490–537; *Paris I*, pp. 213–29, 234–5, 244–5; *Dunstable*, pp. 107, 111, 118, 125, 133; Wolff (pp. 203–20), Van Cleve (pp. 429–62) and Hardwicke (pp. 522–51), *History of the Crusades II*.
23. *HGL VI*, pp. 145–6.
24. *Novare*, p. 194; *Rothelin Continuator*, pp. 39, 41; *Historia diplomatica Friderica Secundi*, V-I, p. 474; Lower, *Barons' Crusade*, pp. 162–3.
25. *Paris I*, pp. 272–3, 314–5; *Rothelin Continuator*; pp. 42–4, 45–51; *Novare*, pp. 194–5; *Joinville*, pp. 204–05; Painter, *History of the Crusades II*, pp. 473–7. The critical Rothelin Continuator says the crusaders fell for the ploy of feigned retreat, but this makes no sense in their situation.
26. *Paris I*, p. 239.
27. *Wendover*, p. 539, 568–92; *Tewkesbury*, pp. 67, 78; *Dunstable*, pp. 91, 136–7; *Paris II*, p. 442; Baker, *The Two Eleanors*, pp. 19–26.
28. *CPR, 1232–47*, pp. 208–09, 222; *Paris I*, pp. 117, 120–3.
29. *CChR, 1227–57*, pp. 242–3; *CLR, 1226–40*, pp. 311, 410; *CPR, 1232–47*, p. 214; *Paris I*, pp. 124, 130, 155, 172.
30. *Paris I*, pp. 194, 236; *Dunstable*, p. 151; Maddicott, *Montfort*, pp. 24–5; Baker, *Montfort*, pp. 49–51; Carpenter, *Henry III*, p. 207.

31. *CR, 1237–42*, pp. 234–5; *CChR, 1227–57*, p. 408; *Paris I*, p. 259; Maddicott, *Montfort*, pp. 103.
32. *Paris I*, p. 273; *Chronica Majora IV*, p. 44, n. 4.
33. *Novare*, p. 196; *Paris I*, p. 308.
34. *Novare*, pp. 197–8; *Paris I*, pp. 337, 362–8; *CPL I*, p. 193.
35. *Paris I*, pp. 368–70; Turner, *Manners*, pp. xviii–xix; *Novare*, pp. 61–170; Edbury, *Kingdom of Cyprus*, pp. 39–73.
36. *Obituaires de la Province de Sens*, p. 225; Grant, *Blanche of Castile*, pp. 175, 227.

Chapter 9: More Crusades and Political Undertakings
1. *Novare*, p. 195.
2. Ibid., pp. 170–2.
3. Ibid., pp. 174–84. Alice was the daughter of Henry II of Champagne and Queen Isabella of Jerusalem, whose mother Maria Comnena took Balian I, the patriarch of the Ibelins, as her second husband. Henry had declared that Champagne should go to his younger brother Theobald III after his death (1197). Although there had been doubts about Alice's legitimacy, she sued and had Theobald IV pay her a huge sum of money that he raised by selling much of his patrimony to King Louis IX. See *Layettes ii*, pp. 272–4. For a full treatment of Theobald IV and his troubles, see Lower, *Barons' Crusade*, pp. 93–115.
4. *Paris I*, pp. 491–500, 522–8, *Melrose*, pp. 186–92.
5. *Paris II*, pp. 37–8, 114, 157, 174–5, 234–5; *Templar of Tyre* (257), p. 20; Edbury, *Kingdom of Cyprus*, pp. 90–1.
6. *Cartulaire de l'abbaye de Porrois*, pp. 236–7; *Seventh Crusade*, pp. 74–83; *HGL VI*, p. 74. After consulting his son-in-law John I de Montfort, Geoffrey and his men attempted to flee for Acre but were restrained by Louis.
7. *Obituaires de la Province de Sens*, p. 225; *Excerpta Cypria*, pp. 44–5; *Paris II*, p. 323; Strayer, *History of the Crusades II*, pp. 493–5; Jeffrey, *Monuments of Cyprus*, pp. 40–1. The memorial service for John I at Hautes-Bruyères gives the date of his death as 5 December 1249.
8. *Joinville*, pp. 169–70; *CPL I*, p. 305; *Obituaires de la Province de Sens*, p. 301.
9. *Letters from the East*, pp. 147–51; *Necrologe de Port-Roial des Champs*, p. 139.
10. *Joinville*, pp. 172–232, 274, 278–82; *Paris II*, pp. 333–5, 360–4, 366–86; *Puylaurens*, pp. 115–6; Edbury, *Kingdom of Cyprus*, pp. 75–6.
11. *CPL I*, p. 239; *Paris II*, pp. 252, 369–72.
12. *Paris I*, pp. 394–402, 404–06, 413–43; *Clairambault 1188*, f. 80; Stacey, *Politics*, pp. 160–200.
13. *CLR, 1240–45*, p. 153; *Paris I*, pp. 421–2; Bémont, *Montfort*, pp. 65–6; Powicke, *King Henry III*, p. 215.
14. *Paris I*, pp. 425, 432–4, 436–7.
15. *CChR, 1227–57*, p. 278; *CPR, 1232–47*, pp. 419, 433; *CR, 1242–47*, pp. 159, 185; *Paris I*, p. 459; Baker, *Montfort*, p. 228.

16. *Paris II*, pp. 7–13.
17. *CLR, 1245–51*, p. 2; *Paris II*, p. 52; Maddicott, *Montfort*, p. 51.
18. *Paris II*, pp. 119–22; Maddicott, *Montfort*, pp. 127, 130, 132, 137, 145.
19. *Paris II*, pp. 231; *Letters of Adam Marsh II*, (no. 135) pp. 328–9, (no. 160), pp. 387–8; Maddicott, *Montfort*, pp. 85–7; Baker, *Montfort*, p. 228.
20. *CR, 1247–51*, pp. 3–4, 22; *CPR, 1247–58*, p. 5.
21. *CPL I*, p. 248; *Paris II*, p. 491; Maddicott, *Montfort*, pp. 109–10.
22. *CPR, 1247–58*, p. 31; *Paris II*, p. 243; Bémont, *Montfort*, pp. 75–6. Henry had sent Simon to Paris on 'very secret business' in the autumn of 1247. The most likely reason was Louis's well publicised intention to do justice to everyone before leaving on crusade and Henry naturally wondered if that included returning the lands seized from him and his father by Louis's father and grandfather.
23. *Layettes iii* (3713), p. 47; *CPR, 1247–58*, p. 23; *Paris II*, p. 37; Bémont, *Montfort*, pp. 76–9.
24. Bémont, *Montfort*, pp. 79–81.
25. *CR, 1247–51*, pp. 343–4; *Letters of Adam Marsh I*, (no. 25) pp. 58–9; *Paris II*, p. 312; Bémont, *Montfort*, pp. 82–5.
26. *Puylaurens*, pp. 111–12, 113–14; Bémont, *Montfort*, pp. 81, 87.
27. *CPR, 1247–58*, pp. 56–7; *Paris II*, pp. 331–2.
28. *Royal Letters II*, pp. 52–3.
29. *Paris II*, pp. 329, 340, 343, 420–2, 451–2, 453–6; Bémont, *Montfort*, pp. 93–6.
30. Bémont, *Montfort*, p. 37; Maddicott, *Montfort*, pp. 102, 104.
31. *Paris II*, pp. 464–5, 476, 487; *CPR, 1247–58*, pp. 56–7, 124; *CR, 1251–53*, p. 207; Bémont, *Montfort*, pp. 97–8; Howell, *Eleanor of Provence*, p. 63.
32. *Royal Letters II*, pp. 68–85; *Paris II*, pp. 477, 485–6; Bémont, *Montfort*, pp. 98–102.
33. *Letters of Adam Marsh I* (no. 30) pp. 78–91; *Paris II*, pp. 486–8, 493, 507; *Dunstable*, p. 184.
34. *Paris II*, pp. 507–08, 509–10; *CPR, 1247–58*, p. 161; *Letters of Adam Marsh I* (no. 134), pp. 326–7. Richard II de Montfort is said to have been born a year earlier in October 1251 on account of Marsh writing that Eleanor went abroad with Simon and their son after his trial in 1252, which would have made her five months pregnant. Paris, however, writes that Simon and Eleanor returned from Gascony in November 1251. It is highly unlikely she would have made such a long journey just weeks after giving birth.
35. *Paris II*, pp. 527, 530; *Paris III*, pp. 15–6, 27–8; Bémont, *Montfort*, pp. 113–6. Montauban was the same castle where Raymond VI of Toulouse had his brother Baldwin hung in 1214. See p. 90.
36. *Paris III*, pp. 16–7, 20, 21–2, 30–1, 34–5, 40–2, 52, 56–7; Bémont, *Montfort*, pp. 118–20; Maddicott, *Montfort*, pp. 120–1.
37. Maddicott, *Montfort*, pp. 122–3.
38. *CPR, 1247–58*, p. 321; *Paris III*, pp. 61–3, 75, 79–80, 83.

Chapter 10: Realpolitik and Revolution

1. *Paris III*, pp. 89–92, 100–04, 122–4, 137, 141–2, 225; *Foedera I*, pp. 297, 301, 312, 316, 319, 321, 322; Strayer, *History of the Crusades II*, pp. 491, 504.
2. *Seventh Crusade*, pp. 229–31.
3. *Templar of Tyre* (268–70), pp. 23–4; Hill, *History of Cyprus*, p. 148; Runciman, *History of the Crusades II*, pp. 568–9.
4. *Templar of Tyre* (279–86); pp. 26–8; Wolff, *History of the Crusades II*, pp. 230–1.
5. Hill, *History of Cyprus II*, pp. 154–5; Edbury, 'The De Montforts of the Latin East', p. 3; Cook, 'The Bezant in Angevin England', p. 258; *Itinéraires a Jerusalem*, p. 137. Matthew Paris reports he took this figure of £50,000 for Acre from Richard of Cornwall, who heard it from the Templars and Hospitallers—'*[C]este vaut à sun seignur chescun an cinquante mile livres d'argent. Co en quist li quens Ric[ars] de Templers e Hospitalers.*'
6. *Cartulaire de l'abbaye de Porrois*, pp. 260–1.
7. *Layettes iii* (4476), p. 456; *HGL VI*, p. 105, 145; Labarge, *Montfort*, p. 131–7.
8. *Paris III*, pp. 98, 104–10, 115, 166–7, 207–09, 252–3; Denholm-Young, *Richard of Cornwall*, pp. 87–96; Powicke, *King Henry III*, pp. 245–6.
9. *Layettes iii* (4416), p. 411–3; *CPR, 1247–58*, pp. 628, 663; *CPR, 1258–66*, p. 24; *Paris III*, pp. 306–07.
10. *Paris III*, pp. 255–6, 265–6, 283, 291; Maddicott, *Montfort*, pp. 125–8, 138–9.
11. *Paris III*, pp. 233–4; Ridgeway, 'Foreign Favourites', pp. 596, 598–9; Baker, *Two Eleanors of Henry III*, pp. 74–6.
12. *Clairambault 1188*, f. 10; Baker, *Montfort*, p. 216–7.
13. *CPR, 1247–58*, p. 627; *Paris II*, p. 260, 269, 278–80; Baker, *Henry III*, pp. 259–60. *Tewkesbury* (pp. 163–4) gives a highly colourful but ultimately too problematic account of the barons marching on the king in his chamber, wearing full armour and demanding he expel the Lusignans and 'all aliens'. This is after he asked for a tax worth one-third the total value of the whole realm.
14. *Paris III*, pp. 285–8; *Dunstable*, pp. 208–09; *Tewkesbury*, p. 165; *DBM*, pp. 96–113.
15. *Paris III*, pp. 292, 294–5; *DBM*, pp. 116–7.
16. *Clairambault 1188*, f. 80 (translation in Baker, *Montfort*, p. 227); *Paris II*, pp. 488.
17. *CPR, 1247–58*, p. 638; *Paris II*, pp. 395–8; *Paris III*, pp. 291–2, 307. Winchester Castle was originally handed over to William de Clare, but he died in an epidemic that swept through Winchester in July after parliament moved there in pursuit of the Lusignans. Clare's brother Richard was also affected and lost all his hair and nails. His steward William Scotenny was accused of being paid by the Lusignans to poison the Clare brothers and

other nobles (see *Tewkesbury*, p. 165; *Paris III*, pp. 291, 293–4, 310–11, 321). His execution by hanging in the spring of 1259 marks the last entry in Matthew Paris's chronicle (*Paris III*, pp. 329–30) .

18. *Clairambault 1188*, f. 10v; Maddicott, *Montfort*, pp. 174–5.
19. *Clairambault 1188*, f. 81 (translation in Baker, *Montfort*, p. 221–3); *Melrose*, pp. 229–30; *Rishanger Barons' War*, pp. 6–7; Maddicott, *Montfort*, pp. 88–99.
20. *Paris III*, pp. 326–7; *CPR, 1258–66*, pp. 18, 19, 25; *Flores*, p. 365; Treharne, *Baronial Plan of Reform*, pp. 99–100.
21. *CLR, 1251–60*, p. 460; *CChR, 1257–1300*, pp. 18, 20; *CPR, 1258–66*, pp. 25–6, 34–5; *DBM*, pp. 196–9; Maddicott, *Montfort*, p. 183.
22. *CPR, 1258–66*, pp. 25, 317; *DBM*, 194–7; Maddicott, *Montfort*, pp. 190–1.
23. *DBM*, pp. 94–5; *Burton*, p. 471; Treharne, *Baronial Plan of Reform*, pp. 160–4; Carpenter, *Reign of Henry III*, pp. 241–51.
24. *CPR, 1258–66*, pp. 106–07; *Mayors and Sheriffs*, p. 46; Maddicott, *Montfort*, pp. 187–8.
25. *CPR, 1258–66*, pp. 25, 106–07; *Foedera I*, p. 386; *Flores*, p. 370.
26. *DBM*, pp. 204–05.
27. *CR, 1259–61*, p. 228; *CPR, 1258–66*, p. 122, 123; *DBM*, pp. 166–7, 170–3, 180–3, 186–9; *Mayors and Sheriffs*, pp. 46–7; *Dunstable*, pp. 214–7; *Flores*, pp. 378–9; Ridgeway, 'Lord Edward and the Provisions of Oxford', pp. 97–8.
28. *DBM*, pp. 194–211; *Flores*, p. 384.
29. *Mayors and Sheriffs*, p. 48; *Flores*, p. 386; Treharne, *Baronial Plan of Reform*, pp. 244–9.
30. Maddicott, *Montfort*, pp. 200–03.
31. *CPR, 1258–66*, pp. 113–14; *Flores*, p. 389; Labarge, *Montfort*, pp. 191–3.
32. *DBM*, pp. 210–47; *Flores*, pp. 391–4; Ridgeway, 'King Henry III's Grievances', pp. 231–2, 239–40, 241–2.
33. *DBM*, pp. 248–51; *Royal Letters II*, pp. 188–92; *CPR, 1258–66*, pp. 162–4; *Dunstable*, p. 217; Maddicott, *Montfort*, p. 212; Ridgeway, 'What Happened in 1261?', pp. 104–05; Runciman, *Sicilian Vespers*, p. 54.
34. *DBM*, pp. 246–9; *CR, 1259–61*, pp. 489–90; *CPR, 1258–66*, pp. 178, 189, 191, 193; *Royal Letters II*, p. 194, 196; *Dunstable*, p. 217; Clanchy, *Memory to Written Record*, p. 62; Ridgeway, 'What Happened in 1261?', pp. 105–06; Maddicott, *Montfort*, p. 217.
35. *Royal Letters II*, pp. 157–8; Denholm-Young, *Richard of Cornwall*, pp. 172–3; Maddicott, *Montfort*, p. 216.
36. *Paris I*, pp. 50, 73–4; *Paris II*, pp. 124–7, 435; *Grosseteste Letters*, pp. 367–73.
37. *CR, 1261–64*, p. 281; *Mayors and Sheriffs*, p. 53; *Paris I*, p. 117; Baker, *Montfort*, p. 226.
38. *Royal Letters II*, pp. 234, 242–3; *CPR, 1258–66*, p. 241; *Gervase II*, p. 217; *Mayors and Sheriffs*, p. 56.
39. *Gervase II*, pp. 214, 215–6, 220–1; Ridgeway, 'Politics of the English Royal Court', pp. 388–99; Maddicott, *Montfort*, p. 220.

40. *Mayors and Sheriffs*, pp. 54–5; *Tewkesbury*, pp. 163–4; *Dunstable*, p. 220; Carpenter, *King Henry III*, pp. 253–4.

41. *Dunstable*, pp. 221–2; Denholm-Young, *Richard of Cornwall*, pp. 86–97, 118–9.

42. *DBM*, pp. 116–17; *Oxendes*, p. 226.

43. *Dunstable*, pp. 222–4; *Flores*, pp. 404–08; *Wykes*, pp. 134–6.

44. *CPR, 1258–66*, pp. 273, 291; *CPL I*, pp. 400–01, 417; *DBM*, pp. 284–5; *Gervase II*, p. 224; *Wykes*, p. 136. Simon would later write to his reclusive great-aunt Loretta de Beaumont, whom he might have visited with his brother Amaury back in 1235, for information on the powers of the steward as exercised by her husband Robert, the 4th earl of Leicester (*CR, 1264–68*, pp. 115–16).

45. *CPR, 1258–66*, p. 275; *Dunstable*, p. 225; *Tewkesbury*, p. 176; *Mayors and Sheriffs*, p. 61; *Gervase II*, pp. 224–5.

46. *Dunstable*, p. 225; *Tewkesbury*, p. 176; *Mayors and Sheriffs*, p. 62; *Wykes*, p. 137; *Rishanger Barons' War*, pp. 17–18.

47. *Dunstable*, pp. 225–6; *Gervase II*, pp. 229–31; *Wykes*, p. 137; *Flores*, pp. 409–10; *DBM*, pp. 280–7.

48. *Rishanger Annals*, pp. 11–12; *Dunstable*, pp. 226–7.

Chapter 11: Tried and Tested in the World

1. *Gervase II*, p. 232; *Dunstable*, p. 227; *Wykes*, p. 138; *DBM*, pp. 252–79.

2. *DBM*, pp. 287–91; *CPR, 1258–66*, p. 378; *Mayors and Sheriffs*, pp. 63–4; *Gervase II*, pp. 232–3.

3. *Dunstable*, p. 227; *Tewkesbury*, p. 177; *Wykes*, p. 139.

4. *Dunstable*, p. 227.

5. *Flores*, pp. 410–11, 412; *Robert of Gloucester*, ii, pp. 740–1; *Mayors and Sheriffs*, pp. 64–5; *Dunstable*, pp. 228, 230. *Flores* credits John Giffard, a Marcher who remained loyal to Simon, with the capture of the earl, William Manduit.

6. *CPR, 1258–66*, pp. 240, 307, 308; Powicke, *King Henry III*, pp. 458–9.

7. *Mayors and Sheriffs*, p. 65; *Wykes*, pp. 140–1; *Flores*, pp. 411–12.

8. *Dunstable*, p. 229; *Rishanger Barons' War*, p. 24; *Wykes*, p. 144; *Gervase II*, p. 234. *Flores*, on the other hand, says Simon raged 'like a lion at the capture of his cubs' (p. 432).

9. *Wykes*, pp. 141–3; *Mayors and Sheriffs*, p. 66; *Dunstable*, p. 230; *Gervase II*, p. 235.

10. *Tewkesbury*, pp. 179–80; *Dunstable*, pp. 230–1; *Wykes*, pp. 140, 146–7; *Gervase*, pp. 235–6; *Rishanger Barons' War*, p. 25.

11. *Rishanger Barons' War*, p. 30; *Wykes*, pp. 148–9; *Mayors and Sheriffs*, p. 66; Maddicott, *Montfort*, pp. 268–70.

12. *Rishanger Barons' War*, pp. 27–9; *Flores*, pp. 414–15; *Oxendes*, p. 222; Blaauw, *Barons' War*, pp. 168–9.

13. *Rishanger Barons' War*, p. 31; *Flores*, pp. 416–19; *Wykes*, pp. 150–1; *Melrose*, pp. 217–19.
14. Maddicott, 'The Mise of Lewes, 1264', pp. 588–603; Carpenter, *Reign of King Henry III*, pp. 281–91.
15. *Mayors and Sheriffs*, p. 67; *Wykes*, pp. 152–3.
16. *DBM*, pp. 292–3, 295–9; *CPR, 1258–66*, p. 326; *Mayors and Sheriffs*, p. 69; *Dunstable*, p. 34; Maddicott, *Montfort*, pp. 286–7.
17. *CPR, 1258–66*, p. 366; Maddicott, *Montfort*, pp. 294–5; Homer's *Odyssey*, Book XI, lines 488–91.
18. *Flores*, pp. 420–1, 423; *Wykes*, p. 154; *Robert of Gloucester*, pp. ii, 751–2; Ridgeway, 'Sir Warin de Bassingbourn', p. 9.
19. *CPR, 1258–66*, pp. 360–1, 362; *Mayors and Sheriffs*, pp. 71–3; *Dunstable*, p. 233.
20. *CPL I*, p. 396; *CPR, 1258–66*, pp. 370–1, 474; *Wykes*, pp. 155–7; *Gervase II*, p. 239; *Flores*, p. 435.
21. *CPR, 1258–66*, pp. 320–1, 322, 323, 325, 350, 398, 421–2, 431; *Mayors and Sheriffs*, pp. 77–8; *Wykes*, pp. 157–9; *Rishanger Annals*, p. 29.
22. *Flores*, pp. 423–4; *Dunstable*, pp. 234–5; *Mayors and Sheriffs*, p. 75.
23. *Flores*, p. 424; Baker, *Henry III*, p. 318. Henry knighted his son-in-law Alexander III on Christmas day in York (*Paris II*, p. 468).
24. Kingsford, *Song of Lewes*, pp. xviii–xix, 33.
25. *CPR, 1258–66*, pp. 273, 393, 394, 404; *Wykes*, pp. 140, 158–9; Maddicott, *Montfort*, pp. 324–5. Teenager Richard de Montfort also held land somewhere because he was given deer for it.
26. *CR, 1264–68*, pp. 84–7; *Mayors and Sheriffs*, p. 75.
27. *Mayors and Sheriffs*, pp. 75–6.
28. *CChR II*, p. 54; *CPR, 1258–66*, p. 409; *Robert of Gloucester*, p. ii, 753; *Wykes*, p. 160.
29. *CPR, 1258–66*, p. 406; *Rishanger Annals*, pp. 31–3; *Dunstable*, pp. 235, 238; *Wykes*, pp. 161–2.
30. *CPR, 1258–66*, pp. 412, 414; *Mayors and Sheriffs*, pp. 76–7.
31. *CPR, 1258–66*, p. 425; *Manners*, p. 15; Labarge, *Montfort*, p. 94.
32. *CPR, 1258–66*, p. 423; *Mayors and Sheriffs*, p. 77; *Wykes*, p. 162–4; *Robert of Gloucester*, ii, pp. 756–7; *Flores*, p. 437.
33. *Royal Letters II*, pp. 284–8; *Manners*, pp. 41–2; *Wykes*, pp. 166–8.
34. *Mayors and Sheriffs*, p. 78; *Melrose*, p. 227; *Wykes*, p. 169; *Flores*, p. 437; *Robert of Gloucester*, ii, p. 760; Maddicott, *Montfort*, p. 339.
35. Laborderie, Maddicott, Carpenter, 'The Last Hours of Simon de Montfort', pp. 378–412.
36. *Robert of Gloucester*, ii, pp. 763–4; *Wykes*, pp. 172–3. The Melrose chronicler says (pp. 222–3) Simon and the barons decided that if they had to die, so too the king.
37. *Mayors and Sheriffs*, p. 80; *Robert of Gloucester*, ii, p. 765; *Wykes*, pp. 173–4; *Melrose*, pp. 226–7.

38. *Osney*, pp. 175–7; *Dunstable*, p. 61; Prothero, *Life*, pp. 371–3; Valente, 'Simon de Montfort, Earl of Leicester, and the Utility of Sanctity in Thirteenth-Century England', pp. 27–49; Turton, *Honor and Forest of Pickering*, pp. 225–6.

39. *CPR, 1258–66*, p. 470; *Wykes*, pp. 175–6; *Mayors and Sheriffs*, p. 87; *Gervase II*, pp. 243–4.

40. *CR, 1264–68*, p. 136; *CPL I*, p. 432; *Wykes*, pp. 178–9; *Mayors and Sheriffs*, p. 88; Powicke, *King Henry III*, pp. 528–9.

41. *CPR, 1258–66*, p. 674; *CPL I*, p. 434; *Gervase II*, pp. 244–5; Wilkinson, *Eleanor de Montfort*, pp. 130–2.

42. *CPR, 1258–66*, p. 678; *CPR, 1266–72*, pp. 130, 140–1; *Royal Letters II*, pp. 304–05, 315; Powicke, *King Henry III*, pp. 535–6.

43. Bémont, *Montfort*, pp. 163–5; Runciman, *Sicilian Vespers*, pp. 79–96; Powicke, *Ways of Medieval Lives*, pp. 76–7; Maddicott, p. 370.

44. Bémont, *Montfort*, pp. 264–5; Powicke, *Ways of Medieval Lives*, pp. 78–81; Runciman, *Sicilian Vespers*, p. 124. In his *Divine Comedy*, written forty years later, Dante famously stuck Guy in the seventh circle of hell as his punishment for the murder of Henry of Almain, submerged up to his neck in a river of boiling blood (*Inferno*, XII 119–20). Almain's bones were carried back to England and interred in Hailes Abbey, which his father had built and became his tomb as well.

45. *Puylaurens*, pp. 120–2; *HGL VI*, p. 146; *Mayors and Sheriffs*, pp. 136–8; Strayer, *History of the Crusades II*, p. 46; Powicke, *Ways of Medieval Lives*, p. 85.

47. *Templar of Tyre* (370), pp. 61–2; Edbury, *Kingdom of Cyprus*, pp. 90–1.

48. *Templar of Tyre* (374), pp. 63–6.

49. Ibid. (376, 378, 382), pp. 67–9; *Wykes*, pp. 248–50.

50. *Wykes*, p. 241–2; *Flores*, p. 452. The statement of the *Flores* chronicler that Simon VII 'during the latter part of his life being, like Cain, accursed of the Lord, was a vagabond and fugitive on the face of the earth' is refuted by the favour and enfeoffment he found in Charles's service.

51. *Mayors and Sheriffs*, pp. 138–40; *Flores*, pp. 455–6; Blaauw, *Barons' War*, pp. 341–8. Gregory X was Teobaldo Visconti, whom Edward got to know after he was sent to England to assist the papal legate Ottobono Fieschi. Teobaldo was then appointed legate himself, to serve Edward's crusade in the Holy Land. He left Acre in November 1271 after being informed of his election.

52. *Nangis I*, p. 259; Bémont, *Montfort*, pp. 265–73; Waley, *Mediaeval Orvieto*, p. 56.

53. *Templar of Tyre*, sections 334–8 as translated by Peter Edbury in 'The De Montforts in the Latin East', pp. 28–31.

54. *Templar of Tyre* (369, 371, 375, 398, 420, 423), pp. 61–3, 67, 74, 82–4; Edbury, *Kingdom of Cyprus*, pp. 93–5; Holt, *Early Mamluk Diplomacy*, pp. 106–17.

55. *Trivet*, p. 294; *Wykes*, pp. 267–8, 277; Smith, *Llywelyn ap Gruffudd*, pp. 393–9, 445, 448–9; Wood, *Letters of Royal Ladies*, pp. 54–5.

56. *Letters of Medieval Women*, pp. 138–9; Maddicott, *Montfort*, p. 43; Smith, *Llywelyn ap Gruffudd*, p. 399.

57. *Wykes*, p. 287; Smith, *Llywelyn ap Gruffudd*, pp. 399–400, 510; Powicke, *King Henry III*, pp. 684–5; Blauuw, *Barons' War*, pp. 334–5; Morris, *Great and Terrible King*, p. 195.

58. Bémont, *Montfort*, p. 262; Powicke, *King Henry III*, p. 610, n. 1; Maddicott, *Montfort*, p. 93. *Flores Historiarum III*, p. 67, says that Amaury had in fact swapped the priesthood for knighthood and fought alongside his brother and cousin in Italy, dying in the same year as Guy. Such a move would not seem out of place for this man of all seasons.

59. Dunbabin, *French in the Kingdom of Sicily*, pp. 144–5; Dunbabin, *Charles I of Anjou*, p. 61. Runciman, *Sicilian Vespers*, p. 264. The regent for Charles's son Charles of Salerno, who was also imprisoned, was Robert of Artois, the nephew of the king. He was married to Amicia de Courtenay, the granddaughter of Amicia de Montfort (Maddicott, *Montfort*, p. 190, n. 126).

60. *Nangis I*, p. 273; Bémont, *Montfort*, pp. 272–3; Powicke, *King Henry III*, pp. 612, 684–5, n. 3; Waley, *Mediaevel Orvieto*, pp. 60, 70.

61. Dunbabin, *French in the Kingdom of Sicily*, p. 145.

Bibliography

PRIMARY SOURCES

Abbot Suger, The Deeds of Louis the Fat, trans. R. Cusimano and J. Moorhead (Washington: Catholic University Press, 1992)

Actes de Simon et d'Amauri de Montfort, ed. A. Molinier (Paris, 1873)

Alberic of Trois-Fontaines, *Albrici monachi Triumfontium chronicon*, ed. P. Scheffer-Boichorst, *MGH SS. 23*: pp. 631–950.

Albert of Aachen, *History of the Journey to Jerusalem, vol. 2: Books 7–12: The Early History of the Latin States, 1099–1119*, trans. S. Edgington (Farnham: Ashgate, 2013).

'Annals of Burton', *Annales Monastici*, Vol. I, ed. H.R. Luard (London, 1864)

'Annals of Dunstable', *Annales Monastici*, Vol. III, ed. H.R. Luard (London, 1866)

Annals of Nicholas Trivet, ed. T. Hog, Historical English Society, ix (London, 1845)

'Annals of Tewkesbury', *Annales Monastici*, Vol. I, ed. H.R. Luard (London, 1864)

'Annals of Waverley', *Annales Monastici*, Vol. II, ed. H.R. Luard (London, 1865)

'Annals of Winchester', *Annales Monastici*, Vol. II, ed. H.R. Luard (London, 1865)

Calendar of the Charter Rolls, 1903 (CChR)

Calendar of the Liberate Rolls, 1930 (CLR)

Calendar of Papal Letters, 1893 (CPL)

Calendar of the Patent Rolls, 1908 (CPR)

Cartulaire de l'abbaye de Notre-Dame des Vaux de Cernay, Vol. I (Paris, 1857)

Cartulaire général de Paris, Vol. I, ed. R. De Lasteyrie (Paris, 1887).

Chronica Albrici Monachi Trium Fontium, ed. P. Scheffer-Boichorst, in *Monumenta Germaniae Historica*: Scriptorum, vol. 23 (Hanover, 1874)

Chronicle of John of Oxendes, ed. H. Ellis (London, 1859)

Chronicle of Lanercost, ed. J. Stevenson (Maitland Club, 1839)

Chronicle of Melrose, trans. J. Stevenson (1856)

Chronicle of the Mayors and Sheriffs of London, 1188–1274, French Chronicle of London, ed. H.R. Riley (London, 1863)

'Chronicle of Oseney', *Annales Monastici*, Vol. IV, ed. H.R. Luard (London, 1869)

Chronicle of Ralph of Coggeshall, ed. J. Stevenson (RS, 1875)

Chronicle of Robert of Torigni (de Monte), trans. J. Stevenson (London, 1856)

'Chronicle of Thomas Wykes', *Annales Monastici*, Vol. IV, ed. H.R. Luard (London, 1869)

Chronicle of Walter of Guisborough, ed. H. Rothwell (Camden Society, 1957)

Chronicle of William de Rishanger, ed. J.O. Halliwell (1840)

Chronicle of William of Puylaurens: The Albigensian Crusade and Its Aftermath, trans. W.A. Sibly and M.D. Sibly (Woodbridge: Boydell, 2003)

Chronique d'Ernoul et de Bernard Le Trésorier (Paris, 1871)

Chronique Latine de Guillaume de Nangis, Vol. I and II (Paris, 1843)

Close Rolls of the Reign of Henry III, 1932 (CR)

Contemporary Sources for the Fourth Crusade: Registers of Innocent III, Count Hugh of Saint Pol's Report, Devastatio Constantinopolitana, Anonymous of Soissons, Deeds of the Bishops of Halberstadt, Chronicles of Ralph of Coggeshall and Alberic of Trois Fontaines, trans. A.J. Andrea (Leiden: Brill, 2008)

Crusade of Richard Coeur de Lion, Richard of Devizes and Geoffrey de Vinsauf (London, 1882)

Crusader Syria in the Thirteenth Century: The Rothelin Continuation of the History of William of Tyre with Part of the Eracles or Acre Text (Crusade Texts in Translation), trans. J. Shirley (London: Routledge, 1999)

Diplomatic Documents, 1101–1272, ed. P. Chaplais (1964)

Documents of the Baronial Movement of Reform and Rebellion (DBM), ed. R.F. Treharne, I.J. Sanders, Clarendon Press (Oxford, 1973)

Documents of the Christian Church, ed. H. Bettenson, C. Maunder (Oxford, 1963)

English Coronation Records, ed. L.G.W. Legg (London, 1901)

Excerpta Cypria, trans. C.D. Cobham (Cambridge, 1908)

Flores Historiarum, trans. C.D. Yonge (London, 1853)

Foedera, Conventiones, Literae, ed. T. Rymer (London, 1816)

Guibert de Nogent, *The Deeds of God through the Franks*, trans. R. Levine (Woodbridge: The Boydell Press, 1997)

Historia diplomatica Friderica Secundi, ed. J. Huillard-Bréholles (Paris, 1859)

Histoire générale de Languedoc (HGL), eds. C. Devic and J. Vaissète, Vol. V, VI, VII and VIII (Toulouse, 1872)

Historical Works of Gervase of Canterbury, Vol. II, ed. W. Stubbs (London, 1880)

History of William Marshal, trans. N. Bryant (Woodbridge, 2018)

Inventaire de pieces de Terre Sainte de l'ordre de l'Hopital (Paris, 1895)

Itinéraires a Jerusalem et Decriptions de la Terre Sainte, ed. H. Michelant and G. Raynaud (Paris, 1882)

Joinville's Chronicle of the Crusade of Saint Louis, trans. F. Marzials (London, 1908)

Layettes Du Trésor Des Chartes, ed. M. Alexandre Teulet (Paris, 1863)

Les Registres de Gregoire IX, ed. L. Auray and others, 4 volumes (Paris, 1896–1955)

Letters from the East: Crusaders, Pilgrims and Settlers in the 12th–13th Centuries, trans. M. Barber and K. Bate (Abingdon, 2013)

Letters of Adam Marsh, Volume I and II, ed. and trans. C.H. Lawrence (Oxford, 2006)

Letters of Medieval Women, ed. A. Crawford (Gloucestershire, 2002)

Letters of Robert Grosseteste, Bishop of Lincoln, ed. F.A.C. Mantello and F.M. Goering (Toronto, 2010)

Letters of Royal and Illustrious Ladies, Vol. I, ed. M.A.E. Wood, (London, 1846)

Manners and Household Expenses of England in the Thirteenth and Fifteenth Centuries, ed. T.H. Turner (Roxburghe Club, 1841).

Matthaei Parisiensis, *Monachi Sancti Albani, Chronica Majora*, ed. H.R. Luard (RS, 7 volumes, 1872–83)

Matthew Paris' English History from 1235 to 1273, Vol. I, II, III, trans. J.A. Giles (London, 1854)

Metrical Chronicle of Robert of Gloucester, ed. W.A. Wright (London, 1887)

Necrologe de l'Abbaie de Notre Dame de port-Roial des Champs (Amsterdam, 1723)

Obituaires de la Province de Sens, Vol. III, ed. A. Vidier and L. Mirot (Paris, 1909)

Odericus Vitalis, The Ecclesiastical History of England And Normandy, Vol. I, II, III, IV, trans. T. Forester (London, 1853)

Philip de Novare, The Wars of Frederick II Against the Ibelins in Syria and Cyprus, trans. J.L. La Monte (New York, 1936)

Political Songs of England, ed. T. Wright (London, 1839)

Recueil Des Historiens De La France, Obituaires, Vol. III (Paris, 1909)

Robert of Clari, Li Estoires De Chiaus Qui Conquisent Coustantinoble (Paris, 1868)

Roger of Howden, Vol. II, ed. W. Stubbs, (London, 1869)

Roger of Wendover's Flowers of History, Vol. I, II, trans. J.A. Giles, (London, 1859)

Royal Letters, ed. W.W. Shirley (London, 1866)

The History of the Albigensian Crusade: Peter of les Vaux-de-Cernay's 'Historia Albigensis', trans. W.A. Sibly and M.D. Sibly (Woodbridge, 1998)

The Honor and Forest of Pickering, ed. R.B. Turton (London, 1895)

The Seventh Crusade, 1244–1254 (Crusade Texts in Translation), trans. P. Jackson (Abingdon, 2009)

The Song of Lewes, ed. C.L Kingsford (Oxford, 1890)

The Song of the Cathar Wars: A History of the Albigensian Crusade (Crusade Texts in Translation), trans. J. Shirley (London, 2000)

The 'Templar of Tyre': Part III of the 'Deeds of the Cypriots' (Crusade Texts in Translation), trans. P. Crawford (London, 2003)

Villehardouin's Chronicle of the Fourth Crusade and the Conquest of Constantinople, trans. F. Marzials (London, 1908)

William the Breton, La Philippide (Paris, 1825)

SECONDARY SOURCES

Baker, D., *Henry III* (Stroud: The History Press, 2017)

———, *Simon de Montfort and the Rise of the English Nation* (Stroud: Amberley, 2018)

———, *The Two Eleanors of Henry III* (Barnsley: Pen & Sword, 2019)

Baldwin, J.W., *Government of Philip Augustus: Foundations of French Royal Power in the Middle Ages* (Berkeley: University of California Press, 1991)

Barber, M., *The Cathars: Dualist Heretics in Languedoc in the High Middle Ages* (London: Routledge, 2014)

Bémont, C., *Simon de Montfort* (Oxford: Clarendon Press, 1930)

Biller, P., 'Heresy and Dissent', in *The Routledge History of Medieval Christianity: 1050–1500*, edited by R.N. Swanson (London: Routledge, 2015)

Bird, J., 'Paris Masters and the Justification of the Albigensian Crusade', *Crusades* 6 (2007), pp. 117-55

Blaauw, W.H., *The Barons' War* (London: Bell and Daldy, 1871)

Carlin, M., Crouch, D., *Lost Letters of Medieval Life: English Society, 1200–1250* (Philadelphia: University of Pennsylvania Press, 2014)

Carpenter, D., *Henry III, 1207–1258* (New Haven: Yale University Press, 2020)

———, *The Reign of Henry III* (London: The Hambledon Press, 1996)

Crouch, D., 'The Battle of the Countesses: the Division of the Honour of Leicester, March–December 1207', *Rulership and Rebellion in the Anglo-Norman World, c.1066–c.1216: Essays in Honour of Professor Edmund King*, eds. P. Dalton and D. Luscombe (London: Routledge, 2015)

Chaplais, P., 'The Making of the Treaty of Paris (1259) and the Royal Style', *The English Historical Review*, Vol. 67, No. 263 (1952), pp. 235-53

Church, S., *King John and the Road to Magna Carta* (New York: Basic Books, 2015)

Clanchy, M., *England and its Rulers, 1066–1307* (Chichester: Wiley-Blackwell, 2014)

Cockayne, G., *Complete Peerage of England, Scotland, Ireland, Great Britain and the United Kingdom* (London: George Bell, 1895)

Cook, J., 'The Bezant in Angevin England', *The Numismatic Chronicle* (1966–), Vol. 159 (1999), pp. 255-75

Cox, E., *The Eagles of Savoy* (Princeton: Princeton University Press, 1974)

Denholm-Young, N., *Richard of Cornwall* (New York: William Salloch, 1947)

Duffy, P., 'Ung sage et valent home: Hugh de Lacy and the Albigensian Crusade', *The Journal of the Royal Society of Antiquaries of Ireland*, Vol. 141 (2011), pp. 66–90

Dunbabin, J., *Charles I of Anjou: Power, Kingship and State-Making in Thirteenth-Century Europe* (London: Routledge, 1998)

———, *The French in the Kingdom of Sicily, 1266–1305* (Cambridge: Cambridge University Press, 2011)

Edbury, P., 'The De Montforts of the Latin East', *Thirteenth Century England VIII: Proceedings of the Durham Conference, 1999*, eds. M. Prestwich, R. Britnell, R. Frame (Woodbridge: The Boydell Press, 2001)

_____, *The Kingdom of Cyprus and the Crusades, 1191–1374* (Cambridge: Cambridge University Press, 1993)

Ellis, C., *Hubert de Burgh* (London: Phoenix House, 1952)

Grant, L., *Blanche of Castile*, (New Haven: Yale University Press, 2016)

Harcourt, L.W.V., *His Grace the Steward and Trial of Peers* (London: Longmans, 1907)

Hill, G., *A History of Cyprus: Vol. 2* (Cambridge: Cambridge University Press, 2010)

Holt, P.M., *Early Mamluk Diplomacy, 1260–1290: Treaties of Baybars and Qalawun with Christian Rulers* (Islamic History and Civilization) (Leiden: Brill, 1995)

Hutton, W.H., *Simon de Montfort and His Cause, 1251–1266* (London: David Nutt, 1907)

Jeffrey, G., *Historic Monuments of Cyprus* (Nicosia, 1918)

Kay, R., *The Council of Bourges, 1225: A Documentary History* (Farnham: Ashgate, 2002)

Labarge, M.W., *Simon de Montfort* (London: Eyre & Spottiswoode, 1962)

Laborderie, O.D., D.A. Carpenter, and J.R. Maddicott, 'The Last Hours of Simon de Montfort: A New Account', *English Historical Review*, Vol. 115, No. 461 (2000), pp. 378–412

Lippiatt, G.E.M., 'Duty and Desertion: Simon of Montfort and the Fourth Crusade', Leidschrift, Historisch Tijdschrift, 27 (3), pp. 75–88.

_____, *Simon V of Montfort and Baronial Government, 1195–1218* (Oxford: Oxford University Press, 2017)

Lloyd, S., *English Society and the Crusade, 1216–1307* (Oxford: Clarendon Press, 1988)

Lower, M., *The Barons' Crusade: A Call to Arms and Its Consequences* (Philadelphia: University of Pennsylvania, 2005)

Maddicott, J.R., *Simon de Montfort* (Cambridge: Cambridge University Press, 1994)

_____, 'The Mise of Lewes, 1264', *English Historical Review*, Vol. 98 (1983), pp. 588–603

Marvin, L.W., *The Occitan War, A Military and Political History of the Albigensian Crusade, 1209–1218* (Cambridge: Cambridge University Press, 2008)

Meier, C., *Preaching the Crusades: Mendicant Friars and the Cross in the Thirteenth Century* (Cambridge, Cambridge University Press, 2008)

Messer, D.R., *Eleanor De Montfort, Princess and Diplomat*. Dictionary of Welsh Biography (2017)

Mitchell, S.K., *Studies in Taxation under John and Henry III* (New Haven: Yale University Press, 1914)

Morris, M., *A Great and Terrible King* (London: Windmill Books, 2009)

Mundill, R.R., *The King's Jews: Money, Massacre and Exodus in Medieval England* (London: Continuum, 2010)

O'Callaghan, J.F., *A History of Medieval Spain* (Ithaca: Cornell University Press, 1983)

Oldenbourg, Z., *Massacre At Montségur: A History of the Albigensian Crusade* (London: Phoenix Press, 2000)

Peters, E., *Heresy and Authority in Medieval Europe* (Philadelphia: University of Pennsylvania Press, 1980)

Power, D., *The Norman Frontier in the Twelfth and Early Thirteenth Centuries* (Cambridge: Cambridge University Press, 2009)

Powicke, F.M., 'Guy de Montfort' in *Ways of Medieval Lives and Thought: Essays and Addresses* (New York: Biblio and Tannen, 1949)

———, *King Henry III and the Lord Edward*, Vol. I, II (Oxford: Clarendon Press, 1947)

———, 'Loretta, Countess of Leicester', *Historical Essays in Honour of James Tait*, eds. J.G. Edwards et al. (Manchester: Butler & Tanner, 1933)

———, *The Loss of Normandy (1189–1204)*, (Manchester: Manchester University Press, 1913)

Prothero, G.W., *The Life of Simon de Montfort* (London: Longmans, Green and Co., 1877)

Queller, D., and Madden, T., *The Fourth Crusade: The Conquest of Constantinople* (Philadelphia: University of Pennsylvania, 1997)

Ridgeway, H., 'Henry III (1207–1272)', *Oxford Dictionary of National Biography* (2004)

———, 'King Henry III's Grievances against the Council in 1261', *Historical Research*, Vol. 61 (1988), pp. 227–42

———, 'The Lord Edward and the Provisions of Oxford (1258)', *Thirteenth Century England I*, eds. P.R. Coss and S.D. Lloyd (Woodbridge: The Boydell Press, 1986)

———, 'What Happened in 1261?', in *Baronial Reform and Revolution in England, 1258–1267*, ed. A. Jobson (Woodbridge: The Boydell Press, 2016)

Robinson, J.A., *Gilbert Crispin, Abbot of Westminster* (Cambridge: Cambridge University Press, 1911)

Runciman, S., *The Sicilian Vespers* (Cambridge: Cambridge University Press, 1992)

Smith, D.J., *Crusade, Heresy and Inquisition in the Lands of the Crown of Aragon, c. 1167–1276* (Leiden: Brill, 2012)

Smith, J.B., *Llywelyn Ap Gruffudd: Prince of Wales* (Cardiff: University of Wales Press, 1998)

Stacey, R., 'Crusades, Crusaders and the Baronial *Gravamina* of 1263–1264', in *Thirteenth Century England III: Proceedings of the Newcastle upon Tyne Conference, 1989* (3), eds. P.R. Coss and S.D. Lloyd (Woodbridge: The Boydell Press, 1991)

————, *Politics, Policy, and Finance Under Henry III, 1216–1245* (Oxford: Oxford University Press, 1987).

Sumption, J., *The Albigensian Crusade* (London: Faber and Faber, 1999)

Treharne, R., *The Baronial Plan of Reform* (Manchester: Manchester University Press, 1932)

Tyerman, C., *God's War: A New History of the Crusades* (Harvard: Belknap Press, 2008)

Valente, C., 'Simon de Montfort, Earl of Leicester, and the Utility of Sanctity in Thirteenth-Century England', *Journal of Medieval History* (1995), pp. 27–49

Waley, D., *Mediaeval Orvieto* (Cambridge: Cambridge University Press, 2013)

Warren, W.L., *King John* (Berkeley: University of California Press, 1978)

White, G., 'The Career of Waleran, Count of Meulan and Earl of Worcester (1104–66)', *Transactions of the Royal Historical Society Vol. 17* (1934), pp. 19–48

Wilkinson, L.J., *Eleanor de Montfort, A Rebel Countess in Medieval England* (London: Continuum Books, 2012)

Wolff, R.E., and Hazard, H.W., editors of *A History of the Crusades: Later Crusades, 1189–1311*, Vol. 2, contributors: Evans, A.P., 'The Albigensian Crusade'; Hardwicke, M.N., 'The Crusader States, 1192–1243'; Painter, S., 'The Crusade of Theobald of Champagne and Richard of Cornwall, 1239–1241'; Runciman, S., 'The Crusader States, 1243–1291'; Strayer, J.R., 'The Crusades of Louis IX'; Van Cleve, T.C., 'The Fifth Crusade'; Wolff, R.E., 'The Latin Empire of Constantinople, 1204–1261' (Philadelphia: University of Pennsylvania, 1962).

List of Illustrations

1. De Montfort Family Tree, author's work.
2. Montfort l'Amaury, author's collection.
3. Bertrade de Montfort, British Library, MS Royal, f. 271.
4. British Library, MS Royal, f. 286, Henry I.
5. Image of Amaury VII at Chartres Cathedral, author's collection.
6. Image of Simon VI at Chartres Cathedral, author's collection.
7. Siege of Zara, Andrea Vicentino (1539–1614) – Sala del Maggior Consiglio.
8. Sack of Constantinople, BNF Arsenal MS 5090, f. 205r.
9. Innocent III calling for the crusade, launch, MS Royal 16 G VI, f. 374v.
10. Carcassonne, author's collection.
11. Battle of Muret, BNF Français 2813 Grandes Chroniques de France, f. 252v.
12. St Dominic accompanied by Simon de Montfort raising the crucifix against the Cathars, Daniel van den Dyck (1610–1670).
13. Burning of heretics, MS Royal 20 E III, f. 177v.
14. Henry III at Salisbury cathedral, James Redfern, 1868–9.
15. Civil war in England, MS Royal 16 G VI, f. 427v.
16. Simon de Montfort on the Clocktower of Leicester, Samuel Barfield, 1868.
17. King John Ancestry, MS Royal 14. B. VI, membrane 6.
18. Charles of Anjou, MS Royal, f. 429v.
19. Charles of Anjou, MS Royal 20 C VII, f. 1v.
20. Chiesa di San Silvestro, Viterbo, author's collection.
21. Assault on Tyre, Yates Thompson 12, f. 75.
22. Assault on Acre, Bibliotheque Municipale de Lyon, MS 828, f. 33r.
23. Coins of Philip I de Montfort, Coins of the Crusaders, David Ruckser.
24. Coins of John II de Montfort, David Ruckser.

Index

Acre, 12, 139, 142, 162–3, 176, 207, 208, 210–1, 236

Agenais, 44, 48, 70, 72–74, 4, 91, 93, 113, 117

Agnes, 3rd wife of Simon I de Montfort, 2–3

Aimery, king of Jerusalem and Cyprus (d. 1205), 23, 24

Albigeois, 45, 52, 60, 67, 70, 121, 164

Aldobandesca, Margherita, wife of Guy IV de Montfort, 205, 209, 214–5

Alexander II of Scotland (d. 1249), 130, 136

Alexander III of Scotland (d. 1286), 156, 159, 174, 239

Alexander IV, pope (d. 1261), 161, 165, 176

Alfaro, Hugh de, mercenary commander, 70–1, 107

Alfonso X of Castile (d. 1284), 158, 159, 160, 181

Algai, Martin, mercenary commander (d. 1212), 64–5, 66, 71

Alice of Champagne (d. 1246), 143, 144, 234

Alphonse of Poitiers, son of Louis VIII (d. 1271), 121, 146, 153

Amiens, Mise of (1264), 184, 186–7, 188, 192

Anonymous poet of Toulouse, 90, 102, 111, 230, 231

Arnaud-Amalric, papal legate (d. 1225), 38–9, 40–1, 42, 48, 49, 52–4, 61, 69, 77, 79, 84, 91, 95–6, 98, 100, 113, 115, 118, 119, 120, 192, 194, 224

Arthur of Brittany (d. 1203), 26, 219

As-Salih Ayyub, sultan of Cairo (d. 1249), 135, 143–4, 145, 146

Aubrey, archbishop of Reims (d. 1218), 70, 71

Baldwin I, first Latin Emperor (d. 1205), 13, 14, 15, 23, 25, 128, 132

Baldwin II, last Latin Emperor (d. 1273), 132, 145, 163

Baldwin of Ibelin, seneschal of Cyprus (d. 1267), 142, 146

Baldwin of Toulouse, brother of Raymond VI (d. 1214), 58–9, 60, 73, 90, 92, 235

Balian of Beirut (d. 1247), 142, 162

Balian of Sidon, half-brother of Philip I de Montfort (d. 1241), 24, 67, 142

Barres, William III des, 2nd husband of Amicia de Montfort (d. 1234), 8–9, 10, 14, 90, 219

Barres, William IV des, half-brother of Simon V de Montfort (d. 1249), 84, 86, 93, 113, 121, 144

Bartholomew of Roye, brother-in-law of Simon V de Montfort (d. 1237), 10, 93

Baybars, Rukn ad-Din, sultan of Cairo (d. 1277), 143, 163, 207, 208, 210

Béarn, Gaston VI de (d. 1214), 62, 74, 78, 81, 102

Béarn, Gaston VII de (d. 1290), 152–3, 153–4, 156, 158, 159, 164, 175

Beatrice, daughter of Henry III and countess of Richmond (d. 1275), 173

Beatrice of Vienne, wife of Amaury VII de Montfort (d. 1248), 91, 105, 123, 139, 145

Beaucaire, 100–01, 102, 103, 112

Beaumont, Amicia de, wife of Simon IV, later William III des Barres, countess of Leicester (d. 1215), 7, 8, 27–9, 38, 48, 54, 84, 99, 233

Beaumont, Loretta de (née Braose), wife of Robert IV (d. 1266), 27, 130, 238

Beaumont, Petronilla de (née Grandmesnil), grandmother of Simon V (d. 1212), 27–8

Beaumont, Robert IV de, 4th earl of Leicester (d. 1204), 9, 13, 14, 27, 28, 130, 219

Beaumont, Waleran de, count of Meulan and husband of Agnes II de Montfort (d. 1166), 5, 6, 7, 218

Becket, Thomas, archbishop of Canterbury (d. 1170), 37, 131